ALSO BY MIKE BYNUM

High Tide, A Story of Class and Courage
Bryant — The Man, The Myth
Never Say Quit
Aggie Pride
We Believe
Bound for Glory
Bear Bryant's Boys of Autumn
Knute Rockne: His Life and Legend
Many Autumns Ago: The Frank Leahy Era
  at Boston College and Notre Dame
Vince Lombardi: Memories of a Special Time
Woody Hayes: The Man & His Dynasty

Pop Warner
Football's Greatest Teacher

The Epic Autobiography of
Major College Football's Winningest Coach,
Glenn S. (Pop) Warner

Pop Warner
Football's Greatest Teacher

The Epic Autobiography of
Major College Football's Winningest Coach,
Glenn S. (Pop) Warner

Edited
by
Mike Bynum

GRIDIRON
FOOTBALL
PROPERTIES

Pop Warner Football® and its logo are registered service marks, which are owned by Pop Warner Little Scholars, Inc. of Langhorne, Pa. The use of this service mark and logo are being used under a license granted by Pop Warner Little Scholars, Inc.

Jacket and Book Design: Debra Schrampfer

ISBN: 1-878839-03-9
Library of Congress Catalog Card Number: 93-079682
Copyright © 1993 by Michael J. Bynum

"The greatest game that a coach can win is the one that develops boys into men."

GLENN S. (POP) WARNER

Contents

Acknowledgements

The research, development, writing and completion of Pop Warner's epic life story has been a journey with many surprises, thrills, frustrations and wonderful discoveries en route.

Yet after a two-year effort, the pieces all came together.

This book, however, would not have been possible without the input and assistance of a large number of people from the sports and academic world whose contributions — both small and numerous — aided greatly in filling in the much-needed details that were woven together for the final presentation of Warner's amazing tale.

First, I would like to thank Pat Harmon, the historian at The College Football Hall of Fame in King's Island, Ohio, who always promptly answered my many research inquiries and provided much invaluable advice while I tried to decipher and fully understand both Warner's coaching record and the frontier era of college football in the late 1800's and early 1900's.

Also, I would like to express my sincere thanks to the many fine folks at six of the schools which Warner was so intimately associated: Dave Wohlhueter, Sports Information Director, Cornell University; Greg Bell, Alumni Office, Cornell University; Ms. Pat Bishop, Registrar's Office, Cornell University; Dr. Gould Coleman, Rare Books & Manuscript Collection, The Carl A. Kroch Library, Cornell University; Ms. Mary Warren, Assistant Researcher, Rare Books & Manuscript Collection, The Carl A. Kroch Library, Cornell University; Ms. Mary Ellen Brooks, Acting Department Head, Hargrett Rare Book & Manuscript Collection, The University of Georgia Library; Ms. Nancy Stamper, Research Assistant, Hargrett Rare Book & Manuscript Collection, The University of Georgia Library; Claude Felton, Assistant Athletic Director/Sports Information, The University of Georgia; Dave Starr, Sports Information Director, Iowa

State University; Lance Ringler, Student Assistant, Iowa State University Sports Information Dept.; Larry Eldridge, Sports Information Director, The University of Pittsburgh; Sam Sciullo, Assistant Sports Information Director, The University of Pittsburgh; Ms. Becky Abromitis, Associate Archivist, The University of Pittsburgh Archives; Steve Raczynski, Sports Information Director, Stanford University; Bob Vazquez, Sports Information Director, Stanford University; Ms. Debbie Kenney, Staff Assistant, Sports Information Dept., Stanford University; Ms. Patricia White, Special Collections Dept., Green Library, Stanford University; Al Shrier, Sports Information Director, Temple University; Gerry Emig, Associate Sports Information Director, Temple University; Steven Glassman, Student Assistant, Temple University Sports Information Dept.; Tom Tucci, Registrar, Temple University; George Brightbill, Assistant Curator, Urban Archives, Samuel Paley Library, Temple University; Bill Stout, CIBARS, Temple University Library; Ms. Theresa Davis, Special Collections Dept., Temple University Library; Ms. Edith Bensville, Alumni Office, Temple University; and Larry Shenk, Sports Information Director, Dickinson College, and Bob Royce, a sports historian from Pasadena, Calif., who both researched Warner's record at the Carlisle Indian School.

In addition, there is a long list of others who aided me during my research: David Vest of *The Arizona Republic*; Ms. Bev Powers, Auburn University Library Archives; Ms. Janet Hocker, Librarian, Cumberland County Historical Society, Carlisle, Pa.; Ms. Pat La Fond, the Baseball Hall of Fame, Cooperstown, N.Y.; Bill Dean, The National Baseball Library, Cooperstown, N.Y.; Ms. Bev Shirley, The University of Texas Library Archives; Pete Cava and Tom Surver, the U.S. Track & Field Association; Ms. Margaret Mayerat, Historian, The Concord Historical Society, Springville, N.Y.; Ms. Judy Hamilton, The Paul W. Bryant Museum, The University of Alabama; Ms. Patricia Jones, The W.S. Hoole Special Collections Library, The University of Alabama Library; Steve Gietchier, Director of Historical Records, *The Sporting News*; Ms. Hannes Combest, Assistant to the President, The Haskell Indian School; Glenn Schwarz, Sports Editor, *The San Francisco Examiner*; Dean Jutilla, Assistant Public Relations Director, The Pac-10 Conference; *The San Francisco Chronicle*

Library; Randy Andrada, a sports author from Oakland, Calif., who had written a wonderful history of St. Mary's football; David Housel, Sports Information Director, Auburn University; Ms. Karen Franscona, Assistant Sports Information Director, Auburn University; Kevin Reneau, Sports Information Director, The University of California; Mark Dellins, Sports Information Director, U.C.L.A.; John Veneziano, Sports Information Director, Harvard University; Tim Bonang, Assistant Sports Information Director, Harvard University; Mike Pearson, Sports Information Director, The University of Illinois; Ms. Betty Erickson, Iowa State University Library Archives; Vernon Tyler, Research Associate, The State of Iowa Historical Society; Ms. Barbara Tinklenberg, Librarian, Eldora Public Library, Eldora, Iowa; Ms. Becky Schulte, Librarian, The Kansas Collection, Lawrence, Kansas; Andrew Hartzock of *The Lawrence Journal-World*; Mike Garcia of *The Albuquerque Tribune*; Harry McKown, Reference Dept., The Walter R. Davis Library, The University of North Carolina; Ms. Gail Stasulli, Sports Information Director, The University of Pennsylvania; Ms. Lanie Moore, Student Assistant, The University of Pennsylvania Sports Information Dept.; Doug Vance, Sports Information Director, The University of Kansas; Ben Boyle, Sports Information Director, Kansas State University; Ms. Tracy Thornton of *The Montana Standard*; Pete Abitante, Director of Information, The National Football League; Steve Hellyer, Sports Information Director, The University of Oregon; Hal Cowan, Sports Information Director, Oregon State University; Joe Klueg, Public Relations Office, The Philadelphia Flyers Hockey Club; Jim Young, Sports Information Director, Santa Clara University; Larry Kimball, Sports Information Director, Syracuse University; Tim Tessalone, Sports Information Director, The University of Southern California; Tod Spieker of Atherton, Calif., whose sports memorabilia collection provided background information on Warner's record at Stanford; Steve Janisch, Sports Information Director, St. Mary's College; Ms. Nancy Masar, Registrar's Office, St. Mary's College; Kurt Kehl, Sports Information Director, Princeton University; Mike Jackman, Student Assistant, Princeton University Sports Information Dept.; Ms. Jeanne Pardee, Assistant to the University Archivist, Special Collections Dept., Alderman Library, The University of Virginia; Jim

Daves, Sports Information Director, The University of Washington; Paul Kirk, Student Assistant, The University of Washington Sports Information Dept.; Steve Malchow, Sports Information Director, The University of Wisconsin; and Ms. Beth Black, of Omaha, Neb., who owns one of my favorite bookstores and researched the popular songs of the 1920's for me.

Finally, I would like to express my sincere thanks to Jon Butler, the Executive Director of Pop Warner Little Scholars, Inc., and his assistant, Ms. Bernadette Portmann, who frequently assisted me in my research of Warner's football-coaching career and his devoted support of Pop Warner Football during its early years; Tom Koreschell, Assistant Sports Information Director, Iowa State University, who meticulously dug through the Iowa State University Archives to research and reconstruct Warner's record at his first coaching post; Bo Carter, Media Relations Director, The Southwest Conference, who guided me through the maze of confirming Pop Warner's actual coaching record; Gordon Smith, my good friend from Los Angeles, Calif., who originally suggested the idea for the Pop Warner book; and Mary Dunn, who patiently and faithfully transferred my long-hand — and often scribbled — manuscript draft into a word processing format so that this wonderful story could, at last, be told.

Introduction

In the early 1900's there were only a few great sports heroes. Yet these men and women seemed to be bigger than life.

One of these individuals that all of America looked up to was Glenn S. (Pop) Warner, who along with Knute Rockne, Amos Alonzo Stagg, Walter Camp and Fielding Yost were giants in the early days of college football.

The history books reflect that Pop Warner was a tremendous football innovator and a very successful coach. Among his greatest players were Jim Thorpe and Ernie Nevers. His teams won 341 games and gave us many memorable Rose Bowl thrillers. And now, after a considerable amount of research of his career coaching record during the early years of college football, Warner has finally arrived at the pinnacle that he truly deserves — the all-time winningest coach in major college football.

Pop Warner, however, was much more than just a football coach. He was also a noted scholar, having graduated from law school at Cornell University.

But the lure of football was eventually too strong. His inventive mind constantly sought new and different advantages but always within the rules. His coaching career started almost by accident, yet in a few years he had the distinction of coaching college football teams at Iowa State and Georgia during the same football season! And this was in the mid-1890's when speedy travel was achieved by riding on a Pullman train. He would later coach at his alma mater, Cornell, on two different occasions.

Warner eventually put aside his law career to teach and coach fulltime at the Carlisle Indian School in Carlisle, Pa.

Carlisle was known as an athletic power before Warner arrived there; however, their teams were inconsistent. His discipline and dedication to these young Indian boys served as an example and a great motivator for them. Many of his athletes in football, baseball and track were real stars, but, most importantly, many of these same athletes and their peers graduated from Carlisle and went on to Yale, Princeton, Penn, Harvard and other fine schools. Later, they became successful businessmen, doctors, lawyers and teachers.

Warner's inspiration and incentive held true for many of the young men he later coached at Pittsburgh, Stanford and Temple.

To really understand how great the undertaking and the success of Pop Warner, consider his timing. After World War I, the United States entered a period of great prosperity, increasing leisure time, growing discretionary wealth and expanded mobility. With more time, money and the means to travel more readily, people embraced sports and entertainment for their glamour and glitter. This embrace raised those heroes to a level above any that had preceded them — Babe Ruth, the "Sultan of Swat;" Jack Dempsey, the "Manassa Mauler;" "Big" Bill Tilden; Red Grange, the "Galloping Ghost;" and Bobby Jones. Sports arenas of the day were much larger than ever before. Mega-palaces such as Yankee Stadium and the Los Angeles Memorial Coliseum became the new playgrounds where heroes were born.

The media of the day — newspapers, radio, newsreels on the "talking pictures" and the movies — made these heroes larger than life for most Americans. This manic world and the potential for money and outside influences provided the background against which Warner, Rockne, Stagg, Yost and the other great coaches tried to provide a counterpoint, a stabilizing influence. Sports were suddenly in greater danger of being commercialized or of being bought by gamblers.

These same great coaches were instrumental in keeping athletics intact. They passed along the greatness of the sport we revere today as well as their own unique historical contributions to the game.

Since becoming Executive Director of Pop Warner Little Scholars, Inc. two years ago, I've learned a great deal of new information about Pop Warner — his exploits, innovations and memories. Many old photos and stories have been sent to our office which humanize a name I've always known, but whose history I've not been fully aware of.

Since I was a boy, reading the children's sport books and seeing the old movies, I knew that Warner had coached Jim Thorpe to his great successes in football, baseball and Olympic track and field. One movie that stands out is *Jim Thorpe - All American*, which starred a young actor by the name of Burt Lancaster who was in the early days of what would be a great career. I can't remember the actor who played Pop Warner, but I very much remember the important role he played in shaping Jim Thorpe's success. The coach's dedication, work ethic and motivation provided the background for Jim Thorpe to become an Olympic champion. Thorpe eventually achieved that feat at the 1912 Olympic Games in Stockholm, where he won two gold medals and was crowned by King Gustav V of Sweden as the "greatest athlete in the world."

Such is the making of a hero!

But Jim Thorpe was not Warner's only success story. Nor were his great teams and athletes at Iowa State, Georgia, Cornell, Carlisle, Pittsburgh, Stanford or Temple. His longest-lived success is alive today and it can be seen in his continuing influence in the form of Pop Warner Football and Cheerleading.

This organization was founded in Philadelphia in 1929 as a local youth football league to keep kids busy and out of mischief. Through the Great Depression, the organization struggled. However, during a late winter storm in April 1934, Fate changed their course. A coaching clinic for the children and coaches in the league had been scheduled, but the winter storm forced most of the invited coaches who were to speak at the clinic to cancel at the last minute. One coach, however, braved the elements to make the clinic. His name was Pop Warner, the respected and legendary coach who was now leading Temple University to greatness on the gridiron. His special efforts in traveling through the stormy weather and the hours he spent with the boys that evening impressed the youths and the coaches tremendously.

Pop Warner's enthusiasm and cooperation also helped the fledgling youth league survive and prosper. As a sign of their appreciation and devotion, the boys later adopted his name for their league—"The Pop Warner Football Conference."

Eventually, The Pop Warner Football Conference grew far beyond the boundaries of Philadelphia. The youth league's name would later be changed to "Pop Warner Little Scholars" to reflect its broadened mission with the youth of America. Today, there are Pop Warner teams and leagues now in 35 states and two foreign countries, with approximately 190,000 boys and girls participating each year in Pop Warner Little Scholars' football and cheerleading programs.

Due to Pop Warner's background and influence as a teacher as well as a coach, Pop Warner Little Scholars is unique among youth organizations in requiring scholastic fitness of all participants and in recognizing children individually only for their academic achievements.

I think that all of us involved in this program believe that Pop Warner would be proud of the organization's growth and of his continuing influence on the boys and girls in 1993 and beyond.

We hope that this book, *Pop Warner: Football's Greatest Teacher*, will bring Pop Warner's story to life for the participants and volunteers in Pop Warner Little Scholars to enjoy and learn from.

Today, we know of Pop Warner by his name but very little of the greatness of the man. Fortunately, this new book gives us a chance to get to know him better.

During his coaching days, Glenn S. (Pop) Warner made a tremendous difference in the game of college football and in the lives of many people. Now, nearly 40 years after his death in 1954, Pop Warner continues to have a great influence on thousands of people through his legacy — the youth football program that bears his name.

June 2, 1993   Jon C. Butler, Executive Director
Langhorne, PA   Pop Warner Little Scholars, Inc.

Pop Warner
Football's Greatest Teacher

The Epic Autobiography of
Major College Football's Winningest Coach,
Glenn S. (Pop) Warner

Warner's Date
With Destiny

As the Amtrak *Yankee Clipper* roared down the rails, heading in a southeastern direction to Washington, D.C.'s Union Station, the late afternoon sun was crawling toward the horizon to my right, which would eventually bring a long and eventful St. Patrick's Day 1992 to a close.

This fading glint of illumination, however, provided only a meager amount of reading light as I began to sift through the thick brown file folder of research articles relating to the life and career of legendary football coach Glenn Scobey (Pop) Warner that I had just received from the Temple University Archives, which is now the depository of the old *Philadelphia Evening Bulletin* newspaper morgue.

Earlier in the day, I had traveled these same tracks from Washington to Philadelphia, where I had gone to pick up this extensive packet of articles which were to form the foundation for a book on Warner and would be a part of my continuing series of biographies on great football coaches.

My preliminary research had reflected that only a modest amount of resource materials were available on Warner and, to date, no formal biography had been written on him.

Warner, himself, had written two coaching books — *Football for Coaches and Players*, in 1927, and *Pop Warner's Book for Boys*, in 1934 — and had participated in a 45-part autobiographical series that had been ghost-written and distributed to newspapers all across the country by the Christy Walsh Syndicate during December 1927 and on through January 1928, when Warner's Stanford team was making its third Rose Bowl appearance in four seasons and he was at his zenith in popularity.

Two decades later, Francis Powers, a noted writer of the 1930's and 1940's on that once-formidable *New York Sun* sports staff, would pen an 84-page, paperback mini-book which highlighted Warner's football career and was used as an insert in the 1947 pre-season edition of *The Sporting News*.

And in the years that followed, four of America's foremost sports journalists — Allison Danzig and Red Smith of *The New York Times*, Edwin Pope of *The Miami Herald* and Tim Cohane of *Look* — would each write brief biographical chapters on Warner in books that they authored.

These, however, have been the only major literary efforts that have chronicled some portion or other of Warner's brilliant and highly-successful career.

And for someone who had been one of college football's most well-known and respected figures during its early days, I considered this to be somewhat strange.

While the *Yankee Clipper* proceeded on its journey from Wilmington to Newark, Del., and from there to Aberdeen, Md., crossing through both the meadows and hills of the countryside and the inner and outer limits of suburbia, I became more and more absorbed in the research file folder that lay open in front of me.

Page after page as I read through these photocopied newspaper stories and sentimental memories of long ago, the fascinating details of Warner's career in football began to come alive. It was if a rare picture into the past was suddenly being opened and I was being allowed to follow Warner through that historically-rich period of the early, growing years of college football, when it was a brutal clash of humanity, and onwards as it began to be transformed into a game of skill and entertaining showmanship.

From these newspaper articles, I was also able to learn many important facts about Warner.

First, he had been born on a farm located just a few miles outside of Springville, N.Y., on April 5, 1871, and was the first-born son of William H. and Adaline Scobey Warner. This would have been just two years after the first college football game between Princeton and

Rutgers in 1869.

When Warner was 10, his family moved into town and there he first learned a crude form of the game of football which was usually played with a blown-up cow's bladder. And though he was somewhat intrigued with this hybrid game that resembled both rugby and soccer, Warner would spend much of his teenage years on the baseball fields in and around Springville. There, the large-framed right-hander earned a reputation for having a terrific fastball and being able to pound the longball deep into right-center field.

Warner would eventually move with his parents and brother to Texas after having finished high school. Yet three years later, he would be enrolled at the Cornell University School of Law.

This event, of course, was the first of several occasions in which Fate had stepped in at an unlikely time and directed Warner onto a new pathway that would greatly affect his life. And in most cases, these interruptions were caused by having lost a wager.

While traveling by train to begin his freshman fall term at Cornell, he was recruited to try out for the school's football team. And with only a meager cast of talent to compete against, the oversized Warner was quickly installed as the varsity's starting right guard on the first day of practice. By his third and final season, he would become the team's captain and pick up a law degree.

Cornell, however, was only an East Coast middleweight when compared to the heavyweight stalwarts of Harvard, Yale, Princeton and Penn, who dominated all others in the skills of playing this rough and grind 'em out, but popularly growing game.

Following his final season at Cornell, Warner tried to make a living while practicing law. But his client list was quite small.

A few months later, when Iowa State — a small school in the Midwest — wrote to him offering a temporary job and a salary of $150 to coach their team for 30 days at the beginning of the 1895 season, a somewhat bored Warner must have taken a brief look at his modest bank checkbook balance and clearly realized that coaching might be a good way to temporarily supplement his income while attempting to build a law practice.

But the rather ambitious Warner, who had worked his way through college while selling boardinghouse meal plans and artwork that he had painted, wasn't content with the possibility of having just one coaching job for the fall of 1895. Instead, he continued to look around at what other coaching opportunities might also be available. Eventually, he would find one at the University of Georgia in which the friendly Southerners would allow him to take the Iowa State pre-season prepping position and then travel to Athens and coach their team for the 1895 regular season.

Although overlooked by many at that time and largely forgotten by historians since then, this unorthodox, dual-coaching arrangement would become of great significance nearly 100 years later.

When Warner got off the train in Ames, Ia., in mid-August 1895, he would find a rag-tag football team who had never before had a formal coach and in their brief history of just three seasons had primarily played such in-state lightweights as Grinnell, Cornell (Ia.), the Des Moines Y.M.C.A. and the Fort Dodge military team. The only formidable opponent on their schedule during this time had been the state's primary academic institution and athletic powerhouse, the University of Iowa.

Warner, however, wasn't worried about such things. He immediately rolled up his sleeves and went to work. And in a brief period of four weeks, he taught the Iowa farmboys the many fundamentals and techniques that he had earlier learned at his alma mater, Cornell.

Then something amazing happened. In such a brief passage of time, the Iowa State team was transformed into a respectable, hard-hitting squad.

In mid-September, when his tenure at the Ames campus had almost wound down to an end, an optimistic Warner and his Iowa State team climbed aboard a train bound for Butte, Mont., where they would take on the Butte Athletic Club, a local all-star football squad, in a season-opening contest.

Butte, of course, was not one of those sporting locales that would remind Warner of those idyllic autumn scenes in the East. It was your typical wild west town which came equipped with saloons, barroom dance girls and fast-living cowboys. Here, the football team's cheerleaders didn't use pom-poms. Instead, they wore six-shooters and frequently fired them into the open air when celebrating a big play that had been made by their team.

On the morning of the game, Warner was given the opportunity to watch his competition practice. And from what he was able to see, Warner didn't give the Butte team much of a chance against his much-improved Iowa State squad. So when challenged before kickoff to place a wager on the game's outcome, Warner opted to back this belief by betting $150 that Iowa State would end up the winner in the contest. (Editor's Note: This amount, of course, was his entire salary which had been earned during his 30-day stint there at Iowa State.)

Unfortunately, there were several factors which Warner did not know would be working against him during the game. These were a sandy playing field, a pair of local referees who favored the home team and a highly-excitable game crowd whose continued gunfire was enough to frighten most anyone.

The game was to become a fierce battle. And when it became apparent that he might need to insure his bet a little more, Warner eventually donned a uniform and joined in playing for the Iowa State team.

Finally after three quarters, in which the Butte A.C. was leading, 13-10, an Iowa State squad that had been bullied and thoroughly embarrassed all afternoon proceeded to walk off the field, thus forfeiting the contest.

A few days later following their return to Ames, Warner handed the coaching reins over to a recent Iowa State grad, Bert German, who would oversee the team while Warner traveled to Georgia and began his new coaching duties.

That season, Iowa State would go on to post a dramatic 36-0 upset over Northwestern in a game which was played on the Evansville, Ill., campus and later defeated their powerful cross-state rival, Iowa, 24-0, and earned a record of 3 wins and 3 losses overall.

Warner's Georgia teams in 1895 and 1896 would go on to post an impressive 7-4-0 record. From there, he would build great football teams at his alma mater, Cornell, the Carlisle Indian School, Pitt, Stanford and Temple and he would amass one of the greatest coaching careers in the history of college football. (Editor's Note: Going into the 1993 college football season, N.C.A.A. records ranked Warner in the number-three spot on the all-time win list of major college football coaches with a total of 313 wins, 106 losses and 32 ties.)

But this is only what the history books have recorded.

As my train began to slow down and I looked up to notice the lights of Baltimore in the distance, I realized now that something just wasn't quite right about Warner's career coaching story, especially in regards to his ties with Iowa State. And with this realization, there were two even larger questions looming. What other mysteries about Warner's memorable coaching career were waiting to be uncovered? Also — and perhaps more importantly — why did I have this feeling down deep in my gut that there was something special about Warner?

I had first learned of Pop Warner when I was a freshman at the University of Alabama while working as one of two dozen student managers who assisted Coach Paul (Bear) Bryant's powerhouse Crimson Tide football team in the mid-1970's.

There among the many championship trophies and plaques in Paul W. Bryant Hall, the plush athletic dorm that the Alabama football players live in, is a plaque displayed in a glass trophy case which I will always remember. It is the one that Coach Bryant had received in the 1960's for having written a Pop Warner Huddle Prayer. This plaque had been presented to him by the Pop Warner Football League, the youth football organization that Warner had supported during its early, fledgling years of the 1930's and, consequently, was named after him.

During those salad days of the mid- and late-1970's when I was a college student, Bryant's Alabama teams were an awesome gridiron machine which masterfully employed the wishbone offense to such perfection that no college team at the time could match their prowess. In all during that wondrous decade, the Crimson Tide would win a total of three national championships, finished second on three other occasions and usually finished in the top 5 during the remaining four seasons.

By 1981, while at the age of 68, a much fatigued and battle-weary Bryant, who had endured and overcome many health problems, had finally garnered enough victories to move past both Warner (with 313 wins) and Amos Alonzo Stagg (with 314 wins) on the N.C.A.A.'s all-time win list and become the winningest coach in major college football history. It was a feat that the hard-driving Bryant had almost willed himself to achieve.

However, a season later, in 1982, Bryant would finally run into a nemesis that he could not conquer — old age. Fearing that he might be losing his firm grip on the great dynasty that he had built in 25 seasons while at the helm of the Crimson Tide football team and not wanting to tarnish such a glorious era, Bryant decided to retire from coaching. One of his former players, Ray Perkins, who had gone on to be a popular pro football player and coach, was then picked to take the reins that Bryant had so skillfully handled for such a long time.

Yet in late January 1983, only five weeks after Bryant had coached his last game — and 323rd victory — in the 1982 Liberty Bowl, he was stricken with a heart attack and died a day later.

Suddenly, the world of college football was without one of its greatest coaches. His funeral was to attract a gathering of sports and political celebrities that had not been seen for a long, long time. Bryant's lengthy funeral procession would draw nearly a million people who watched from the roadside as the cortege passed by. A television viewing audience of several million would also join in on this very sad and difficult day. Together, they watched in silence and wept as Bryant went on to his final resting place.

For me, it was one of the longest days that I would ever know. I had lost one of my biggest heroes.

As the *Yankee Clipper* began to put Baltimore behind us, I glared out into the darkness that lay beyond the window next to me.

Occasionally, there were lights from a few houses or a business that might interrupt my thoughts. But mostly, I thought about Pop Warner and the long and, perhaps, winding journey that might be in front of me if I was going to search for the answers to the questions about Warner's record and his real life story. Would this be an elusive effort that would never pan out? Would the passage of time have already destroyed much of the records of long ago? And, just as importantly, perhaps this path had already been properly researched before and I would be only turning over old stones?

Still, something kept tugging at me?

Within a half hour I would finally be arriving at Union Station.

Early the next morning I planned to go over to the Library of Congress' James Madison Building and begin my journey to find out more about Warner.

Little did I realize what an emotional roller coaster this research effort would create.

In time, I would eventually find out why Warner was not given as much coverage by the newspaper writers of his era. His sometimes gruff and to-the-point attitude, which when combined with a frequent winning record, often did not present the kind of aura that sportswriters warmed up to during those years.

Instead, it was two of Warner's colleagues who basked in the limelight. Stagg's gentlemanly statesmanship and Knute Rockne's great wit and enthusiastic flair frequently attracted a larger press following and usually made for better newspaper copy.

As a result, later-day historians have long pointed to both Stagg and Rockne as the voice of this wildly-growing and exciting period.

Yet in my research there was much about Warner that I would eventually uncover and it presented an impressive image.

Warner was a great tinkerer whose creative contributions to football helped bring about a much more safer and enjoyable game. His efforts probably did more to shape the game of football than anyone else. And in today's modern era, these contributions are very much a part of the game that we now enjoy on autumn weekends.

Warner was the first coach to have taught the spiral punt and one of the first to have advocated the use of the spiral pass; he introduced the numbering of plays and the weaving of numbers on jerseys; his Carlisle teams wore one of football's first headgear types; he also introduced the huddle, the three-point crouch stance, the direct center snap to the ballcarrier, the bootleg play, the reverse, the screen pass, the mousetrap play, the rolling body block and the infamous "hidden ball" play.

A large degree of Warner's success was that his quick-thinking and imaginative mind always seemed to be one step ahead of the game's rule makers.

When once asked to describe Warner's keen ability to exploit a loophole in the rules and use it to his advantage, his long-time friend and rival, Amos Alonzo Stagg, once noted: "Glenn was never very active on the Rules Committee. But we'd make a rule and Glenn would think up a way to get around it within the rules and then we'd have to meet the challenge. He kept us on our toes, I can tell you."

Warner's genius also unleashed the powerfully explosive single-wing formation offense against Army in 1912 and almost overnight the game of college football would never again be the same. His installation of a wingback, an unbalanced line and an unbalanced backfield quickly became the vogue of the entire country. He would later unhatch the double-wing formation which was a highly-successful passing attack.

Together these two wide-open offenses, which emphasized maneuvering and deception to mask the direction of the offensive attack, greatly revolutionized the game of football. And in the years ahead, only Rockne's Notre Dame "shifting box" would rival Warner's in being used by other coaches around the country.

Warner's tremendous influence would also affect several less noticeable but just as important areas. His first use of solid-fiber thigh pads and other protective padding and a lightweight uniform designed for speed — as opposed to the clumsy and much heavier version that was used in the early 1900's — are now the standard for use in today's game. He also invented the free-standing tackling dummy and even developed an entire dummy team to run signals against during practice.

Throughout the summer and fall of 1992 and on through the winter and spring of 1993, as I completed my research on Warner and began the actual editing of his autobiography, I began to run into several inaccuracies and some rather interesting discoveries regarding Warner's career coaching record.

The first real tip-off that his record might be incorrect was found on that St. Patrick's Day evening, while traveling on the train from Philadelphia to Washington, as I read through the 45-part autobiographical series that had been syndicated to newspapers all across the country in the late 1920's by Christy Walsh, the widely-respected sports agent of that era, who also represented Babe Ruth, Ty Cobb, Walter Johnson, Knute Rockne and several other sports heroes. This series had two installments that were devoted to Warner's tenure at

Iowa State and had specifically noted that Warner had coached there during his first three years as a college coach.

Later, when I reviewed the N.C.A.A.'s historical records of Warner's coaching career, there was no mention of Warner having ever coached at Iowa State.

A bit perplexed, I then turned to the best possible source for this answer — Iowa State. After receiving a copy of the Cyclones' 1992 football guide, I quickly noticed that they had listed Warner as their coach of record for the 1895-1898 seasons. His record during this tenure was 18 wins and 7 losses.

Knowing that Warner was also supposed to have been coaching at Georgia during the 1895 and 1896 seasons and at Cornell during the 1897 and 1898 seasons, I realized that something didn't quite add up here. But in time, this confusion would eventually lead to an answer that would properly explain this matter.

As I followed Warner to his next coaching stop at Carlisle, I also ran into several inconsistencies with Warner's record there and the season records for the Indian School that had been published by the N.C.A.A.

In an attempt to resolve these inconsistencies I turned to three previous books that had chronicled some portion or other of the Carlisle football story. John Steckbeck's *Fabulous Redmen*, the excellent and thorough account of the Indian School's entire football program from 1893 to 1917, helped paint a more defined record of Warner's tenure there. Jack Newcombe's classic, *The Best of the Athletic Boys*, which is the best biography to date of Jim Thorpe, and Brad Steiger's and Charlotte Thorpe's *Thorpe's Gold* would greatly clarify and answer a lot of my questions concerning the years from 1907 to 1912 when Warner had coached Thorpe.

Subsequent inquiries into Warner's tenure at Pitt, Stanford and Temple would also reveal many new discoveries. Yet with each new discovery that I made in regards to Warner's record, there were also many more new questions.

At each of the schools where Warner had coached, I found their records from this era to have been in different degrees of accuracy. Only at Cornell were the records perfectly complete. At the other schools, I would often find no prior history of their game dates and in some occasions their game sites and game scores were incorrect.

In a couple of occasions, I found their entire roster of games to have been out of order. And in a few places, I was able to find some games that had been forgotten or overlooked entirely.

As this effort continued, I became keenly aware of the fact that Warner's overall career coaching record was going to significantly change. The biggest question that I kept asking myself was "by how much?"

In order to get an accurate picture of Warner's record, I began an exhaustive undertaking in an attempt to verify Warner's record. This meant getting newspaper game stories of each game that he had coached. Much of the work I did myself, while using *The New York Times* as a primary reference.

However, in many cases I had to hire researchers from many different parts of the country to pull copies of game stories from certain newspapers. At times, it seemed to be a maddening process to keep up with. But after a large number of telephone calls and a steady perseverance, the pieces of Warner's *real* overall record came together.

And the new numbers for his career coaching record were rather shocking. Warner's new career total was 341 wins, 118 losses and 33 ties.

This amount greatly exceeded his previously-believed record of 313 wins, 106 losses and 32 ties. More importantly, it also pushed him past the career coaching records of both Paul (Bear) Bryant and Amos Alonzo Stagg, who had 323 wins and 314 wins respectively, and had previously occupied the number one and two spots on the N.C.A.A.'s all-time win list for major college football coaches.

How does one explain this discrepancy?

Perhaps the answer to this dilemma is easier to understand when you step back and see how today's college and coaches' records were earlier compiled. Many years ago, the N.C.A.A.'s records were a real hodgepodge of a mess until Steve Boda, their long-time historian and record-keeper attempted to pull them together in a standard format that was consistent. This Herculean effort was done nearly 25 years ago and greatly stabilized the presentation of information for college football records.

While writing his own book, *Encyclopedia of Football*, which was co-authored by Harold Claassen, Boda even made mention of the fact that Warner had made a brief pre-season appearance at Iowa State in 1895, but did not credit him with being the actual coach there during the regular season.

Little did Boda realize that after Warner's Iowa State team had actually lost the 1895 season-opener to the Butte Athletic Club — the one he had wagered away his entire paycheck of $150 on the game's outcome — he had agreed to continue coaching the Iowa State squad even while he was overseeing the Georgia team that season.

In ordinary times this may sound like a strange and hard-to-believe arrangement. But Warner was a young man who had high hopes of one day becoming a great lawyer and, for him, football coaching was to only be an interim task so that he could continue to pay the bills while awaiting for his law practice to flourish.

However, by having lost the bet on the Iowa State-Butte A.C. game, this twist of Fate actually put Warner into an eventual collision course with destiny and the record books. With only a meager bank account, Warner was, in essence, forced to take the second job of continuing to coach Iowa State from afar during the 1895 season. This was accomplished by reviewing weekly accounts of the team's progress which were sent to him by his assistant, Bert German, and other Iowa State athletic officials. Warner then responded with letters and an occasional telegram.

As it turned out, Iowa State finished the season with a record of 3 wins and 3 losses. Two of these wins were over Northwestern and the University of Iowa, who were both much more powerful teams.

For Iowa State and Warner, this arrangement — although an odd one — proved to be good for both parties. Warner had continued to get an additional paycheck during the season and Iowa State's alums felt that they were beginning to grow in athletic prominence in the Midwest.

This relationship was again renewed in 1896 and continued each year through the 1899 season. As always, Warner would travel to Ames and prepare the team in the pre-season and usually coach the Iowa State squad in their opening game. He would then travel to Georgia or Cornell or Carlisle. During the season, he would continue his long-distance coaching.

It was only after Warner had gone to Carlisle in 1899, and after a successful season there had been offered the permanent position as the school's director of athletics and football coach — along with a much larger paycheck — was this dual-coaching arrangement to finally end.

Warner would later in his career pull off a similar stunt which was just as crazy when he signed with Stanford after the 1921 season, while he was still the coach at Pitt. This event caused quite an uproar at Pitt and would forever haunt him.

However, after having signed the contract with Stanford, Pitt officials decided to not let Warner out of his contract there. So in a clever move, Warner responded by sending two of his assistants, Andy Kerr and Claude (Tiny) Thornhill, out to Stanford to coach the Cardinal team until he would arrive there in 1924. Kerr was to become the coach of record for Stanford during the 1922 and 1923 seasons but Warner kept the telephone and telegram wires between Pittsburgh and Palo Alto, Calif., humming. Warner also traveled westward to oversee the Stanford spring practice drills in 1922 and 1923 and even brought his Pitt squad out there to play in the 1922 season. The Panthers would proceed to win this contest, 16-7.

Finally, by the time Warner arrived at Stanford in 1924, the Cardinal football program was set. They would go on to enjoy to a 7-0-1 record and a Rose Bowl date with Notre Dame that season.

In looking back, I must admit that Warner's methods were definitely unorthodox but highly effective. And in the wild and unruly times of college football's growing years, these antics were more of the norm than the exception.

As this book goes to print, I am saddened a bit to see Warner replace Bryant as the winningest coach in major college football because I had seen firsthand Bryant's struggle to obtain this lofty personal mark.

Yet, if both were still alive today, Bryant would have been the first person to pick up a telephone and place a call to congratulate Warner on achieving this new record. He was that much of a classy winner.

Mike Bynum
July 30, 1993

The
Autobiography

1

Having been born and raised in Western New York, I moved to town with my family when I was ten years old. The town was Springville, N.Y., and it could only boast of a population of 2,500. Yet to a country boy like myself, it seemed like New York City.

And I was probably the greenest and most bashful youngster that ever moved in from the country.

During my youth, I was rather big for my age. Both tall and fat. Because of this fact, the town kids of Springville nicknamed me "Butter." This moniker would follow me from the first week that I arrived in town until I later graduated from high school.

As you can probably imagine, being timid, awkward, overgrown and fat, I was a frequent target of the many childhood pranks being practiced by the other kids in town.

One of the mischievous pranks that the town kids liked to employ involved the use of the slingshot, which was in its heyday of popularity. And my broad dimensions offered a tempting target for both bean-shooters in the summer and snowballs in the winter. I was the recipient of many perfect "slingshot bombs" before I finally got mad and had the spunk to "get even" with my attackers.

This memorable day occurred when I was heading home after school. En route, I was confronted by a town bully who snatched off my hat, threw it in a mud puddle and then stomped on it.

Quickly, my temper got the best of me and I proceeded to give him a good licking, while the other town kids looked on. This battle showed me a new way of looking at life. And after winning a few more of these youthful scraps, I was soon held in respect by my schoolmates.

While living in Springville, I attended Griffith Institute, which was a combined elementary and high school. There were no athletic teams of any kind at Griffith in those days. Nor was there a physical education director or a gymnasium.

During our recess period and after school, we played a crude form of football and a game which was similar to baseball.

The Griffith schoolyard, where we played these games, was a large grassy field located in front of the school. It ran from one street to another. With the distance between these two streets being approximately the length of a football field, the streets became the goal lines in our makeshift football games and the walkway leading up to the school building, which crossed at the mid-point of the schoolyard, was the kickoff line. We used anything that we could for a football. Most of the time we ended up playing with a blown-up cow's bladder. The style of football that we attempted to play was very similar to soccer. Until I later enrolled at Cornell, this is the only exposure to football that I ever had.

In late spring of 1889, I completed my high school requirements and graduated from Griffith Institute.

A few weeks following graduation, one of my teachers asked me to take an exam for appointment to the U.S. Military Academy at West Point, N.Y. Initially, I balked at the idea and told the teacher that I had no interest in attending college. However, after a bit of persuasion, I finally softened my stance and agreed to take the entrance exam.

Forty applicants from my area showed up to take the exam when it was given. Later, four of these young men were chosen to receive a West Point appointment. Needless to say, I was not one of the lucky four who had been picked.

In early fall, I joined my family when they moved to Wichita Falls, Tex., which is located northwest of Ft. Worth and near the Texas-Oklahoma border.

There was no prospecting for oil in Texas at the time. This frenzied fever wouldn't arrive for another 10 years when the gushers at Spindletop came in. In the late 1880's and early 1890's, the large, expansive Texas landscape was primarily frontier cattle country, with only small pockets of the state beginning to be transformed into grain and cotton-growing areas.

On the first full day after our arrival in Wichita Falls, I joined both my father and brother in riding horseback across the pastures and streams near our ranch. In all, this expedition lasted nearly 10 hours and the sights I saw that day were both intensely wild and beautiful.

My father grew wheat and raised cattle on his ranch. During that first year, both my brother, Bill, and I worked with him clearing the land, herding cattle and planting.

The next summer, a local tinsmith, who knew of my interest in both drawing and art, asked me to become his assistant. I had been to his shop several times and watched him fashion tin into lots of unique shapes and designs. After learning that the pay was pretty good, too, I decided to accept his challenge.

Over the next two years, I became a full-fledged tinner and was placed in charge of running the tin shop in town. This additional responsibility also brought an increase in wages to $15 a week, which was considered pretty good money in those days.

Those three years that I lived in Wichita Falls were perhaps the happiest of my life because I loved to hunt, camp and rough it in the open country.

2

While growing up as a youngster, baseball was my favorite sport.

I was a member of a junior baseball team in my hometown of Springville, N.Y., and the trousers of my baseball suit were made by my mother from a pair of old overalls. As I grew older, I became a pretty fair catcher and an even better pitcher. Eventually, I was asked to become a member of the regular Springville team.

After moving to Texas, I was asked to pitch for a local team who was quite good. That first season, we played — and lost to — Waxahatchie in the State amateur championships.

In the summer of 1892, I returned to New York for a summer vacation. While there, I played for the Springville team in a game against John McGraw, who was just starting upon his career as a professional baseball player. McGraw would later become one of pro baseball's greatest players and afterwards the manager of the New York Giants baseball team.

Springville was scheduled to play a late summer, five-game series with Gowanda, a neighboring town and much-hated rival. It was one of those series which started out with each team having all home-grown talent in the first game. By the second game of the series, each team had imported some additional strength to beef up their rosters. Then toward the end of the series, both squads were fielding teams that consisted almost entirely of professional players, or "ringers."

By some stroke of luck, I was able to keep my spot on the Springville team and not displaced by any of the hired players. That is how I happened to find myself on the same field with McGraw, who had been imported from a minor-league team in Western Pennsylvania to play shortstop for Gowanda in the deciding game of the *amateur* series. As it turned out, Gowanda had better imported talent than we did and ended up winning the series, 3-2.

Following the baseball series, I opted to travel to Buffalo, which was the nearest big city — some 30 miles away. Buffalo was a great place to visit during my vacation. With the Grand Circuit harness races in town, I decided to use some of the money which I had saved from my work as a tinsmith, back in Texas, and test my luck at the harness track. My plan was to bet small amounts on each race that I wagered. This strategy proved quite successful and after a week I had cleared a net profit of $50.

Unfortunately, my early success also gave me a false sense of security because I quickly jumped to the conclusion that I must be an excellent judge of horseflesh. And with nothing else planned during my remaining vacation, I quickly decided to follow the Grand Circuit harness races until the end of the summer. At the rate of my early success, I figured that I would be able to have both a good time and clean up on profits of $50 to $100 a week.

However, my vision of frolicking and sure-fire plan for financial success were to soon meet up with reality.

The next week, I followed the Grand Circuit races on to Rochester, N.Y. And, to cut a long story short, I wound up losing all my recent "profits" and the extra money that I had with me, except for a small amount to pay for my return train fare back to Texas. Thus, my budding and brief career as a race-track gambler came to an end before I ever really got started.

But this wasn't the first setback that I had ever encountered while trying the fast-paced life of betting on horses.

My other experience occurred nearly two years earlier in Texas. At the time, I had a cow pony which I thought could outrun a mustang that belonged to a friend of mine. I wound up losing the first $20 that I had ever earned as a tinner by backing this belief. Following the race, I realized that it was not my horse's fault that I had lost the bet, but, instead, it was probably due to the extra load he had to carry. In this race, I had been my own jockey and I weighed about 200 pounds. My opponent had weighed only 140.

Having lost all of my gambling profits and remaining vacation money at the Rochester harness track, and with only enough funds to get back to my job in Texas, I soon became depressed and was forced to do some serious thinking. While returning to Springville by train, I began to review my options, which were limited. I dared not write to my father and tell him that I was broke because I would have had to explain what had happened to the money he knew I had when I left home to begin my trip. There was, of course, no compelling reason that I could use to explain my decision to remain in Springville for awhile longer. However, by the time that my train reached Springville, I had figured out a plan that perhaps could help me resolve my predicament.

Knowing that my father wanted me to study law, I sent him a catalog of the Cornell University Law School, along with a letter explaining that I had decided to pursue a career in law. I noted in my letter that I thought the best way to achieve this task was to go to law school rather than to study under a practicing law office, which was also a popular route at the time. I explained in my letter that the expenses to begin law school — tuition, books, etc. — were somewhat more than I could raise. Being a good son, I wasted no time in asking him for some help.

A few weeks later, my father wrote back and expressed that he was glad that I had decided to study law. In his letter, he also enclosed a check for $100. This initial amount allowed me to enroll at the Cornell University Law School soon thereafter. More importantly, it allowed me to escape the embarrassment of having to admit to my parents the fact that I had lost my vacation money while gambling on harness races.

Now while looking back, I must admit that it is rather odd how Fate sometimes works. Following my graduation from Griffith Institute, I had no thoughts of going on to college. Then later on, I made a sudden decision to enter Cornell because of the failed result of a horse race.

At the time, I considered this event to be a great misfortune. But, instead, it turned out to be about the luckiest thing that ever happened to me.

3

On the train from Buffalo to Ithaca in September 1892, prior to the beginning of the fall term at Cornell, I was fortunate to meet Carl Johanson, the captain and coach of the Cornell football team. Johanson had played football at Williams College for several seasons before arriving at Cornell for the 1891 season.

Football in those days was a comparatively new game. Having been originated in the East in the 1860's, colleges in that section of the country were the first to become familiar with the game. Yale, Harvard and Princeton — who were often referred to as the "Big Three" — were the supreme football powers and practically all of the college football coaches in the country came from those three schools.

Seldom did any of the so-called minor schools in the East ever score upon the Big Three. Whenever one of the smaller fry did manage to cross the goal line belonging to one of their more powerful brethren, this was considered a wonderful feat.

And though Williams College was not in the same class with Princeton, Yale or Harvard, it was also among the first colleges to have taken up football in the East. With this kind of football background, Johanson was just the man that Cornell had needed to continue building their fledgling program which had begun only a few years earlier, in 1887.

At this time, Cornell's football manager (now referred to as the team's business manager or athletic director) was Burt Hanson, who had earlier played football at Yale under Walter Camp. Hanson also played center on the Cornell team and served as an assistant coach to Johanson.

A boyhood friend of mine, who was also traveling on the train to attend Cornell, was the person who actually had introduced me to Johanson. And since I was of good size and looked like football material, Johanson inquired if I had any football experience. When he learned that I had never seen a football except the one which had been made from a cow's bladder, he then asked if I had played any other sports. After I told him of my background in baseball, he told me to report to football practice that afternoon and he would make sure that I was issued a uniform. At this point of my young life I had never seen a real game of football played before, much less ever had a thought of trying to play in one.

Later that afternoon, I went over to the Cornell football stadium, which was a modest structure called Percy Field. There I received my uniform and pads. At the beginning of practice, Coach Johanson took one look at me and put me at the guard position on the varsity squad. He gave me some simple instructions: "Keep anyone from getting through my position when our team had the ball, and to get through and tackle the runner when the other side had the ball."

I remember that in our first scrimmage the varsity was forced to punt because I had botched up an important play.

The punt was a high one which went downfield, deep into the scrub team's territory. The scrub safety, who had been set to receive the punt, instead, let it hit the ground. Which it did. The ball then bounced high in the air and I jumped and batted it across the scrub team's goal line.

In doing this, I broke two pivotal rules: 1) I was not supposed to touch the ball during this play, and 2) it was illegal to bat the ball forward.

The scrub team demanded — and got — a penalty on the play which advanced their cause. I felt horrible for making these mistakes but one of the team's seniors just laughed at the matter. Afterwards, he pulled me aside and explained how the rules applied during a punt.

Although my attempt on the punt was illegal, it showed Coach Johanson that I was both eager and determined to get the ball over the opponent's goal line — and it made a hit with him.

Following a long preliminary drill of tackling, falling on the ball and a strenuous scrimmage on this first day of practice, the squad was ordered to begin their daily run around the track. Moments before the running drill began, Coach Johanson called me aside and told me that I wouldn't have to do this since it was my first day of practice. However, *because* it was my first day of practice, I thought it would make a greater impression on the coach if I did all of the work — just like all of the other players. So I followed the team around the track, while thinking that it would only be for one lap and I knew that I could make that.

After the leaders passed the Percy Field gates following the first lap, I didn't know whether I could last for another lap or not; but I hung on. Following the second lap, I nearly collapsed when I saw the leaders again lead the squad past the gates for another lap. This almost wiped me out. But I kept up the pace with the others on the team. As it turned out, I not only completed that lap, but also completed a fourth lap to make it a 1-mile run.

The next day, which was registration day for those who were entering the new school term, Cornell was scheduled to play their opening game of the 1892 football season. Our opponent for this game was the Syracuse Athletic Club. And with only one day of practice on the varsity under my belt, I was put at left guard and played that position the entire game.

In the late September heat, Cornell won, 16-0. A week later — and with more experience under our belt — we put on a more powerful offensive display, and walloped Syracuse, 58-0, who was a new contender on the Eastern football scene.

Little did I realize that this was just the beginning of my lifelong association with the gridiron game.

4

During the fall of 1892, which was my first football season at Cornell, we played eleven games and won ten. Our only setback was a 20-14 defeat by Harvard. This game was played at Springfield, Mass., and was lost primarily due to the phenomenal punting skills of Harvard's fullback, John Corbett.

Midweek games were quite common early in the season, which accounts for the large number of games on Cornell's schedule. Charles Courtney, who was Cornell's famous crew (rowing) coach, acted as a trainer for the football team. Consequently, many of Cornell's best football players in the 1890's were also members of Courtney's championship crews.

Courtney was an extraordinary conditioner of athletes and was of great assistance to the coaches in the early days of football at Cornell. The football players were obligated to maintain strict diets which were prescribed by Courtney for the training table. We weren't even allowed to have an apple on our Sunday afternoon hikes, on which he accompanied us. And if we were not at breakfast promptly at 7 a.m., we had to have a very good excuse.

Eating a piece of pie or drink an ice cream soda meant being dropped from the team. On one occasion, when his crew was training at Poughkeepsie, N.Y., several days before the intercollegiate crew races, Courtney found out that his entire varsity crew had eaten strawberry shortcake. He then suspended the whole crew right on the spot and put his second varsity crew in the race. With an excellent display of both courage and skill, they won the intercollegiate title. That crew is still famous in Cornell rowing history and has since been known as the "Shortcake Crew."

The Cornell football squad did not lack for material in those days because Courtney developed some husky athletes and he encouraged his oarsmen to play football in the fall. A few years later, Cornell hired a track coach who was also to take on Courtney's assignment as trainer for the football team. In response, Courtney initiated fall crew practices. From that point on, only a few crew members came out for football.

Although I originally had no thoughts of playing football when I entered Cornell, there was nothing modest about my baseball ambitions. I had considerable experience in this sport and had made what I thought was quite a reputation as a small-town pitcher. Neighboring teams had often had sought my services and, like most young amateur ballplayers, I had visions of someday being a big-league baseball star.

There were the days of Cap Anson, Willie Keeler and Ed Delahanty, and I followed their exploits like baseball fans of the 1920's followed Babe Ruth or Ty Cobb.

The captain and coach of the Cornell baseball team in the spring of 1893 was Harry Taylor. He had played on the Cornell team a few years earlier and following graduation had enjoyed a successful career as a professional player on the Louisville and Baltimore major league baseball clubs. After giving up pro baseball, Taylor returned to Cornell to study law.

There were no eligibility rules in those days and Taylor was unanimously elected captain of the baseball team. He later became a long-time judge on the New York State Supreme Court.

During the winter prior to the beginning of the 1893 baseball season, a notice was put up on the campus bulletin boards which stated that all candidates for the Cornell baseball team were to report for indoor practice. I was among the first to arrive there.

On that initial day of practice, Coach Taylor had me throwing to him. I was anxious to show him both my curveball and fastball. And, although cautioned against too much exercise at such an early point prior to the season, I was careless.

"I'll show this bird something," I remember saying as I let loose a roundhouse curve. The ball caught Coach Taylor on the fingertip of his glove and he dropped it. This flashy display of skill, spurred me to try more foolishness, more speed and, of course, more curveballs. The next day, when I started to throw to him again, my arm felt so bad that I could hardly throw the ball.

Instead of taking it easy or quit throwing when I saw I wasn't getting any speed, I tried to throw the ball even harder. Right there, I ruined my arm and any chances of making the Cornell baseball team. My pitching arm was never any good after that. Following college, I did briefly try to pitch again while using a special harness device that I had invented, but I didn't have much success.

Prior to enrolling at Cornell, I had some previous experience with boxing. And in my freshman year there, I was encouraged to enter the school's winter boxing and wrestling tournament. My knowledge of the rules of formal boxing were somewhat limited and I had not trained for this tournament. But I was bigger and stronger than my opponent and won the heavyweight boxing championship. By sheer strength and awkwardness I defeated the man who had held the tournament's title for the past two years.

The next winter the faculty employed a professional referee and cautioned him against all swinging and slugging, since the previous year's meet had resulted in some bloody noses and a couple of knockouts.

When I started my "rushing at the opponent" tactics, the referee stepped in and shoved us apart. We were required, instead, to stand up and in a tight circle throw our punches at each other. The result was that I lost to a much lighter and clever boxer. Soon thereafter, I retired from boxing.

During the spring of my freshman year in 1893, I also tried out for the Cornell track team. I won a varsity monogram for competing in the field events that season. I put the shot nearly 35 feet and threw the hammer 84 feet. But don't laugh at that last stat. The hammer in those days had a wooden handle and a participant was not allowed to perform a full turn while throwing it. The record in those two events at Cornell in 1894 was 35 feet, 3 inches in the shot-put and 86 feet, 3 inches in the hammer throw.

By using these comparisons, my efforts were pretty good.

5

The football season of 1893, which was my second year at Cornell, was one of the most disastrous in Cornell's gridiron history. George Witherbee, who had been an outstanding halfback and an oarsman on the crew team at Cornell, had been elected in the spring as the new captain of the football team for the 1893 season. Unfortunately, during the summer prior to his return to Cornell, he drowned. Witherbee was so well-liked by the students, faculty and alumni at Cornell that the athletic fieldhouse at Percy Field was later christened The Witherbee Memorial Club House.

In addition to the loss of our team captain, the other regular halfback in our offense decided to leave Cornell and transferred to the University of Pennsylvania. This was Winchester Osgood, who was one of the most elusive ballcarriers that I have ever seen play.

Osgood's athletic career is one that took an interesting path. He had arrived at Cornell as an undersized young man who looked like a weakling. Without a doubt, he was the last man one would ever expect to become a famous athlete. But he was determined to become strong and worked very hard to develop himself, physically. In time, Osgood became a fine oarsman on the Cornell crew, an accomplished gymnast and tumbler and a great football player.

Although he only weighed 170 pounds, Osgood was one of the hardest men to tackle that ever played football. But Osgood was valuable only as a ballcarrier. He later left Cornell to play for two seasons at Penn when the Quaker teams were good ones. After graduation, Osgood joined the Army so that he could fight in the Spanish-American War. There, he was killed while in combat.

Besides the death of George Witherbee and the loss of Winchester Osgood, the 1893 Cornell football team was also hit with numerous graduation losses. We lost both of our tackles, a guard and two other regular players. This, of course, made me one of the few veterans left on the squad. The team also suffered many casualties in pre-season practice. Our coach, Carl Johanson, had also departed and team captain, C.J. Barr, was now overseeing the squad. In an effort to put together a competitive team, Barr overworked and overtrained us. The end-result of Barr's coaching strategy was a series of disastrous defeats, which concluded in a season-finale 50-0 licking at the hands of Penn.

This experience later helped me in my coaching career, because I learned how easily good players could be ruined by overworking them. We scrimmaged every day during the 1893 season. And as it turned out, our Cornell squad was probably a better football team on the first day of fall practice than we were at the end of the season.

Our record proved it, too. During the 1893 season, we won only 2 games, lost five and tied one.

Following the conclusion of the 1893 season, a temporary team captain was elected for the 1894 season. This was done because there was much uncertainty over which ballplayers would be returning for the following season. For me, the law school curriculum which I had taken while at Cornell had required only two years to complete and I was set to graduate in the spring of 1894 and begin practicing law afterwards. However, during the summer following my graduation, the Cornell football manager visited me and persuaded me that I should return to Cornell for another year of post-graduate studies. Without much hesitation, I agreed to his request.

Previously, my father had helped me by paying for my law school education. In an attempt to cover my living expenses during this period, I had also waited on tables, organized boarding clubs and performed lots of other odd jobs.

In addition, I had developed a little talent for painting landscapes while using water colors. This brought in extra revenue. Remarkably, it was the sale of several of these paintings in the summer of 1894 which enabled me to return to Cornell for the upcoming season.

That fall, when the school term began and we reassembled on Percy Field to practice for the upcoming season — my third year on the Cornell varsity — I was elected the team's captain.

There were also some new changes at the coaching helm for Cornell. Marshall Newell, who had been a great tackle at Harvard as well as one of Walter Camp's all-America selections for the previous four years, was hired to be the Redmen's new football coach for the 1894 season. He was a good one, too. In the 1894 season, our record greatly improved to a respectable six wins, four losses and one tie.

We scored two touchdowns on both Harvard and Princeton that season but still lost these games by rather narrow margins. This was a great feat for a so-called "minor" Eastern college like Cornell to score upon two of the Big Three schools. And Cornell, athletically speaking, was definitely considered to be one of the minor colleges.

The University of Pennsylvania had fielded a great team in 1894, with that still-famous middle line trio of Charles Wharton, Willy Woodruff and A.E. Bull and a great backfield of Winchester Osgood, George Brooke, Arthur Knipe and Carl Williams.

This stellar combination of players was coached by George Woodruff, who was just starting out on what would become a successful coaching career. He originated the "guards back" style of offense and it proved to be a terror to other teams. Later, this offensive strategy — which permitted linemen to be set back in the offensive backfield — was widely copied. The only defense that slowed down this formation was the college football rules book which eventually outlawed it.

It was also Woodruff who invented the quarterback onsides kick, which has since become outlawed in the rule books, and the smashing style of defensive end play that is still being used by many coaches in the modern era of the game of football.

In 1894, Woodruff's Penn squad defeated mighty Princeton in the last game that was to be played between those two schools until 1935.

The style of play which Woodruff's teams used was typical of that era. Their potent offense was called the "flying interference" formation. In employing this attack, the Penn offensive team would line up in a regular formation. Then and on signal, the entire backfield and the three linemen from the opposite side of the center (from which the play was being run) started on a run behind their own line. The ball was then snapped to a runner-in-motion, who was behind the mass of flying interference. Together, they led him in a sweep around end.

During the 1894 season, while attending the Yale-Princeton game, I saw the flying interference utilized to achieve its maximum potential. The entire team, with the exception of the center, gathered at a spot about ten yards behind the line of scrimmage. They then took off on a dead run, moving like a battering ram. As they neared the line of scrimmage, the ball was snapped to a back who was following the flying mass of interference just before it began to bulldoze over the opposing defense.

It was an awesome offensive strategy. But as usual, the rule makers soon adopted a way to stop or greatly slow down a play that most great defenses were never able to.

6

During the 1890's and the early portion of the twentieth century, it was quite common in colleges and universities throughout the country to give an athlete the nickname of "Pop." Usually the athlete who is given this honor is either prematurely bald or is considerably older than the other players or has a good-natured disposition.

I had only been at Cornell for a very brief period when I acquired this nickname, which has stuck with me ever since.

I had been blessed with plenty of hair while in college so this wasn't the reason for such a nickname. Instead, it was because I had not begun college until three years after I had graduated from high school. This, of course, made me older than most of those who were in my freshman class.

And when one of my teammates pinned that label on me at practice one day, the other players laughed and from then on they kept calling me "Pop."

7

In my final season at Cornell in 1894, our football coach, Marshall Newell, was asked to return to Cambridge, Mass, for a two-week period to help his alma mater, Harvard, prepare for their upcoming game against Yale. Since I was the team captain, I was put in charge of the team while he was away.

My first act as the *interim* coach was to put in a new play which we would use in our upcoming game against Williams College. The new play was based on deception and, if properly used at the right time in the game, our chances for being successful were pretty good.

The new trick play required for all of the backs to fake an end run to the left while the quarterback, instead, kept the ball and then handed it off to the left guard, who ran with the ball to the right without interference.

My keen interest in the play is that I would be the left guard who would be carrying the ball. And since being a ballcarrier was a privilege which is usually entrusted to the backs, this new trick play gave me my long-awaited chance.

By the time that the Cornell-Williams game had arrived on Saturday, we had practiced the new trick play several times and felt confident in our ability to pull it off when the appropriate time came around.

As expected, the game turned out to be a close one. Toward the end of the fourth quarter, I decided the timing was right for me to whisper "No. 39" to the quarterback while we were in the offensive huddle. This was the special play that I had earlier installed.

Without hesitation, the quarterback then told the others in the huddle that the special play would be run next.

As the play began, the backfield faked the end run to the left as required, the quarterback then faked a toss to the last back for the intended end run and, at the precise moment, pivoted around and handed the ball off to me. Remarkably, the play was working so well that suddenly I had a clear field in front of me to run in.

I, of course, was not a fast runner and had never been coached on how to properly carry the ball. While running in the open field, I had the ball hugged close to my chest with both hands. After gaining 25 yards, I was finally tackled from behind by one of the Williams defensive backs who had been initially tricked by the fake end run and had since recovered to catch up with me. In a beautiful saving tackle, he prevented me from scoring.

As I fell to the ground I attempted to use the football and both of my elbows to cushion my fall. But on impact, the football shot straight up in the air such that it resembled a punt. Soon afterwards, one of the Williams' players jumped on the loose ball and recovered it to give them possession.

A few minutes later, the game ended in a 0-0 tie.

As it turned out, my first play as an interim coach proved to be a successful one, but I put the wrong player — me — in the game to run with the ball.

8

One of the last few games that I played for Cornell was against
Penn, whose 1894 team was one of the greatest gridiron machines
that the Quakers ever had. Penn had been picked to win the contest
rather easily. Their team was much heavier than Cornell and, since
the game was played on a wet field, this was a decided advantage.

Cornell averaged 164 pounds per player, which was light for a
first-class football team. Even football squads of today, which stress
speed and cleverness more than poundage, are bigger than our 1894
Cornell squad.

The Redmen team that year consisted of several good players
including Hawley Taussig, Tommy Fennell, Joe Colnon, Tom Hall,
Charley Rogers and myself on the line, with Joe Beacham, George
Dyer, Billy Ohl and Clint Wyckoff, our great all-America quarterback, rounding out the backfield.

We kicked off to open the game with Penn, but the Quakers
couldn't sustain their drive and eventually punted the ball back to
Cornell. Our offense then hit the Penn line hard with a series of quick-
hitting plays that advanced the ball to the Penn 5-yard line. It was at
that point that Paul Dashiell, the referee, gave the ball to Penn on a
penalty. Dashiell claimed that the Cornell line was holding on the
play. (Editor's Note: During this era the penalty for illegal-use-of-
hands, or holding, was loss of the ball.)

Penn, however, was unable to move the ball and was forced to
punt, with the kick going to midfield. Again, the Cornell offense
moved the ball to Penn's 5-yard line and ended up losing the ball on
the referee's decision. Our confidence was almost shot by then. We
had given our best against Penn's great team and twice had been
denied a touchdown — but not by Penn's vaunted defense. Instead,

we had been stopped on both occasions by a zealous referee's flag.

As the game continued, Penn kept getting stronger and finally defeated us, 6-0.

In these final weeks my college football career, I played my best ever. I realized afterward that my efforts prior to the Penn game had been mediocre in comparison. Besides, I was just getting wise to what I could do and I regretted greatly that I did not have another season to play.

My case, of course, was considerably different from most of today's college players. The modern era players are fortunate to play in high school and prep school leagues and look forward all through their pre-college days to making their varsity team.

I, however, had virtually no preparation prior to my playing the game of football. I had never dreamed in my high school days of later playing college football because we did not formally play the game in high school. And when I did finally begin to play at Cornell, the talent on our team was so scarce that I was placed on the varsity on my first day of practice. It was because of these fortunate breaks that I did not have to work too hard to earn for my place on the team and was not spurred on to achieve great efforts. And it wasn't until I was almost finished playing at Cornell that I had learned the game's primary fundamentals such as blocking and tackling.

Sometimes, I wonder if I could have been selected to Walter Camp's all-America team had I only gotten more football experience while in high school.

9

After graduating from Cornell in the fall of 1894, I had no thoughts of taking up a career in coaching football. After staying to play a third football season, I had decided to begin my legal career at the earliest opportunity.

During this time, I had passed the State of New York legal examination and was admitted to the bar to practice law. Then in January 1895, I accepted an offer from a law firm in Buffalo, N.Y., and immediately went to work there.

Later that spring, the business manager of the Cornell football team sent me a letter that he had received from Iowa Agricultural College at Ames, Ia. (which is now known as Iowa State University). The letter asked if he could recommend a football coach for their school who would be able to begin coaching that fall.

At that time, I was just starting my legal career and I had yet to build a stable of clients whose legal fees would provide me with a respectable salary. After receiving this letter the thought occurred to me that I might supplement my legal career in these early lean years by coaching football part-time.

The Iowa State graduate football manager's letter stated they wanted to start practice in the middle of August. When I contacted them about their offer, the Iowa State officials responded that they would pay a salary of $25 per week, plus all expenses for the season.

If you can imagine a poor young lawyer who was a prospective football coach listening to such an offer, then you will understand how tempting such an offer was for me. A dollar then looked as large as a balloon tire does today. And with Iowa's farmers' corn selling that fall for ten cents a bushel, the $25 a week coaching salary sounded like big money to me.

However before committing to the Iowa State offer, I decided to find out if there were other openings which would pay better. I then got a list of nearly 100 colleges and sent my applications to several of them in the South and West to inquire about vacant positions at their schools. One of the replies which I received was from the University of Georgia. They offered me a salary of $35 per week, plus expenses for ten weeks beginning on September 15th. I quickly sent a telegram to them to accept their offer.

Next, I wrote to the officials at Iowa State to tell them that I had accepted the coaching position at Georgia but would be willing to coach their squad for four weeks beginning in early August and then would leave in mid-September to take the coaching job at Georgia. In my letter, I told them that I would like the opportunity to do this if they were unable to find another coach. I also told them that I felt that I could greatly help their program during my brief stay there.

The Iowa State officials favorably accepted my proposal and offered me a starting salary of $150, plus expenses for thirty days of coaching. Their letter also noted that an alumni player, Bert German, would work as an assistant during my 30-day tenure and afterwards would fill in for me during my absence.

In early August 1895, I arrived in Ames, Ia., to begin my coaching career in football. Little did I know that this would be the beginning of a profession that I would continue in for the remainder of my life until retiring in the late 1930's and one which I wouldn't have traded for any other in the world.

Upon inspection, I noticed that the Iowa State squad had some pretty good athletes but they lacked the fundamental knowledge and experience of playing football. Ames, of course, was a small town and the school's athletic finances did not allow for paying very much for a football coach, which may explain their decision to take my offer of a 5-week stint as opposed to the entire season.

The Iowa State squad had not received much in the way of coaching prior to my arrival and perhaps didn't learn too much from this rookie coach who was straight out of college.

Those initial practices were just as rough for me as they were for my players. I felt that I knew how to teach the guard position quite well, but I soon found out that playing end or a backfield position was another chore. I learned more football in those 5 weeks in Iowa and later during that first season at Georgia than I had previously learned in three years as a player at Cornell.

What little football knowledge I did possess, I imparted fairly well to the players. The Iowa State players were mostly farm boys who had never played any football before entering college, but they were all good pupils. I worked them hard during those five weeks.

In mid-September, on the final weekend that I was there at Iowa State, we were scheduled to play an exhibition against the Butte Athletic Club of Butte, Mont.

We had received the offer to come to Butte shortly after I had arrived in August. A letter had been sent to the Iowa State graduate football manager with an offer "of a financial guarantee sufficient to cover the team's expenses" for a game at Butte. The game was scheduled to be played on a Sunday in order to attract a large crowd.

Both myself and the team members wanted to take the game, but we knew that the school's faculty would be against a game which was to be played on Sunday. So in order to gain the faculty's approval, I told them that the game would be played on Saturday. Without hesitation, we received their sanctioning for the trip to Butte.

10

Butte, Mont., was a mining town which was one of the wildest, wide-open roughneck sporting towns in the United States during this era. The mines ran three eight-hour shifts each day and just as many people were on the streets and in the saloons and hotels at 4 a.m. as at any other time.

There was considerable betting on the Butte Athletic Club-Iowa State game. I even let my youthful gambling spirit get the better of my judgment and wagered my entire salary of $150 — for the 5 weeks of coaching at Iowa State — that we would win the game. During my brief stay there, we had improved to become a good college team so I figured that no athletic club in a dinky mining town could show us any tricks.

My judgment regarding the athletic ability of both teams was sound. However, I had not figured on the condition of the Butte playing field, the officials and several other distractions.

In explaining the setting for this game, I should first note that this was the kind of place where the cheerleaders for the Butte Athletic Club were wearing old-fashioned revolvers and frequently shot them into the air while on the sidelines instead of leading cheers with their pom-poms.

In the stands, the spectators often would fire their six-shooters in a frenzied state of excitement after a big play or a score occurred. These moments of wild behavior often sounded much like a large fireworks display.

Also, the Butte players were the roughest characters that I have ever seen. And the playing field was nothing more than hardened, sun-dried clay.

The Butte A.C. squad was composed of former college football stars from the Montana area along with some local players. They were an extremely talented bunch and had made a strong reputation for themselves in the Northwest and on the Pacific Coast.

Prior to the contest, Butte picked the game's referee and we chose the umpire. The game was played on a field which was absolutely bare because the fumes from the ore smelters in the town prevented grass from growing. Everywhere I looked I only saw shades of brown.

In this era, it was customary to snap the ball back from the center on one bounce or on a roll to the quarterback. But on this sand-covered field, the ball merely slipped and slid and didn't bounce at all like it did on grass. It was almost impossible getting the ball snapped back to the quarterback without a fumble.

During the game, if Iowa State threatened to score on Butte's goal line, the referee, a local man who had been picked by Butte A.C., would make some penalty call that would cause us a setback. On one occasion, we threatened to leave the playing field because of a bad decision which was made by the local referee. The Butte A.C. officials, however, quickly reminded us that we had not been paid our financial guarantee for the game yet — and wouldn't be if we left without completing the contest.

At halftime, I decided to join the Iowa State team in playing against the Butte A.C. team. It was such a rough game that almost all of my clothes were ripped or town by the middle of the third quarter.

As it turned out, the game was called after the third quarter. And eleven pretty good football players who made their own rules — and were aided by the referee — won the game by the score of 13-10 that afternoon. We left Butte that day a sadder but wiser bunch.

Upon our return, the graduate football manager explained to the faculty that the weather had prevented the game from being played on Saturday and that we had to stay an extra day and play on Sunday or not get paid our "financial guarantee." The faculty bought this explanation without an objection from anyone.

The $150 which I had lost on the game was a lot of money to me. I felt bad about losing it, especially since the game was not fairly won. But that wager was a good investment because it taught me a valuable lesson. Since that day, I always made sure I knew a lot more about my competition before betting on one of my teams.

11

Following nearly five weeks of hard work during the hot, late-summer weather and the emotional encounter at Butte, my players' vitality was so sapped that they had no pep.

Fortunately, there were no games scheduled until the last Saturday in September, which would be two weeks away. Before my departure to leave for Athens, Ga., I instructed my assistant, Bert German, who would be filling in for me in coaching Iowa State during my absence, to give the players a whole week of absolute rest in order to prepare for their next opponent, Northwestern.

German agreed to this plan and when the Iowa State team arrived in Evanston, Ill., to meet Northwestern on Sept. 28th, they were a well-rested and much-spirited team.

Northwestern was one of the top teams in the Midwest at this time and were expected to apply a licking to the Iowa farmboys.

However early in the game, Iowa State drove the ball downfield in steady gains for a touchdown. Undoubtedly, this feat filled their hearts with joy. But it spread dismay in the camp of their boastful opponents, who were now silent.

Shortly thereafter, Iowa State scored another touchdown and their superior talent began to shine through on this early autumn afternoon. Still, the Iowa State players did not believe that they could luck up and win this contest against a team which had scheduled them just for an easy workout.

The Iowans then scored a third touchdown. After the point-after goal was kicked, the Iowa State team captain, Ed Mellinger, suddenly realized that with 18 points on their side of the scoreboard his team perhaps had a chance to win this game.

At halftime, Mellinger began to encourage his teammates, patting them on the back and shouting: "Now, let's go back out there and beat them."

With this being an early season game, the halves were also shortened, which was customary in this era. During the halftime break, the Northwestern coach came over to the Iowa State locker room and requested that the second half be shortened by an additional ten minutes to prevent a runaway game from occurring, which was agreed to.

However, in spite of this request, the Iowa State team scored three more times in the second half against Northwestern while en route to a 36-0 victory.

The next day, a Chicago newspaper called them "the cornfed giants from Iowa."

So in order to show that their great Northwestern victory was no fluke, nor a flash in the pan, these game cornfed lads went on to wallop the University of Iowa, 24-0, later in the season.

12

My train arrived in Athens, Ga., in mid-September 1895, after having traveled nearly a thousand miles from my 30-day coaching stint at Iowa State. This was to be the first of my early season commutes over the next five seasons between Ames and my other coaching posts at Georgia, Cornell and the Carlisle Indian School.

I was met at the train station by the graduate football manager at the University of Georgia, who wasted no time in loading my bags into the back of a horse-drawn wagon and then proceeded to take me over to the school to show me the campus and their athletic facilities.

It was one of those dog days of late summer that the South was famous for. The sun was making its presence well known, with the temperature in the 90's and the humidity near one hundred percent.

Upon our arrival at their football field, I stood up in the wagon and looked around in dismay. All around me was a large pasture area that was mostly covered with a red-clay surface that had a few parched spots of grass. Their wooden bleachers probably could seat no more than 150 fans.

It was this point that I seriously considered sending a telegram to Iowa State to let them know that I would be returning for the remainder of the season.

But the graduate football manager of the team was a great salesman and told me that the schools' lack of facilities would be overshadowed by their tremendous football talent.

After hearing those words of encouragement, I decided to stay.

However, on the first day of practice only a dozen players reported. And these didn't look too promising.

I later told the team's graduate football manager, "Looks like I'm up against pretty tough opposition out there. We've got to drum up some players with a bit more talent."

Soon afterwards, I found the Southern boys to be game fighters who possessed much more fiery tempers than Northern players. They were inclined to be more jawboned with less surplus weight than Northern players. This example still holds true today, although the Southern teams are a lot heavier than they once were.

Recently, I saw two fine Southern teams, Alabama and Georgia, play in a game in Birmingham, Ala. Alabama, which had played my Stanford team in the 1927 Rose Bowl, was just as heavy and as husky as the other great teams in any section of the country. But the Georgia squad, who played against a great Alabama team that afternoon, still had players who were built similar to their predecessors over a generation ago (in the 1890's).

In the old days, Georgia and Alabama Polytechnical Institute, who was generally referred to as Auburn (and now called Auburn University), which is where the college is located, were bitter rivals. They usually completed their seasons with a knockdown battle that would be played in Atlanta.

During my initial season at Georgia, I was often told by well-wishing fans of the significance of this new rivalry and that a victory over Auburn was an important goal of the Georgia alumni.

Knowing this, I frequently asked the graduate football manager and other prominent Georgia alums if perhaps we shouldn't send someone to scout some of Auburn's games.

But each time, I got the usual reply: "Georgia defeated Auburn last year and since Georgia has a much stronger team this season there is no need to worry. Our only concern is *how big the score is going to be?*"

Auburn had played a rather easy schedule that season and there was no indication that they were any better than a year ago.

Finally, the big game arrived and we traveled to Atlanta a very confident and somewhat cocky outfit. Auburn entered the contest with a record of 1-1-0. Georgia's record to date was 3 wins and 3 losses.

Before the game, many Georgia students went around to the Atlanta hotels and saloons trying to make wagers with the visiting

Auburn fans. They were offering odds of 2-to-1 or 3-to-1 on an Auburn defeat at the hands of the mighty Georgia team. In addition, some even wagered even money that Auburn wouldn't even score. However, because there was scarcely any money being placed on the game, the Georgia college boys became all the more confident of a victory.

In this season, Auburn was playing under a new coach, John Heisman, who would later become a well-known coach at Georgia Tech. Heisman had been a player at the University of Pennsylvania and afterwards had coached for a couple of years in Ohio at Oberlin College and Buchtel (which later became the University of Akron). He was both a wise and capable coach and showed it by keeping his team's talents from being highly publicized during the season. Heisman also knew that if his Auburn team could lick Georgia then it would be a real feather in his cap.

Unfortunately, we didn't realize the trap that Heisman had set for us. His Auburn team decisively whipped us, 16-6, that afternoon. And the Auburn faithful danced in the saloons in Atlanta until late that evening. Of course, if their fans had had any confidence in their team on that day, they could have won all of the Georgia alums' betting money.

The final outcome of this game provided a great lesson to me in my first year as a football coach. In my strong desire to turn out a winning team, I had brought the boys up to their final game in an overtrained condition. This, along with their over-confident and self-satisfied feeling coupled with the uncertain knowledge of our opponent's strength, brought us to football's version of Waterloo.

Heisman had developed a smooth-running football machine at Auburn. His plays were good and they had great teamwork. Their field general, a 130-pound quarterback named Reynolds Tichenor, was someone who I have never forgotten.

After the game, the Georgia alums assured me that they — and not the coach (me) — were responsible for the unexpected defeat against Auburn because they had told me not to send a scout to observe Auburn's team in other games as I had originally planned to.

They then asked me to return to coach the next season. The Georgia alums made it quite clear that even if the team lost all of the games on their schedule but one — that victory should be over Auburn.

With their newly-spirited enthusiasm and determination backing me as the team's coach, I accepted their offer to return for another season, along with a raise in my salary from $35 to $40 per week.

In my second season at Georgia, we won all of our games prior to the long-awaited contest with Auburn. We had assembled a clean string of victories against some of the best teams in the South that season. Auburn had a fine team, too, and a good record, but we had scouted them in several games and were ready for them. As it turned out, the Georgia-Auburn game was a barn-burner.

In scouting the Auburn team during the season, I had noted that when they lined up to receive a kickoff, there was only one player — the center — who was up close. He was set 10 yards from the ball. The other players were spread out well behind him.

Consequently, I had the Georgia players practice a short, dribbled kickoff to the left side of the field. I also placed two of my fastest players out near the left sidelines to beat the Auburn players in getting to the ball.

In addition, I devised a series of plays to be used without a signal if we succeeded in getting the ball on the kickoff. These were trick plays to throw the opposition for a loop.

On the first play, which would be run if we had recovered the surprise kickoff, the entire team was to be set up on one side of the ball, with the player who had recovered the kick acting as the center, or snapper back. The center would then toss the ball out sidewards to one of the backs who would begin to run toward the side of the field that his teammates had lined up on. This back would then toss the ball to another back who was running behind the rest of the team as his interference. On the next play of this series, the same play was to be run to the opposite side of the field.

In the Auburn game, our plans turned out perfectly. The short kickoff, or onsides kick, was made to the left side of the field and one of our Georgia players recovered the ball before any Auburn players could arrive on the scene. The entire Georgia team then moved into position on the right side of the ball, which was done both quickly and unexpectedly.

This caught the Auburn defense off-guard.

The Georgia player, who had recovered the ball on the kickoff, then snapped the ball back to a back and we were off to the races.

This trick play netted 25 yards on the first play. And before the Auburn boys had recovered, the same play was made to the left side and went for a touchdown. Following our point-after kick conversion, Georgia led, 6-0.

The trick kickoff and the two trick plays following it won the game for us. But it is only once in a lifetime that such a series of three trick plays can be run without something going wrong. However, since everything turned out perfectly and we went on to win the game over Auburn, 12-6, we were called a smart team. But, if luck had been against us, then I—being the football coach — would have been branded as being stupid.

Such is the life of a football coach.

13

John Heisman, whose well-coached teams at Auburn had given our teams at Georgia such difficult games during my first two years of coaching, was just beginning what would be a long and successful coaching career. He coached for over 25 years in the South, while turning out great teams at various schools.

After five years at Auburn, he coached at Clemson for four years and then later went to Georgia Tech, where he remained for 16 seasons. His Georgia Tech teams attracted attention from all over the country and their whirlwind — and almost unstoppable — attack won them the nickname of the "Golden Tornado."

I did not coach in the South beyond my initial two seasons at Georgia and did not have an opportunity to go up against a Heisman-coached team again until 1918, when the "Golden Tornado," who after cleaning up against everybody in the South, came up to Pittsburgh to tangle with my great Pitt team.

Much had been written about this great Georgia Tech team and the game attracted a large amount of interest among the newspaper sportswriters and college football fans around the country.

I had my Pitt squad primed for this battle because I realized how hard those Southern boys would fight to win. Georgia Tech had brought along their band and a large number of their fans, but the lengthy train trip, the climate and a tough Pitt squad proved to be too great of an obstacle to overcome. They were soundly defeated, 32-0.

A year earlier, in 1917, the University of Pennsylvania had played Georgia Tech in a game in Atlanta. Heisman's team ran over Penn that afternoon, defeating them 41-0.

Penn later hired Heisman to return to his alma mater at the end of the 1919 season. Afterwards, Heisman coached successfully at Washington & Jefferson and at Rice University. He eventually became the athletic director for the Downtown Athletic Club in New York City, where he worked until his death in 1936. In an attempt to honor Heisman's many accomplishments in college football and his memorable leadership at the Downtown Athletic Club, the Club's membership voted to rename its Downtown Athletic Club Trophy to The Heisman Memorial Trophy. This award is given now each season to the best college football player in the country.

During my two-year coaching tenure at Georgia, there were many amusing and interesting incidents. One of the more memorable ones involved a football player's attempt to attract a considerable amount of *attention* to himself, which is known among athletes as "playing to the grandstand."

Our dilemma involved a Georgia player who appeared to be getting injured — almost severely — on a daily basis during spring football practice. Yet when I attempted to put a substitute player in his place, he would protest and ask to remain in the practice session.

His response in wanting to continue practicing in spite of his injuries seemed to indicate his gameness and great fighting spirit.

For several days, this player's injury routine continued, then one day I stumbled onto the cause of it all.

Over in one corner of the practice field was an area with some big shade trees. And each afternoon, a few young ladies from a local girls school would gather there, sit on some benches beneath the shade trees and enjoy the beautiful spring weather as well as observe some of the college boys engaging in football practice.

In what seemed to be more than coincidence or fate, the player who was always getting injured usually put on his act when the ball had been spotted over near this admiring audience.

Realizing, of course, what was being put over on me, I waited until the next practice scrimmage to call this player's bluff. When the ball had been moved close to the shade trees and the female observers, I suddenly interrupted the scrimmage and made a brief suggestion to my quarterback. I told him: "Change your signals. Don't you see that we are over near the girls again? Give the ball to our good-looking halfback. It is time for him to break his leg again."

Knowing that I had caught on to him, the player carried the ball on that play with great effort and amazingly didn't get hurt. It seems that my actions also quickly put an end to the player's rash of daily injuries.

A second memorable incident involved one of our Georgia players from the backwoods of rural Georgia. Without a doubt, he was the greenest, backwoods specimen I had ever seen in college. This young man was a brainy chap and knew his schoolbooks, but he had evidently never strayed too far away from the Georgia hills because when he arrived at the University of Georgia, I eventually found out that he had never ridden in a Pullman train car before, nor had he ever stayed in a hotel.

When our team went to Atlanta to play Auburn in 1895, we checked into our team headquarters, The Kimball House Hotel. This young country chap would take his first ride on an elevator that day.

After the elevator arrived at his floor in the hotel, he stepped off the elevator and stated to the elevator attendant: "Mr. Stubbs (the team captain) will pay my fare."

Although this story makes for a nice laugh, it does have a happy ending. This green farmboy had the proper stuff in him and eventually became one of the best football players in the South. Following his graduation from Georgia, he became a prominent lawyer.

14

My early success in those initial two years of coaching football at the University of Georgia had attracted the attention of my alma mater, Cornell, where I had first learned the game as a player.

I was eventually asked to return there as head coach of the Cornell team for the fall of 1897. After much consideration — and a sweetened salary offer of $600 for the season — I finally accepted their offer.

Joe Beacham, who had been a teammate of mine, joined me as an assistant and we turned out a good team that season with a record of five wins, three losses and one tie. Our final game of the season was against Penn and we lost, 4-0, in a heartbreaker.

One of the memorable players on the squad that year was a young man who had been unjustly judged as being "yellow" or chicken by some of the other players and Cornell alums. His name was Mark Faville and he was a well-built and husky player who was trying to make the team roster. Faville made such a favorable impression on me in his initial practices that I soon placed him at the guard position on the Cornell varsity.

Following this move, several people came up to me and asked whether I intended to make Faville a starter on the varsity. When I informed them that as long as he continued to play with great determination and showed progress that he would retain his position on the varsity.

These same individuals then suggested that Faville would not do well at the guard position because he lacked the proper stuff. They said that as a player on a nearby high school team that he had shown a yellow streak and was not to be depended upon.

I thanked them for this information but quickly told them that I would judge each player on the Cornell team by what he had shown on the field and not by what I had been told by outsiders.

Afterwards, I told Faville what I had heard about him because I figured he would try even harder to overcome such an impression, — which he did.

This, of course, was the era of close offensive formations and defenses in which three middle linemen were assigned to dive under the "flying wedges" mass of players in order to stop such plays. There were no helmets with ear protectors then and like many players of this era, Faville developed a case of cauliflower ears.

This was extremely painful for Faville and the others, and his condition grew more painful when he came in contact with the opposing team during a game. Faville, however, continued to diligently play his position as a defensive lineman and always dived at the "flying wedge's" mass of players. He never complained or alibied. And though he was unable to finish his studies at Cornell, Faville was one of the best guards that I ever coached.

Prior to my return to Cornell in 1897, Princeton had been a powerhouse and had run roughshod over every team they met, including Yale. They had been using a new close formation called "the turtleback" which had been the basis for their great success.

In this era, there were no rules which governed how an offensive team should line up while on the field. Princeton used this loophole to their advantage and devised an offense in which the players lined up in a very tight formation with each player slightly overlapping each other.

In this new "turtleback formation," the ends were set slightly behind the line with their shoulders upon the outside hip of their tackle. The halfbacks and fullback were then set very close together and less than three yards behind the linemen. There was just enough room between them and the line for the quarterback to stand behind the center and take the snap.

With this formation, a back went through the line with the other backs helping push him in tandem. This play was called "the revolving wedge."

It was almost impossible for the defensive linemen to break through this formation. The only way to stop it was to dive into the feet of the charging players and then start grabbing all of the legs that they could. Most of the time, this effort would cause a pile-up and stop the play from advancing.

End runs were seldom attempted in this era. Only five yards had to be gained to secure a first down, and in those days no plays were attempted which stood a chance of losing yardage. Straight-ahead running plays or off-tackle plays to either side of the line were the rule and the spectators seldom saw the ball during a play except when it was punted.

Princeton had a lot of success in their first year of using this new turtleback formation. None of the opposing coaches were able to figure out a way to defense it. However, by the next season, a lot of schools copied Princeton's new offense as more coaches began to become familiar with it. These opposing coaches made a more thorough study of the turtleback formation and were able to eventually devise a more effective defense for it. Afterwards, this formation began to lose its mysterious appeal and was no longer the great deadly offensive weapon that it had once been. It was gradually discarded.

There has never been an instance in the history of college football when a coach has been able to invent an unstoppable play or an unstoppable offense. Either his fellow coaches were eventually able to find a way to defense it or the rule makers would change the rules to allow them to stop it.

15

While coaching, I never liked to see a football player shed tears. I have been a firm believer that if a football player starts crying during a game, then it is an admission of defeat. And after a game there is no need for a player to start crying.

I have always encouraged the players that following a bitter defeat they should cheer up, forget the loss and think about the next game. If a player has done the best he can, he should take defeat philosophically and profit by the lessons to be learned.

I, myself, have had several setbacks during my coaching career and I have always found the unexpected defeats were the hardest to swallow. Only once in my career have I ever shed tears because of a game. It was in my first year as head coach at Cornell. The tears were not because of a defeat but because I was angry at an unexcusable error of judgment which was made by one of our players.

Princeton had defeated Cornell by a large score a year earlier, in 1896, with their close formation. Now, the press was noting that this year's Cornell-Princeton contest would be another runaway win for Princeton.

This, of course, was a big game for me because it was my first year at Cornell as the football coach. Also, it was still early in my coaching career and I was most anxious to build a good record.

Prior to the game, I thoroughly prepared my team to meet this human tank which had been crushing every team in its path.

We did not have any inflated dreams of beating this mighty Princeton team, yet I did hope to hold them to a low score. Cornell, however, did so well that with only two minutes remaining in the first half, they had held Princeton to a 4-0 lead. Cornell also had the ball on the Princeton 30-yard line.

On third down and with two yards remaining for a first down, I instructed the Cornell offense to punt, because with only two minutes remaining in the first half Cornell could not hope to score. However, by punting the ball deep into Princeton's territory — near the goal line — it would be a miracle for the Tigers to score.

But instead of punting, the Cornell offense tried to gain the few yards needed for a first down and failed, thus losing the ball on downs. Princeton then struck like lightning and quickly marched downfield and scored just before halftime. Princeton now led, 10-0.

This was the score at the end of the game, too. Cornell had played valiantly and given a creditable performance. Still, the 4-0 score would have looked so much better. Our squad had foolishly given away the other six points to Princeton. I was so disappointed that following the game I locked myself in a room and cried.

This game is an example of how poor judgment on the part of a team's field general can lead to another team's scoring or perhaps a game-winning (or game-losing) play. A coach who is on the sidelines sometimes must helplessly watch as his team is scored upon or beaten through a mistake which is made on the field. Many times, his input could have changed the play's outcome.

It is no great wonder that a coach often exhibits great nervousness during a game.

Later, when I look back on the 1897 Cornell-Princeton game, I realize that I should not have blamed the quarterback for the mistake of going for the first down which was made in the game. We were fortunate to have been close enough to win. My tears were based on youthful ambition and my own desire to win. It was a mistake to have faulted our quarterback, because he was playing to win — which is the only way I would have wanted him to have played.

In the 1897 season, we also had on our team a good player who seldom got hurt, but when he did one day he made a terrible fuss over it. He was not grandstanding either.

The player was then carried to the sideline on a stretcher and carefully covered with a blanket. It was a close game and Cornell soon scored a touchdown. However after the touchdown, the injured player was so elated that he threw off his blanket and turned several handsprings.

After seeing this, I concluded that such idiosyncracies with players were due not to their gameness to play and to win but, instead, to simply being a case of more or less sensitive nerves.

16

My first season in coaching at Cornell proved to be a successful one and I was asked to return to coach the squad for the 1898 season. My meager salary was also increased to $800 for the season.

Unfortunately, my assistant, Joe Beacham, was unable to remain with me. He was replaced by a former Cornell player.

Cornell had a great team that season. Our record was ten wins and two losses, but we again lost the final game of the season to Penn. The score this time was 12-6.

Cornell had a much better team than Penn that season, but we were not prepared for the conditions under which we were to meet. The game was played in Philadelphia, where all Cornell-Penn games were played during this era.

It cannot be denied that a lengthy train trip and an opponent's home field are a handicap to a visiting team. But these are to be expected as part of college football and playing against rivals. The handicaps that were not expected were primarily weather-related.

When our train had departed Ithaca, N.Y., the weather was reasonably good for late November. However, upon reaching Philadelphia we were met by an icy rain and thunderstorm which had set in over the city and would last for nearly two days.

The playing field at Penn quickly became a sea of mud, and during the game both sleet and rain were being driven by such strong winds that they seemed to be of hurricane proportions. It was perhaps the worst weather conditions and muddiest field that I ever saw in a game.

I was still quite young at the coaching game and had never before met such adverse conditions of both stormy weather and a rain-ravaged playing field. To compound my problem, I had neglected to bring a change of spare uniforms for my players.

The first half of the game ended with Cornell leading, 6-0. During the halftime break, we retired to an unheated, old barn which was used during the winter for indoor baseball practice. The icy, cold wind which whistled in between the barn's wooden slats made the intermission almost unbearable. The Cornell players who were sitting on stacks of hay or on the dirt floor suffered terribly. Often I looked around to notice my players, who were still wearing their water-soaked uniforms, shivering or their teeth would be chattering. There was no spare dry clothing for us this side of Ithaca.

In the Penn locker room, their players were resting in warm, comfortable surroundings. They had removed their heavy, wet uniforms and were given an alcohol rub to increase their blood circulation. Afterwards, they then put on fresh, dry uniforms without pads for the second half.

Cornell returned for the third quarter while still dressed in their regular padded uniforms, which were mud-soaked and weighed an extra 20 pounds.

Penn was late in returning to the field for the third quarter because of all of the special extra attention which they had been receiving. This additional treatment was a benefit to the Penn squad but it was a severe handicap to the Cornell team. We would have been much better off by not having an intermission at all.

In the second half, Penn came back and scored two touchdowns and won the game, 12-6. They scored both times on their famous "delayed pass" play.

The Penn game, of course, taught me another valuable lesson as a young coach. Afterwards, I made a rule for myself and my equipment manager that we would never go on an out-of-town trip without an extra set of uniforms so that we could be prepared for bad weather.

17

After our return to Ithaca following the Cornell-Penn game, I had intended to practice law during the off-season. I had done this following my first season at Cornell and it had been a nice change of pace for me. My Cornell teams had been blessed with two very good seasons and a 15-5-1 record during my brief tenure there and I fully anticipated being asked to return to coach there for a third season.

However, I did not reckon on dealing with local college politics.

Following our return from the Cornell-Penn game, I found out that my assistant was trying to land the head-coaching job for himself. This was a surprise to me because he had repeatedly told me during the course of the season that he did not expect to be coaching after this season.

Although now warned of the activities of this rival for my job, I felt that my record as head coach was such that I did not need to pull any strings to be retained. Most importantly, I tried to stay out of the controversy which was developing.

The team captain had a great deal to say in those days as to who should be the team's coach. When it came time for the election of a new team captain for the next year's squad, one candidate favored retaining me as the team's coach while the other candidate favored my assistant being made the new coach.

The fight began to grow bitter and I soon realized that one faction of the team would be pitted against the remainder of the squad no matter what the outcome. In an attempt to silence this controversy, I then postponed the elections for team captain. However, when this controversy cooled down, I knew that the faculty would probably recommend a new coach who had not been involved in this scrap. It was at this point that I began to look elsewhere for a new coaching job.

One of the schools that I looked at was the Carlisle Indian Industrial School, whom we had played earlier in the 1898 season and defeated, 23-6, by using several trick plays to win.

The Indian boys appealed to my football imagination and I decided to apply for the job at Carlisle. Walter Camp, the great coach at Yale, wrote a letter of recommendation for me to the Carlisle superintendent, Major Richard H. Pratt, which must have done the trick. A few weeks later, Carlisle sent me a telegram with an offer to take the head-coaching job. I wasted no time in accepting their offer.

The Cornell situation turned out as I anticipated. Percy Haughton, who later became a great coach at his alma mater, Harvard, was brought in to take the head-coaching job.

It was with great regret that I left Cornell. I had visions of eventually becoming as an important contributor to Cornell football as Charles Courtney had been for the Cornell crews. But the change was a good move because Carlisle was an up-and-coming nationally-known football power and it exposed me to the American Indian culture.

18

Prior to my agreement to accept the position of head coach at Carlisle, the school's superintendent, Major Pratt, asked for my terms to coach the Indian's football team.

When I set my price at $1,200 for the season, plus expenses, Pratt didn't blink an eye. After a bit of discussion on the contract's fine points we then shook hands on a deal. I was scheduled to begin coaching at Carlisle for the fall of 1899.

Major Pratt had built Carlisle into an excellent school. He was a veteran of the Civil War and had been a career officer. Following the war, he had been stationed on the western frontier where the Indians were causing trouble.

It was there on the frontier that Pratt was put in charge of a tribe of Indians who had been rounded up and were to be sent to Fort St. Augustine in St. Augustine, Fla. These Indian warriors were being sent there along with their wives and children.

Pratt, who was then a captain in the U.S. Army, became interested in the welfare and education of the young children in these tribes. When the Indians were relocated from Fort St. Augustine and sent to the Oklahoma Territory, Pratt obtained permission from the U.S. Government to take these Indian children along with Indian children from other tribes which were being relocated and then take them to the Carlisle Barracks in southeastern Pennsylvania to establish a school for them. This was in 1878.

Carlisle Barracks was an abandoned military post which had been established nearly 125 years earlier when Carlisle was a frontier town and continually threatened by hostile Indians. Later in the Revolutionary War, Hessian prisoners were confined there as prisoners of war.

Under Pratt's direction, the old Carlisle Barracks was transformed into a school campus and the Carlisle Indian Industrial School was started. During the course of my tenure there, it had an enrollment of nearly 1,000, who represented over 70 different Indian tribes.

Carlisle fielded its first football team in 1894. Vance McCormick, a former Yale quarterback and team captain from nearby Harrisburg, Pa., had begun to take a great interest in the Indian School and later offered to teach the Carlisle students the game of football, which had been predominantly played in eastern colleges — such as Yale, Harvard and Princeton — up to that point.

Being impressed with the Indian boys' gridiron abilities, McCormick persuaded his former coach at Yale, Walter Camp, to take on the Carlisle team in a practice game. Yale ended up having their hands full with the Indian team and barely pulled off a victory.

William Hickok of Yale was the first paid coach at Carlisle, and under this tutelage Carlisle made impressive showings against Princeton and Yale in 1896. William Bull and John Hall, both Yale grads, coached at Carlisle for one year, in 1897 and 1898, prior to my arrival at the Indian School.

My approach to coaching the Indian boys was similar to the style that I had used at Georgia, Iowa State and Cornell, which was to push my players to become a successful team.

Football coaches in that era were a pretty tough lot. As a player and a coach, I was quite accustomed to hearing a lot of profanity and swearing by coaches in their efforts to push players to achieve a greater performance from them. After becoming a coach, I, too, adopted these same tactics and style of coaching.

However, when I arrived at Carlisle and had begun fall football practice, my coaching style almost caused a team mutiny.

Toward the end of the first week of practice, I noticed that several of my better players had not reported to practice after having attended the first two or three daily sessions. Then each day afterwards, more and more players began to not show up for practice.

I had a difficult time trying to get at the root of the problem. Then one day, I found out that the Indian players loved to play football but they did not like to be the object of my "cussing," or swearing, at practice. They took such humiliations as being personal and were greatly offended at this practice.

I finally called a team meeting of all the Indian boys who had been at practice, including the ones who had been missing team practice for several days. Once we were all together, I told them that I meant nothing personal toward them by my outrages of profanity and swearing at them and that this was being done to simply impress certain things more forcibly upon them. I then concluded our meeting by telling them that in the future I would tone down my swearing and cussing at them.

The next day, the Indians returned to practice and I went on to coach without using a lot of profanity to motivate my team. I soon found out that I would get better results from them by this method.

Once this problem was settled, the Carlisle team began to concentrate on football. And the results were impressive.

19

The 1899 season at Carlisle was a great beginning for the football program which I was trying to develop there.

The prior successes of the teams which had been coached by Vance McCormick, Bill Hickok, William Bull and John Hall gave me a foundation to build upon with the Indian boys who had been well-tutored in the fundamentals of the Yale-style of playing football. It also gave us a good reputation while trying to schedule *name* opponents.

In that first season of coaching at Carlisle, we put together a record of 9 wins and 2 losses, which included victories over Penn and Columbia.

At the end of the regular season, Carlisle was invited to play the University of California in a post-season game on December 22nd in San Francisco. I put this proposition up to a vote by the entire team, who wasted no time in accepting the offer. Afterwards, I sent a telegram to the game's promoters notifying them that we would accept their invitation.

I am not sure if we were the first Eastern team to play an intersectional game on the Pacific Coast, but we were at least one of the first to do so.

California had a fine team that season and had amassed a 7-0-1 record. They were coached by Gerry Cochran and Ted Kelly, who had been a pair of Princeton star players. Earlier in the season, Cal had defeated a very good Stanford squad, 30-0, and was now anxious to compare their prowess against a formidable Eastern team.

On the train trip westward, I encouraged the Indian boys to get off the train and take all the exercise that they could whenever the train made a stop.

At one such stop, the Indian boys, who were dressed up in their red monogram sweaters, had exited the train and were limbering up their muscles by passing and kicking the football around in a nearby vacant grassy field.

While I sat on a bench outside the train station watching the Indian boys at play, an older, bewhiskered gentleman, who claimed to be a citizen of this small town, walked up to me and inquired "as to who we were and where we were going."

This town, of course, was located in the Far West and there wasn't much love for Indians there, so you can understand that my team's presence probably raised many eyebrows.

When I told him that this was the Carlisle Indian football team and that we were en route to San Francisco to play the University of California in a few days, he stroked his beard for a moment or two and then remarked, "Well, they are going a darned long way to get the hell kicked out of them."

As it turned out, California was unable to fulfill the old frontiersman's prophecy. In a fiercely-fought contest that was played with much emotion, Carlisle managed to win, 2-0.

The game was played on a sandy field which had been rolled, but it was still loose and gave no secure footing. The Carlisle offensive attack, which was a much lighter squad and depended primarily on speed, was severely handicapped by the slow and insecure footing. Neither team was able to mount much of an offensive that afternoon and the game eventually became a punting duel.

The big break in the game came when a California player mishandled a punt and had to fall upon the ball behind their goal line. This safety decided the game in Carlisle's favor.

At the conclusion of our visit to San Francisco, we returned back to the East via a southern route. Along the way, we stopped and visited several other Indian schools in the West and the Southwest.

One of our first stops was at the Indian School in Phoenix, Ariz. The school superintendent there insisted that we play his team in a football game before we continued our journey back to Carlisle.

It took a bit of coaxing but I finally agreed to the game. We had just completed the game with Cal only a few days earlier and my weary squad probably wouldn't be able to give their best effort.

The Phoenix Indian School was coached by a Harvard grad. And since Harvard had created a big stir that season by wearing leather uniforms, this Harvard disciple had decided it would be only appropriate to issue his squad the same kind of uniforms — leather pants and close fitting leather jackets.

Harvard had used leather uniforms while believing that they would not absorb much moisture from the playing field, which was a frequent obstacle in the East in the month of November.

Unfortunately for Harvard, this idea did not prove to be a correct one. The uniforms which were warmer to wear during the autumn chilly temperatures, became very heavy to wear when exposed to the rain, mud and snow.

In the hot and dry climate of Arizona, those leather uniforms were probably the worst type of clothing which one could wear. The Phoenix players were accustomed to the extreme hot weather of this area, but in the game with Carlisle they wilted in those new red leather uniforms. These uniforms were like an oven for the players and they soon became overheated and exhausted.

Carlisle was able to score on the Phoenix squad at will and ended up winning the game by the lop-sided score of 83-6. In a normal game, Carlisle would have beaten them anyway, but not as much as the scoreboard indicated in this game.

After such a rout, the coach of the Phoenix Indian School team asked us to stay as their guests for a few days and teach the Phoenix team some of our special plays. Which we did.

This was the first long trip that the Carlisle football team had ever taken and our success on this journey gave us an overall season record of 9 wins and 2 losses. However, these trips were to become quite common as the Carlisle Indian School grew in both popularity and national stature. We soon began to play most of our games away from home and took many trips to the West, including a second trip to the Pacific Coast in 1903. The newspaper writers, who were keenly aware of our frequent train travels each season, eventually began to refer to our team in their newspaper stories by calling us "the Nomads of the Gridiron."

Major Pratt, the Carlisle superintendent, sanctioned these trips because he believed that the Indian boys would receive a great education from traveling and their contact with other college men. This experience would more than offset any time that they lost in the classroom. And it was a noticeable fact that the Indian football players were often the brightest students at Carlisle and that their teachers frequently remarked on how much quicker they were to learn than the other students.

On many occasions following a road trip, the Carlisle teachers would ask the football players to tell stories of their travels to the class. These stories proved to be both entertaining for the other Indian students and allowed them to learn from the trips which the football team had taken.

During our football travels, the Carlisle squad always traveled first class by train and stayed at the best hotels. Their good conduct and manners and the quiet behavior they had while out amongst the public, always made us welcome guests wherever we went.

20

After the Carlisle team had returned from their West Coast trip, my duties as the Indian School's football coach were completed. It was at this point that Major Pratt, the school's superintendent, approached me to take over as Carlisle's director of athletics.

His offer was indeed flattering. Prior to this time, I had been coaching football at two schools in the fall and practicing law for the remainder of the year. I had even given serious thought as to possibly giving up coaching and pursuing my legal career full-time.

Suddenly, my career plans were at a serious juncture. If I decided to accept the year-around job as director of athletics at Carlisle, this would mean that I would have to give up my other coaching job at Iowa State and my budding law practice. However, at this particular stage in my legal career, I had not yet developed a great passion for law and it seemed to take a long time to build a law practice.

On the other hand, I did like athletics and had begun to achieve a fair measure of success in coaching. In addition, the new job's $2,500 salary which Carlisle was now offering was a large increase from my coaching salary of $1,200. It was also much more than I would make while practicing law at that time.

After a few days of thinking over Major Pratt's offer, I decided to accept it.

Looking back, I have estimated that in the long run I would have probably made more money while practicing law than in coaching football. Still, I have never regretted making this decision, although at times it has been rather difficult on the nerves.

As director of athletics at Carlisle, I had to oversee as well as coach and train all of the school's athletic teams. This job combined the present-day positions of athletic director, trainer and coach of the school's football, baseball and track teams.

Prior to my arrival there, Carlisle had fielded a strong baseball team. But the Indian School had never competed in competitive track and field against other schools.

I, of course, knew a lot about baseball and felt competent to coach this sport. Track, however, was like a foreign language to me. I knew virtually nothing about coaching track athletes.

Over the next 2-3 months, I proceeded to obtain all of the books that I could on the subject and got as much information as possible from my visits with other college coaches such as Michael Murphy, Jack Monkley and George Connors. Armed with a small bit of knowledge and an eager heart, I formed Carlisle's first track program in the spring of 1900.

The Indian boys, of course, were well adapted for the track and field events and they took to them quite readily.

Although we had no big stars in those first few years after starting the track program at Carlisle, we did turn out some very competitive squads and had increasing success against the small colleges and universities in Pennsylvania.

A few years after this meager start, Joe Pipal, the athletic director at Dickinson College, and I helped form the Pennsylvania Track & Field Athletic Association, which consisted of all of the colleges and universities in the state, except for the University of Pennsylvania. This association held an annual State championship track & field meet in Harrisburg, Pa., each year and Carlisle often had great success in winning this meet.

The Carlisle Indian boys eventually became well-known for their long-distance running. We were also blessed with some pretty good hurdlers and field event athletes, but sprinting was not one of our better events. The only exceptional sprinters that were ever on the Carlisle squad during my tenure there were Frank Cayou, Frank Mt. Pleasant and Jim Thorpe. Jim, however, was outstanding at anything he ever tried in athletics.

Many of the Carlisle boys went on to college after finishing their coursework at the Indian School. One of these was Frank Mt. Pleasant who was a talented sprinter on the Carlisle track team. He had the ability to become a world champion if he had continued to train harder when he went on to Dickinson College. Mt. Pleasant ran the 100-yard dash in ten seconds, the quarter mile in 49 seconds and broad-jumped more than 24 feet. In 1904 and 1908, Mt. Pleasant was chosen as a member of the U.S. Olympic team.

Although he only weighed 130 pounds, Mt. Pleasant was also a great football player. He was perhaps the best quarterback Carlisle ever had as well as being a skilled punter and drop-kicker. He later coached at Franklin & Marshall College.

Frank Cayou, another of my great sprinters, later went on to become a well-known sprinter and an outstanding halfback at the University of Illinois. Following his graduation there, Cayou became a football coach at Washington University in St. Louis. He later entered vaudeville, while working under a stage name, and had considerable success performing an Indian skit. Cayou was also a good singer which was rare for an Indian boy.

Edward Rogers wasn't on our track squad at Carlisle but he was an outstanding end on the Indian football team and went on to play for the University of Wisconsin. There, he became one of the best ends in the Midwest. Rogers later became a prominent lawyer in Wisconsin, which was his native state.

Another of the Indian School's gifted athletes was James Phillips who was one of the best guards that ever graced the Carlisle football field. He later graduated from the Dickinson College School of Law and became a member of the State of Washington Legislature.

Many of the Carlisle boys went on to college after attending the Indian School and later became successful in their careers. I have often been asked whether education was really beneficial to the Indian boys or did they simply return to the reservations and their old way of life after attending Carlisle. My experience at Carlisle convinced me that education was just as important and meaningful to the Indian boys as it was for our own race.

21

The Carlisle baseball teams held their own against the best college teams in the East and Midwest. The Indian boys had very good mechanical skills in batting, pitching and throwing but often displayed poor judgement while fielding or completing a play. This was probably due to their lack of educational training prior to their arriving at Carlisle, where they were finally taught how to think and use their brains.

Yet the Carlisle players loved the game of baseball with a great passion. Many of them had aspirations of developing into big-league players. Several of them were indeed fortunate in achieving this dream.

One of these was Louis Leroy, who was a successful pitcher while playing for Buffalo in the Eastern League (which later became known as the International League).

Leroy was an amusing ballplayer who loved to joke and have fun with his teammates. On one occasion while he was still playing for Carlisle, Leroy came into the locker room before practice. After sitting on a bench, he then began rubbing his arm and remarked to the other Indian ballplayers: "Now this here is a ten thousand dollar arm!"

Not to be upstaged, one of Leroy's teammates quickly responded, "Well, Leroy, you may have a $10,000 arm but you've also got a five-cent head."

This remark towards Leroy had been made in a friendly spirit, but it stung with the taste of the truth because everyone at Carlisle knew that Leroy was rather slow in his schoolwork and had a somewhat exaggerated opinion of his ability as a ballplayer.

However, there was one Indian boy at Carlisle who did possess a "ten thousand dollar arm." And he turned out to be a champion, too.

His name was Charles Albert Bender. He was a Chippewa Indian and had come to Carlisle when he was a small boy. As a youngster, he had often pitched to the Carlisle baseball squad members during the winter while they were getting indoor batting practice in the batting cage. When Bender was 16, his pitching in the indoor practice sessions impressed me such that I decided to put him on the varsity baseball squad.

When spring arrived and we moved outdoors to practice, I moved Bender to center field, where he quickly became a starter. I also placed him in our rotation as a substitute pitcher. Then in his second season on the Carlisle varsity, Bender became one of the team's starting pitchers and had an outstanding record.

In the summer following Bender's second season on the Carlisle team, he joined the Harrisburg Tri-State League and began playing under the name of Charles Albert. By the close of the summer, Bender had attracted the attention of Connie Mack, who wasted no time in signing him to play for the Philadelphia Athletics in the American League. Almost overnight, Bender became one of the star professional baseball pitchers in the country.

Rarely has a ballplayer ever had such a rapid rise to baseball fame as Bender. As a student at Carlisle, he was the brightest boy in his class and one of the youngest to ever graduate from the Indian School. He also held the record for checking out the most number of books from the Carlisle library.

While in the major leagues he became known as "Chief" Bender. He was the star pitcher in five World Series and for many years during his pro baseball career was considered to have been the best pitcher in either the American or National Leagues. In any high-stakes game, Bender could always be counted on to lead the Philadelphia Athletics to victory.

Following a long and successful playing career in the major leagues, Bender eventually retired and became a baseball coach and pitching tutor for several major league clubs. He later became the baseball coach at the U.S. Naval Academy at Annapolis.

During his final year at the Carlisle Indian School, Bender was also a member of the football team. Undoubtedly, he would have developed into a gridiron star if he had not graduated from Carlisle and entered pro baseball while only 17 years old.

Albert Bender was a rare find for any coach. His success made us all proud.

22

Carlisle had been a military school in its early days of existence after being founded by Major Pratt. The students were required to enroll for a five-year period. This commitment was later reduced to three years. However, if a student had not finished his school courses, he was then asked to stay long enough until their completion.

During the summer, the Carlisle students usually did not return to their homes. These students either stayed and worked at the Indian School or were placed in good homes in nearby towns under the "outing system."

In this program, the boys from Carlisle went to work on farms while the girls did housework in the homes. These students were paid for their labor and usually earned a lot of money for their summer's work. They also benefited from learning from those who they had lived with.

Sometimes a problem would crop up when a student became homesick and wanted to return to their home on a reservation in the West. Since they were not permitted to go home during the school year, some of these students would run away while out on a summer job in the outing system. They would then try to get home to their tribe as best they could. Often though, they were usually located and brought back to the Indian School.

We had one ballplayer at Carlisle, Louis Leroy — whom I had previously mentioned having "the $10,000 pitching arm and a five-cent head" — that ran away from the Indian School each spring as soon as baseball season was over. His escape schedule was like clockwork.

Leroy was crazy about playing baseball and was always trying to land a job with a professional baseball team, thus the reason for his annual spring madness.

And each fall, like clockwork, Leroy would return to Carlisle and beg to be able to re-enter the Indian School. On each occasion, he would make penitent promises not to desert again. For three years in a row, he successfully performed this routine while trying to land a major league baseball job.

After the third time that Leroy returned to Carlisle in the fall, Major Pratt, the school's superintendent, made up his mind that the next summer Leroy would have to remain at the Indian School during the summer break and not be given the opportunity to run off and play baseball. This decision was intended to last until Leroy had completed his term of enrollment at Carlisle.

The following spring of 1901 while on our last baseball trip, Leroy jumped off the train during a brief stop in Lancaster, Pa., on the return trip to Carlisle.

When we returned to Carlisle and noticed that Leroy was missing, Major Pratt sent me back to Lancaster to locate Leroy and return him to campus.

After a few days of checking out several false leads, I finally located Leroy when I went to visit a minor league pro baseball team that was in a nearby town. The team's manager told me that he hadn't seen a boy named Louis Leroy but that he had, however, just signed up a young Italian pitcher. The manager's signing of a new pitcher seemed to be more than a coincidence.

With a bit of detective work, I was soon able to locate where this red-skinned Italian pitcher had bunked in town for the evening.

I then went to see him.

When the young man answered my knock at the door of his boardinghouse room, his eyes lit up as he stood there in shock to see who was calling on him.

Yes, it was Leroy and he knew why I was there in his doorway.

"Come along with me, kid," I said as I yanked him out into the hallway. "You're going back to Carlisle. These summer playdays are over!"

We then went back into his room, got his gear and headed for the train station.

Upon our return to Carlisle, Leroy was placed in a dungeon

beneath the Barracks' old guard house for punishment.

The old guard house at Carlisle was originally built as an old frontier post to protect early settlers against the Indians in the French and Indian Wars. Later during the Revolutionary War, the post was expanded to become the Carlisle Barracks and it was used as a prison for captured Hessian soldiers. The walls in the old guard house were made of stone which were four feet thick. Downstairs, there were four dungeon-type cells which received no sunlight.

Leroy ended up spending the entire summer in one of these dungeon cells. He would not have received such severe punishment if he had not foolishly attacked one of the Indian boys who had carried him his meals each day. The attack occurred when the Indian boy opened the dungeon cell door to pass the food inside to Leroy, who then struck the boy over the head with the heel of his shoe and made a mad dash to escape.

Outside the old guard house, a group of boys who were playing baseball saw Leroy begin his escape and chased after him. Late that afternoon, he was finally discovered in a nearby barn while covered up with hay. Like a chicken, he had buried his head and body deep beneath in the hay but his big feet stuck out from under the hay. Leroy was promptly escorted back to the old guard house where he remained from mid-June until early September, when school began. Upon his release, Leroy vowed never to escape again.

In late September, after being out of the guard house for several weeks, Leroy joined the other Indian boys who were reporting for football practice. On a squad that was weak in overall ability and depth and had a tough schedule ahead in the 1901 season, Leroy made the varsity team as a substitute halfback.

After we were licked by Harvard, 29-0, in the eighth game of the season, and with both of our starting halfbacks having been injured in this fierce licking, we were now facing Michigan in our next game. I decided that it might be best to sacrifice the game against Michigan in an attempt to give both of my halfbacks a chance to get well and hopefully be able to play the remainder of the season.

There was, of course, another factor in my decision to sacrifice the upcoming game against the Wolverines. Two weeks later, we would be playing in Philadelphia against Penn, who was a big powerhouse among the Eastern schools and a school that Carlisle had built up a rivalry with in recent years.

Fielding Yost, the Michigan coach, had a great outfit that season with one of his "Point-a-Minute" teams. They were running up big scores every week on each team they played.

By leaving our two regular halfbacks at home instead of playing against Michigan, I had to move both Leroy and Edward DeMarr into the two starting halfback positions.

However, at lunch on the day of the Carlisle-Michigan game, both Leroy and DeMarr were reported missing from the team's hotel. These two must have figured that Detroit was pretty far West and this trip was a good opportunity to try to run away back to the reservation. As you can imagine, their desertion put us in a pretty tough spot.

In an attempt to even-up the situation I suggested to Yost that we reduce the game's regular 45-minute halves. But he wouldn't listen to me.

Our bad luck continued to mount when one of the Carlisle ends dislocated a shoulder in the first minute of the game. As the afternoon continued, Michigan walloped us, 22-0.

The following summer, Leroy would turn up while playing for the Buffalo team in the Eastern League. I happened to be in the area at that time en route to visit a relative so I stayed over a day in Buffalo to see him play in a game against Providence.

Leroy had no idea of my presence at the game. He was sitting by himself at the end of the player's bench prior to the beginning of the contest.

Unnoticed by him, I slipped into the dugout and went over to where he was sitting, slapped him on the shoulder and demanded: "Come over here for a moment!"

You should have seen Leroy's facial expression upon seeing me. He looked more shocked than at that boardinghouse in the town near Lancaster, Pa., when I had caught up with him before.

Leroy turned as pale as I have ever seen a redskin boy turn. Stammering and nervous, he replied, "Where to?"

"Back to Carlisle," I told him.

Leroy must have thought his chance at a career in the major leagues was all over. However, he soon became one happy Indian when I finally told him that I was only kidding and didn't plan to take him back to Carlisle.

George Stallings was the manager of the Buffalo baseball team at that time and a friend of mine. When Leroy told him that I was here to see him play, Stallings gave Leroy the starting pitching assignment for the afternoon.

Leroy then went out and pitched a phenomenal game that day and his team won over Providence. This, however, was the last time I ever saw the eccentric little Indian with a "ten thousand dollar pitching arm and a five-cent head."

23

When professional football began to get a lot of newspaper headlines in the late 1920's, most people seemed to think that this was some promotor's new invention. Almost overnight, newspaper writers and college football fans became alarmed at the presence of this venture. Their skepticism then created much speculation as to what effect the professionals might have on the college game.

However, most people — those living outside the Northeast — didn't realize that professional football had been around for a very long time. For me, I had already finished my brief pro football career before Red Grange, the famed Galloping Ghost of the University of Illinois and later of the Chicago Bears, had even been born. (Editor's Note: Grange was born on June 13, 1903, in Forksville, Pa.)

I played in my first and only professional football game in New York City in 1902. The game was played in the old Madison Square Garden. And my salary for participating in this game was $23.

Football as a possible big-time box office proposition indeed existed at the turn of the century. Yet it would not be until the late 1920's before it would begin to flourish on a wave of ballyhoo unknown to earlier football generations.

My involvement with professional football occurred because of my younger brother, Bill Warner, who had followed in my footsteps and played left guard at Cornell for four seasons. Bill was a great player there and earned a spot on Walter Camp's all-America team in 1901 and 1902.

It was also at Cornell that he succeeded in earning the nickname of "Little Pop."

Following his last game for Cornell, a promoter had approached him and asked if he would like to play for the Syracuse professional football team which would be playing in an indoor tournament in Madison Square Garden in New York City. The promoter told him that it would be a cooperative affair, with the net profits to be divided among the players on each team. It was estimated that each player's share would be $300, plus expenses.

With his college playing days now behind him and while continuing to work his way through Cornell, I advised Bill that he should accept the promoter's offer but to ask for a guarantee on the $300 salary — which the promoter promptly paid to him.

The promoter later approached me and asked if I would be interested in also playing for the Syracuse team.

Please remember that this was 1902 and it had been nearly eight years since I had played at Cornell. Still, I figured that I was in reasonably good shape and could contribute to the team effort. Besides, the extra pay would be a nice windfall for a short period of work.

After thinking over the offer, I decided to play if the promoter could arrange for me to play while using an assumed name.

With that understanding agreed to, I then traveled to Syracuse and joined in several practices with the Syracuse professional team. From there, we journeyed to New York City for the indoor professional football tournament.

Tom O'Rourke, the old prize fight promoter, was one of the promoters of the Madison Square Garden pro football tournament. The teams who were playing in the tournament were New York City, Philadelphia, Watertown (N.Y.) and, of course, Syracuse. Syracuse and Philadelphia were scheduled to play in the first night of the tournament, and New York and Watertown were to play on the second night. The two winning teams would then play in the final game for the professional football championship of the world.

The tournament's promoters had figured that Philadelphia and New York would be the winning teams in the two preliminary games, with Syracuse and Watertown being considered rather weak opposition. (Editor's Note: The Philadelphia pro team fielded a squad in this tournament which was composed mostly of ex-University of Pennsylvania football stars. Many of these players had earned national reputations and were expected to be a big box-office draw.)

Fate, however, had another plan for the professional football tournament. Our Syracuse squad upset the promoter's strategy when we defeated the ex-Penn stars by a close margin.

During this contest, I ended up playing the entire game and handled all of the team's kicking assignments. My efforts produced several field goals.

The next morning — following the game — I awoke feeling very stiff and could only move my tired body with great difficulty. I even had to call upon my brother, Bill, to help me get dressed that morning because of the tremendous pain that I was suffering.

After that single game, I decided to retire from my career in professional football.

Blondy Wallace, of the Philadelphia professional team, ended up taking my place in the final game. Still, I wound up being paid the magnificent sum of $23 as my share of the player's purse from the tournament's proceeds.

It would take me several weeks before I could move or dress without pain.

And the pro football tournament, well it proved to be a financial "flop" due to the early loss of the team from Philadelphia. My brother, Bill, was the only player in the tournament to receive the full amount that the players had been promised.

24

In 1903, Carlisle had one of the school's great football teams. Although we lost to Princeton, 11-0, and to Harvard by the narrow margin of 12-11, the Indian School won all of its other games that season, including a 16-6 victory over Penn and a 28-0 defeat of Northwestern.

It was in the game against Harvard that the Indians pulled off the now-famous "hidden ball" play. This play has been talked about and written about more than any other play in football history. The game was played at Soldiers Field in Cambridge—just two weeks prior to the opening of the massive Harvard Stadium, which would be the largest steel-reinforced structure in the world and America's first football stadium.

The controversy surrounding the hidden ball play was caused when a Carlisle player, while receiving the Harvard kickoff, concealed the football under the back of another Carlisle player's jersey. This Carlisle player then ran with the ball almost the entire length of the football field through a bewildered Harvard team for a touchdown.

Among the Indian players, the player who had been designated to carry the ball in this most unusual fashion was jokingly referred to as the "hunch back." After being used in the Carlisle-Harvard game, the hidden ball play quickly became famous and created an endless amount of controversy because it had occurred in an important game, but this was not the first time that this play had scored a touchdown.

When I was coaching at Cornell in 1897, I had the scrub team work the hidden ball play against the varsity in a practice game. Then later in the season against Penn State, the hidden ball play was used for the first time in a game. In those days, Penn State was not as strong on the gridiron as they would later become and this game was merely a workout for Cornell.

This play was only used once in the game and this was late in the fourth quarter after Cornell had already secured a big lead on the scoreboard.

After Penn State had scored a touchdown, the referee announced to both teams that there was only 30 seconds remaining in the game. It was late afternoon and the skies were getting somewhat dark so I thought that perhaps now was the perfect time to try the new trick play that we had been successfully using in practice on several occasions. Wasting no time, I then sent in a substitute player with instructions to use the hidden ball play on the ensuing kickoff.

And the play worked like a charm. The Cornell ballcarrier made it through the opposition untouched and scored a touchdown.

Dr. Newton, who was a competent and well-known referee of that era, declared the kickoff runback a touchdown but afterwards said: "I don't know how the ball reached the other end of the field unless there is an underground passage."

During this era, a player's jersey was generally worn outside of his game pants instead of inside the game pants as is the custom now. So by installing an elastic cord through the hem of the waistline of a player's jersey, we were able to place a football under the front of a player's jersey or could shove it up the back of his jersey. In either case, the ball would not easily fall out.

Unfortunately, those kinds of tricks are not seen anymore.

At Carlisle practices, we often practiced this play and other trick plays to liven up the daily grind of scrimmaging. Sometimes these plays worked successfully and sometimes not. But neither the Indian boys nor myself considered the hidden ball play to be strictly legitimate. We did, however, know that the play would work against Harvard and, at least, prove to be a good joke on the arrogant Crimson players.

In the Carlisle-Harvard game of 1903, the Indians led, 5-0, at the end of the first half.

Knowing that Harvard would be kicking off to begin the second half, I went over and explained to Mike Thompson, one of the game's referees and perhaps the best football official in the country, that we were going to attempt the hidden ball play in the second half. I also informed him of the details of how this play would be run.

On the kickoff to begin the second half, the Harvard kicker attempted to kick the ball deep and to one side of the field. In doing so, he booted the ball out of bounds, thus forcing the ball to be kicked again. The second kickoff then sailed far and high down the middle of the field, where it was caught on the goal line by Jimmy Johnson, our quarterback.

Quickly, the Carlisle players gathered together in what would now be called "a huddle" formation, except that everyone was facing outward. Johnson, who was in the middle of the huddle then slipped the ball under the back of Charles Dillon's jersey and shouted, "Go!"

Dillon had been selected to be the "hunch back" because he was a big and fast runner. Playing the position of a guard on the team, he would not be suspected of carrying the ball on a kickoff return.

When Johnson yelled "Go!" this was the prearranged signal for the Indian players to scatter and run upfield and toward both sidelines. As they did, Dillon continued to run straight down the field. The result of this planned confusion was that the Harvard players could not get a side view on the hump of Dillon's back where the football was safely hidden.

Carl Marshall, the famous Harvard quarterback and captain, was playing the safety position on the kickoff. When Dillon came running toward him, with his arms swinging as though to block him, Marshall unsuspectedly stepped aside and allowed Dillon to continue on his journey toward the goal line.

As it turned out, no Harvard player laid a hand on the big Carlisle guard, who crossed Harvard's goal line with the ball still stuffed in the back of his jersey. Afterwards, several Indian players removed the ball from Dillon's jersey and touched it to the ground for the score.

Referee Thompson, while knowing that the play was to be made, and therefore being able to watch it carefully, declared that it was unquestionably a touchdown within the rules.

Afterwards, the large Boston crowd, who had come out to see the popular Indians play, arose to their feet and cheerfully applauded the flying Indian with the hump on his back and who had romped through a bewildered Harvard group of would-be tacklers.

The play, however, was no joke to the Harvard coaches and players, who were now eleven points behind and facing defeat. The Crimson team then began to play desperately from that point on. They eventually blocked a punt and scored a touchdown. Late in the second half, the Crimson broke loose on a long run and scored another touchdown. This gave Harvard the lead, 12-11, and eventually the victory.

In a way, I'm glad that Harvard was able to come back to win because I never liked to win a game on a fluke, although the hidden ball play was within the rules at that time.

25

After the exciting scrapper and near defeat of Harvard, my inspired Carlisle squad began to click off the victories.

A week later, the Indians convincingly smashed Georgetown, 28-6, in a game which was played on their home field in Washington, D.C.

We then traveled to Philadelphia and defeated Penn, 16-6, which was our second straight victory against this mighty East Coast rival.

Feeling perhaps a bit cocky following our win over the Quakers, we didn't take our next game against Virginia seriously and managed to only pull off a 6-6 tie. In this contest, we tried too many daring, crowd-pleasing plays which brought a lot of applause and cheers from the Norfolk, Va., crowd. But in the end result, this exhibition of showmanship didn't help us win.

However, on Thanksgiving Day, we proceeded to get back on track. By returning to our basic offense of counter-bucks, dives and sweeps, the Indians romped over Northwestern, 28-0, in a wind-chilled contest in Chicago.

With our record now standing at 8 wins, 2 losses and 1 tie at the end of our regular season, I accepted an offer for the Carlisle squad to travel to the West Coast in mid-December to play three opponents.

Our first stop on this journey was a match against the University of Utah on December 19th.

On the morning of the game, I had to bench our team captain and all-America quarterback, Jimmy Johnson, over a rule infraction. His replacement, Joe Baker, did an admirable job that afternoon and led us to a 22-0 victory over the Salt Lake City school.

Johnson, however, fumed about being benched.

Upon our arrival in San Francisco, there was a large contingent of newspaper writers on hand to meet our train. They were greatly interested in this nomadic Indian football squad who had earned such an impressive reputation while playing in the East.

In their pre-game stories, the San Francisco sportswriters had heaped large amounts of praise on the gridiron abilities of Johnson, the little Indian quarterback who led our Carlisle team. His stature as a member of Walter Camp's all-America team put him in the focus of all of the limelight which the Carlisle squad had attracted.

Of course, this vast publicity build-up also served to widen the recent strain that had developed between Johnson and me.

Our trip to the West Coast was to include games against two teams from the San Francisco area. The pivotal match in this journey was the Christmas Day contest against the Reliance Athletic Association, which was a team composed entirely of all-star players. The San Francisco newspapers had referred to them as "The All-California Team" because it represented the best former college football talent in the entire state. Our other opponent on this trip was the Sherman Institute, which was an Indian school much like Carlisle.

An hour before the kickoff against Reliance, I pulled both Johnson and Baker over to a corner of our locker room and informed Johnson that he would be the team's starting quarterback that afternoon.

As I continued to give him the pre-game strategy and instructions, Johnson — who must have been still mad at me over being benched at Utah — suddenly flared up at me and shouted: "Listen Pop. I don't care if I never play in one of your ball games!"

Now, while looking back, I must admit that I was upset at Johnson's attitude. However, I was determined to not let him take control of this situation. Without hesitation, I then turned to Baker and told him that he would be taking Johnson's position as the starting quarterback.

Almost immediately, the other Indian players who had overheard Johnson's outburst came over to where we were standing and began to request that I give Johnson a second chance and let him play.

Realizing that this moment could greatly impact our morale heading into the afternoon's contest, I decided to turn up the emotional heat in the locker room by telling them: "Baker really did a fine job for us against Utah. And besides, I couldn't play a player whose heart wouldn't be in the game."

It was at this point that my temperamental redskin quarterback, who was probably beginning to feel the emotional weight of the moment, spoke up. He noted, "Well, Coach. If the other boys want me to play, I will."

Feeling that Johnson was earnest in his intentions, I agreed to let him take his regular position on the field that afternoon.

Next, something truly amazing happened. Whether it was because I had gotten under Johnson's skin by bragging on the football prowess of Joe Baker, his substitute, or perhaps it was because he had been reading of Walter Camp's praise for him in the San Francisco newspapers. Undoubtedly, it was one of these reasons, or probably both, because a now-inspired Johnson went out that afternoon and played the best game of his career.

His deft ballhandling skills and lightning runs proved him to be a truly amazing gridiron magician as he led Carlisle to a 23-0 shutout over California's top football talent.

In the newspaper stories following the contest, the consensus of opinion among the San Francisco sportswriters was that Johnson was "the greatest quarterback that had ever been seen on the Pacific Coast."

A week later, on New Year's Day, the Indians met their redskin opponents from the Sherman Institute. My Carlisle squad didn't view this encounter with the same sort of seriousness as the Reliance game. And though they played well enough to win, 12-6, the Carlisle players much more enjoyed trying to see if they could succeed in pulling off more gadget, or hocus-pocus, plays than their opponents.

Normally, I would have gotten upset at this kind of performance, but since it was at the end of a long season — and as long as we were winning the game — I was glad to see the Carlisle boys having some fun.

26

A few weeks after our return from the West Coast, I received a visit from three Cornell representatives — Professor L.M. Dennis, the faculty football representative on the Cornell Athletic Council; Jim Lynah, the recently-elected captain of the Cornell football squad; and David Hoy, the baseball representative on the Cornell Athletic Council — who wanted me to return to my alma mater as both the school's football and baseball coach.

My brother, Bill, who had a stellar career as an all-America lineman on the Cornell football squads of 1901 and 1902 and graduated from Cornell in the spring of 1903, had served as the school's football coach during the 1903 season.

Bill had posted a respectable record of 6 wins, 3 losses and one tie during his first year at the helm of the Cornell football program. However, in reviewing the flow of the 1903 season I quickly noticed why the Cornell alumni had become a bit disgruntled.

The Redmen had won their first six games of the season and outscored their opponents, 108 to 0. But from that point on until the end of the season, Bill's squad fell into a slump. They then proceeded to lose 3 of their next four games and tied the other one.

And to make matters worse, one of these losses was a 44-0 shutout at the hands of Princeton. Another was a 17-12 loss to Columbia. But the defeat that got the Cornell alumni most disturbed was a season finale, 42-0 blowout loss to Penn.

When the Cornell representatives initially approached me about returning to the Ithaca campus, it was not a flattering salary offer which had turned my head. Instead, it was the fact that I sincerely didn't want to see my brother, Bill, get caught in the middle of any kind of tug-of-war match with the Cornell alumni and administration over the football team's direction. Based on my previous tenure there, I knew that this could be a rather difficult spot to be put in.

Also, knowing that Major Pratt was probably gonna be forced to retire from his post as the superintendent at Carlisle in perhaps the next year or two by certain federal officials and Congressmen who didn't agree with his continued success at the Indian School, my decision became much easier. Finally, a few weeks after the Cornell representatives first approached me, I agreed to take their offer.

That fall, the Cornell football program began to slowly make some strides in the right direction. We pulled off a record of 7 wins and three losses and narrowed the margins of the previous season's losses. Princeton only defeated us by the score of 18-6; Columbia managed to only win by a 12-6 margin; but Penn was still able to pull off a lopsided, 34-0 shutout.

However, I was building for the future. And in the next two seasons, Cornell's football prowess began to reach that level of quality and stability that I had hoped for.

In 1905, the Redmen posted a record of six wins and four losses. After winning our first six games of the season, we lost to Swarthmore, 14-0, and got knocked off by Princeton, 16-6, and by Columbia, 12-6. Against Penn, we lost a heartbreaking, difficult battle by the mere margin of 6-5.

The following season, in 1906, my rebuilding plan started to show off some impressive results as Cornell posted a record of eight wins, one loss and two ties.

Our only loss of the season was to Princeton, 14-5. We also opened the season with a scoreless tie against Colgate and were able to pull off a similar feat against Penn in the season finale.

Needless to say, the Cornell alumni were becoming quite happy with the improvements being made on the gridiron.

But off the field, I began to run into a lot of friction with certain alumni over my handling and the direction of the Cornell football program. And during this era, the alumni played just as a significant part in influencing a school's football program as the fanatic alumni of the modern era.

Unfortunately, it was alumni interference that played a large part in my decision to leave Cornell and return to the Carlisle Indian

School in 1907. But there were also other considerations for my departure from my alma mater.

I had previously left Cornell as head coach following the 1898 season because of an unfortunate mixup over the election of the team's varsity captain for the next season.

During my second term at Cornell, from 1904-1906, I encountered an unpleasant problem that every football coach eventually meets up with during his career — having to discipline a star player on the team.

In this case, I took the extreme course — which was the only one possible for the team's ultimate welfare. I dropped him from the squad.

But my disciplining of this player nearly caused a campus riot. The player was a hero among the school's student body, and naturally my action created an uproar with them and caused a lot of trouble and unrest. I, however, had anticipated the students' response in this problem and was ready to meet it head on.

I had felt in my heart and mind that I was right in regards to my handling of the matter, because I had done what any coach would have done if he has any *backbone* to him. And I wasn't worried about any negative criticism being thrown my way afterwards.

But in the end result, it proved to be the event which forced me to leave Cornell.

After my two terms at Cornell I came away convinced of three important observations: 1) a football coach there had a larger uphill road to overcome than most other schools during this era; 2) Cornell was not very cooperative in allowing for football practice time; and 3) there was also an unusually high academic requirement for all students and a general lack of active alumni support.

Following my departure from Cornell, the football team began to slip down a notch or two in their on-field performance despite the excellent efforts of a highly-efficient coaching staff. For awhile, my replacement, Henry Schoellkopf, was able to continue the success that I had established. But when he left after the 1908 season, the program began to fall apart. It would be nearly another decade, while under Al Sharpe and then later under Gil Dobie, before the Cornell football program would recover and get back on track.

27

In 1906 there was a change in the long-standing football rules. The style of football which had been played prior to then, with its close formations, had continued to grow rougher with its dangerous pushing and pulling. Beefy-sized players were very popular in this era, along with tousled and over-padded hair. Intelligence helped but it wasn't a top requirement.

Yet, I must also note that some of the smartest men who ever trod a gridiron played before 1906. But the lightweight man — no matter how smart and cunning — had little, if any, chance against the revolving wedge, the flying interference and similar old-time strategies of employing weight and momentum.

In the era of football prior to 1906, with only 5 yards to gain in three downs, there was no necessity for anything but the slam-bang method of attack. The ball and the runner was so closely surrounded on every play that the spectators were usually unable to follow it and seldom saw the ball except on a kick.

There was also no open style of offense as you see today, which produced very little variety.

Speed had little place in a team's offensive attack. Big human mountains were sought and valued by every coach and it didn't matter if the behemoths could navigate slowly or swiftly.

The style of play in this era — primarily close up and piling on against the opposition — made the casualty lists long and often serious by the end of every season. And by 1906, a considerable amount of strong agitation had built up against the game and many advocated its complete abolishment.

On the Pacific Coast, many of the colleges there actually did stop playing football and, instead, took up the sport of rugby. This English import game grew in importance and flourished for about 10 years before eventually dying out.

A growing dissatisfaction with the Rules Committee began to erupt at this time. The Rules Committee had pretty much been a closed group of college coaches from the East who had grown up playing and teaching the old style of football and its rough play.

This growing dissatisfaction soon spread from coast to coast and eventually burst into an open antagonism against the Rules Committee and the existing rules. Such an uproar, along with the prodding of President Theodore Roosevelt, finally forced the Rules Committee to react. Radical changes in the playing rules and regulations were soon made and implemented.

Almost overnight, the game of football became less dangerous and more wide open, which made it more interesting for spectators to enjoy. The forward pass was legalized and encouraged as a first radical step in a new direction of playing style. However, it would be another seven years — in 1913 — before the forward pass began to be popularly used.

The pushing and pulling of players was prohibited under the new rules. And the old practice of additional linemen being set in the backfield to carry the ball — such as in the "guards back" or "tackles back" formation — were also curbed by the new rules which required that a minimum of seven players be set along the line of scrimmage.

In addition, the antiquated "5 yards in three attempts to make a first down" was stretched to ten yards to make a first down — and in the same number of attempts. A few years later, a fourth down was added to the 10-yard, first-down requirement.

The onsides kick was legalized by putting every player onsides as soon as the punted ball hit the ground. This rule, however, did not work out among the coaches and players and was soon discarded.

It is important to understand that the losing team in a game seldom had the chance to rush the ball and defense it properly because the stronger team usually was able to smash and grind the ball downfield in short, steady gains until they had finally crossed the goal line. The weaker teams could seldom cope with these steamroller tactics.

However, under the changed rules, it became much more difficult to make a first down. Possession of the ball became less important.

Consequently, all teams began to open up and take more chances.

The old push-and-pull offenses such as the flying interference, the revolving wedge and others had not been developed to gain 10 yards in three tries — at least not in dependable fashion. These age-old methods and systems were soon scrapped and new ones were invented and installed.

The new rules spelled the doom of the big-college, East Coast supremacy on the gridiron and swept in a new era of fresh contenders. Coaches of the younger generation — which I was a member of — were not handicapped by old customs. They were quicker to adapt both themselves and their teams to the new order of the game of football than were the older and more conservative coaches of the large Eastern schools.

Football in the South and the West also began to grow more rapidly because of the rule changes.

28

From 1904 to 1906, while I was back at Cornell, football at the Carlisle Indian School continued to flourish and was strongly supported by the school's new superintendent, Major W. A. Mercer, an Army officer who loved athletics and the Indians' growing prominence as an Eastern football power.

For the first season, 1904, Mercer had recruited a Carlisle alumnus, Edward Rodgers, who had been a famous Carlisle player, to coach the team and the Indians posted a 9-2-0 record. In 1905, George Woodruff, the former Penn coach, took charge and turned out a 10-4-0 record. Then in 1906, another Carlisle alumnus, Bemus Pierce, became the coach of the Indians.

It was in this time, in 1906, that the forward pass came into vogue. I was still coaching at Cornell in my second post there, but Major Mercer asked me to come back to Carlisle for a week in early September to show the Indians my plans on how to adapt from what remained of the old-fashioned running game to the new forward passing game.

The Indians quickly picked up on this new style of offense and went on to enjoy a record of 9 wins and 3 losses under Bemus Pierce.

Later that winter, after I had my falling out at Cornell, Major Mercer invited me to return to Carlisle to coach the Indian team in 1907. I gladly accepted his offer.

At the beginning of the 1907 season, I noted that the material on this squad was quite good and I was encouraged about our prospects. By the end of the season, they would prove to be one of the best Indian teams that I ever coached. Princeton ended up licking us, 16-0, in a game which was played in the rain, but this was our only defeat in the season.

The Indians had been deadly accurate in their use of long passes while on offense during the 1907 season. However, with the bad weather and being forced to handle a slippery ball, the Indians were unable to make full use of their potent passing attack against Princeton. This difficulty helped decide the game in the Tigers' favor.

The forward passing game was still in the experimental stage at this time. There were no rules yet against the offensive team going downfield and knocking over a defensive player or interfering with someone who might be able to intercept or knock down the pass.

With the rules that existed then, the Indians would often go into punt formation and throw long, arching passes down the field with the ineligible players running and knocking over the defensive players so that the eligible offensive players could go downfield and catch the ball.

The Indian players were so successful with this play that it resulted in the rule being changed the next year, in 1908. This new rule change brought in the "pass-interference penalty" which prevented the players of the offensive team from going downfield and interfering with a defensive player during a passing play.

If you put yourself in the position of a defensive safety, you can probably imagine how you might feel — and perhaps where else you might want to be — with ten or eleven speeding Indians bearing down on you with the intention of walloping you en masse — if necessary. The ball being thrown into your defensive territory would have little hope of being intercepted or batted away under these conditions.

Bill Hollenback, who was a famous Penn back, had a taste of this onslaught offensive interference when playing against Carlisle.

"I'd see the ball sailing in my direction," Hollenback would later describe. "And at the same time came the thundering of what appeared to be a tribe of Indians racing at full tilt in my direction. When this gang hit you, they just simply wiped you out and you lost all other interest in the football contest."

Hollenbeck was so banged up following one of the Carlisle-Penn encounters that he had to recuperate at Atlantic City. Both of his arms were in slings and two attendants were required to help him recover to his former self.

29

Jim Thorpe, who was a member of the Sac and Fox Indian tribe and had been raised in the Oklahoma Territory, came to Carlisle in 1904 when he was just 16 years old. He was a scrawny kid who had not developed much. He stood 5 feet, 5 inches and weighed only 115 pounds.

However, after spending nearly 18 months in the "outing system" while working as a foreman on the farm of Harby Rozarth in Robbinsville, N.J., Jim returned to Carlisle in the spring of 1907 and looked a lot different. He was now 19 years old and had gained nearly thirty pounds and five inches in height. More importantly, Jim also displayed a more grown-up attitude.

It was after his return that I first met Jim.

In late April 1907, Jim was walking across one of the twin, grass practice fields with some of his schoolmates en route to play a late afternoon football game with some of the other Indian boys. While walking near the track that covered this upper grassy practice field, Jim noticed several boys from the varsity track team practicing the high jump. The bar kept going higher and higher until it finally reached 5 feet, 9 inches. None of the Carlisle track boys were able to make it at that height.

The track boys were ready to call it quits when Jim approached them and asked if he could have a try at it.

The track boys were amused at Jim's request but consented to give him a shot. They then reset the bar at 5 feet, 9 inches. Jim was dressed in a pair of overalls, a hickory shirt and a pair of gym shoes that belonged to someone else, yet on his first attempt he cleared the bar with great ease. He then walked away laughing to rejoin his friends in a football game, while the track boys were left with a look of astonishment on their faces and some heavily bruised egos.

The following day, I was told of Jim's impressive accomplishment by a Carlisle student, Harry Archenbald. I immediately sent for Jim so that I could see who this mystery athlete was.

When Jim arrived in my office an hour later, he asked, "You wanted to see me, Coach. Have I done anything wrong?"

I then told him, "Son, you've only broken the school record in the high jump. That's all."

Jim responded with a sigh of relief at my statement. He quickly noted to me, "Pop, I didn't think that very high. I think I can do better in a track suit."

Putting my arm around his shoulder, I told Jim that we'd make sure he got a track uniform because beginning that afternoon he would be on the Carlisle track team.

30

In the fall of 1907, Jim Thorpe reported for football practice and immediately attracted a lot of attention on a Carlisle team that would prove to be one of the best teams in the history of college football.

Jim began his football career as a substitute halfback on the Carlisle varsity team, but this eventual Pro Football Hall of Fame member was rather fortunate to have ever been issued a uniform.

I was originally against Jim joining the Carlisle football team because he was still rather on the skinny side at 145 to 148 pounds. He was also my best track man and I didn't want to see him get hurt.

But Jim didn't like to take "no" for an answer. He kept pestering me to allow him to suit up and prove himself. Finally one day, when I had grown weary of his continued requests, I told him: "All right. If this is what you want, go out there and give my varsity boys a little tackling practice. And believe me, kid, that's *all* you'll be to them."

That afternoon at football practice, Jim ran through the Carlisle varsity defense and made them look like a bunch of old maids. He easily outran most of them. And those who happened to get close enough to tackle him, they either bounced off his hard-pumping legs or fell on their faces while grabbing at him in an attempt to make a tackle.

Standing on the sideline, I gazed in amazement while watching Jim perform his magical run through the Carlisle defense.

Afterwards, he jogged back to where I was standing and tossed the ball to me. He had a big grin on his face.

"I gave them some good practice? Right, Pop?" Jim noted.

One of my assistants, who was standing nearby, jokingly told him, "You're supposed to let them tackle you, Jim. You weren't supposed to run through them!"

Jim's big grin then began to disappear. Instead of being praised for his great run, he was now being laughed at. This made him quite mad.

"Nobody going to tackle Jim," he quickly proclaimed.

By now, my face was flush with anger at being shown up by this young Indian and his display of cockiness. I took the football and slapped it into his mid-section and told him: "Well let's see if you can do it again, kid!"

As Jim ran back out onto the field for another offensive play, I yelled out to the players on defense: "This isn't a track meet. Who does this kid think he is? Hit him so hard that he doesn't get up and try it again!"

Needless to say, on the next play Jim ran through the entire Carlisle defense with ease. No one could get a firm grasp on him and he gracefully strode into the end zone for another touchdown.

After crossing the goal line for the score, Jim circled back in my direction. When he got close, he tossed the ball to me and proudly noted: "Sorry, Pop. Nobody going to tackle Jim!"

I cussed at both him and my varsity defense for a few moments. After calming down, I told one of my assistants: "He certainly is a wild Indian. Isn't he?"

My assistant shook his head and added, "Yeah, untamed and one of a kind."

Now, after a lifetime of football coaching, I must admit that Jim's performance at practice that afternoon on the Carlisle varsity playing field was an exhibition of athletic talent that I had never before witnessed, nor was I ever to again see anything similar which might compare to it.

31

Following Jim Thorpe's impressive showing at football practice, I decided to permanently move him up to the Carlisle varsity. Our season was soon approaching with only 10 days remaining until the first game, but I figured that with a lot of work Jim could learn our system of plays and polish his blocking, tackling and passing skills so that he might could help us later that fall.

The 1907 Carlisle team was a powerhouse that boasted of a starting eleven which consisted of such great players as Albert Exendine and William Gardner at the end positions; Emil Hauser (Wauseka) and Antonio Lubo (Wolf) as tackles; Samuel McClean (Man-Afraid-of-a-Bear) and William Winnie as guards; Little Boy at Center; Frank Mt. Pleasant as the quarterback; Albert Payne and Fritz Hendricks as halfbacks; and Peter Hauser as the fullback.

Our squad was smaller and lighter than most of the opponents, but our great determination and speed allowed us to defeat Penn State, Syracuse, Penn, Harvard, the University of Minnesota and the University of Chicago.

The biggest win for us that season was against the University of Chicago, who was coached by Amos Alonzo Stagg — the great coach who would later retire with 314 wins. (Editor's Note: Stagg held the record as the winningest football coach in major college football until 1981 when Paul "Bear" Bryant broke it. Bryant later retired with 323 wins. However, the recent finding of Pop Warner's additional wins at Iowa State, Carlisle and Pittsburgh have caused this record to be corrected to reflect Warner as the all-time winningest coach.)

Stagg's team was undefeated at the time and were led by Wally Steffen, who was a great runner with amazing cutting ability. Stagg had called this Chicago squad "his best team ever," but both Exendine and Gardner kept Steffen fenced in all afternoon and Carlisle won, 18-4.

Our only setback that season was at the hands of Princeton. The game was played on the Princeton campus and in a downpour of rain.

The foul weather hampered the Carlisle team greatly. And for some reason, the Indian boys always seemed to lose interest if they were forced to play in soggy or snowy conditions.

Little Boy, who was one of the best linemen to ever play for Carlisle, following this game gave me an explanation for the Indians' halfhearted play in foul weather. He told me: "Football no good fun in mud and snow."

A similar problem had occurred for Carlisle nearly two years earlier in 1905 when their opponent, the Canton Athletic Club of Canton, Ohio, had learned that the Indians did not like to play in the mud. Before the game, some of their fans fire-hosed the Canton A.C. playing field for three consecutive days. The game looked like a comedy of errors and Canton won the contest easily, 8-0.

In the 1907 contest against Princeton, the weather was our only enemy. However in the end, Princeton won the game, 16-0, and put a bit of a damper on what had been a memorable season.

For Jim Thorpe, the 1907 season was anything but a memorable season. He had spent a great deal of the season while sitting on the Carlisle bench as an understudy for our right halfback, Albert Payne. Yet it was there that he was able to learn the rules of the game of football. His understudy role also pushed Payne into having a great season.

Carlisle finished the year with a splendid mark of 10 wins and one loss and outscored our opponents, 267 to 62.

32

While at Carlisle, I had developed a theory that the Indian boys had been trained by their forefathers to be keen observers. Often when the Indian boys were exposed to a new sport or game they would usually refuse to participate. Instead, they would stand and watch the older, more experienced Indian boys, who were participating in the new sport or new game, demonstrate how it was to be played.

Then after having studied the play or actions of their elders, they would attempt to mimic those same actions, or motions, and would usually be almost as accomplished as those who they had just observed.

While sitting on the bench as a substitute in 1907, Jim Thorpe was able to observe the great kicking skills of Peter Hauser and Frank Mt. Pleasant, the formidable passing abilities of Mt. Pleasant and the excellent blocking and tackling example of Albert Exendine.

Jim proved to be a fast learner and eventually got to play in a few games that season. He was also invited to eat at the Carlisle football team's dining table and move into their special dormitory.

In the spring of 1908, Jim continued his steady improvement in track. He won the high-jump event by clearing six feet at the Penn Relays, then in a triangular track meet with Dickinson and Swarthmore he set a school record for the 220-yard hurdles at 26 seconds. (Editor's Note: Jim Thorpe would eventually lower his time to 23.6 seconds for this event.)

In a meet with Syracuse, Jim captured five events and placed second in another. He won both the high and low hurdles, the broad jump, the high jump and the shot-put and was the runner-up in the hammer throw.

At the Intercollegiate Meet at the Harrisburg, Pa., Jim triumphed in the high and low hurdles, the hammer throw, the high jump and the low jump.

Then in a big meet in Philadelphia, the Middle Atlantic Association Meet, Jim placed first in all five of the events that he entered — and this was against the best athletes on the East Coast.

After a trip home to Oklahoma during the Indian School's summer break, Jim returned to Carlisle with great enthusiasm and a determined attitude. He was much more disciplined in his schoolwork and training and began to serve as a leader for the other Indian boys to look up to.

While now weighing 175 pounds and in excellent physical shape, Jim stepped into the left halfback starting position to replace Frank Mt. Pleasant who had graduated.

Exendine and Lubo had also graduated but many of the stars from the 1907 squad remained. Among those returning were Wauseka, McClean, Little Boy, Hauser, Hendricks, Payne and Winnie.

The 1908 Carlisle team posted a record of 10 wins, two losses and one tie that season, with the two defeats being at the hands of Harvard, 17-0, and Minnesota, 11-6.

Thorpe was the headline grabber all season for the Indians, but his most memorable run was in a sixty-yard romp for a touchdown against Penn. He also added the extra-point kick to tie the game, 6-6.

Jim's running and kicking prowess continued to excite the packed stadiums that came to see the Carlisle Indians play. Newspaper writers found him to be great copy for their stories.

And as Thorpe's legend began to grow, his loving fans in each town or city began to toast him in the local saloons in post-game celebrations. This new-found success and the many invitations for free drinks of whiskey or beer, however, would eventually begin to cause problems off the field for the Carlisle star.

33

Jim Thorpe's five-year term of enrollment at Carlisle concluded in the spring of 1909 and he returned to his home in Oklahoma.

Or, at least, that is where the school administrators at Carlisle thought he had gone to.

Except for a visit by Jim to see the Carlisle-St. Louis game, which was played in Cincinnati, Ohio, on Thanksgiving Day in 1909, and a trip by Jim and some friends to visit Carlisle at Christmas — when Jim had promised to return to Carlisle for the spring semester, but never did — we had little contact with him until the summer of 1911 when the Olympic Games of 1912 were beginning to be discussed.

I had thought that if Jim would return to Carlisle, he would stand an excellent chance of making the American Olympic team. It was then that I wrote to him and pitched him on the idea. Jim jumped at my suggestion and quickly returned to Carlisle. He arrived just in time for the kickoff of the 1911 football season.

This edition of the Carlisle team turned out to be the best in the school's history — even better than the 1907 squad. They defeated both Harvard and Penn and lost only one game of the season.

For one reason or another, the Indians were never able to go through an entire season without at least one defeat. And this defeat usually came at the hands of some team which the Indians should have beaten.

As often happens to other great teams, the Indians' only loss of the 1911 season was to Syracuse and it came about because they had underestimated their opponent and lost through sheer overconfidence.

But the Indians' greatest moment of the season came against Harvard on November 11th in a game at Cambridge, Mass. Before a crowd of 30,000 fans jammed into the concrete behemoth beside the Charles River, also known as Harvard Stadium, Carlisle took on their powerful Eastern foe in a game which had been heavily publicized for weeks in the Boston newspapers.

Percy Haughton, the Harvard coach who had previously followed me at Cornell when I had gone to coach Carlisle the first time, had dressed forty Crimson players for the contest. He had also added fuel to the game's growing publicity when he had told the newspaper writers that "he may not have to use his first team for the game."

The Carlisle-Harvard game would prove to be one of Jim Thorpe's greatest college games. (Editor's Note: The other game would be against Army in 1912.) Carlisle destroyed both Harvard's first and second teams that afternoon and gave the large crowd much to cheer about.

Jim led the Carlisle effort all day and showed to everyone in Harvard Stadium that he had the heart of a lion. With a heavily-bandaged leg and a badly swollen ankle, he kicked four field goals, including one from the 48-yard line.

Although every movement must have been in agony, not once did he ask for a time-out. Because of these injuries — and also because I figured that Harvard expected Jim to carry the ball on every play — I switched the Carlisle offensive plan of attack and began to use him mostly as a decoy or a blocker through the remainder of the first half.

The game continued to be bitterly fought in the second half, with Haughton, the Harvard coach, putting in his well-rested first team — for the first time in the game — in the fourth quarter while Carlisle's starting lineup continued to hold their ground valiantly.

When Jim saw that the game was turning into a tight struggle, he forgot about both his injured leg and sprained ankle and told the Carlisle quarterback to begin feeding him the ball once again.

And how that Indian did run! His courageous effort carried us to a 18-15 victory over Harvard that afternoon.

Following the game, one of the Harvard players told me that trying to tackle Jim was like trying to stop a steam engine.

Against Harvard on that memorable day, Jim was a one-man wrecking crew.

The Harvard game also brought in $10,400 to Carlisle as our share of the contest's gate receipts — the largest amount that Carlisle had ever received up until that time.

Upon our return home to Carlisle, Pa., we were met by the entire Carlisle student body, the school band and most of the townspeople. This large welcoming celebration soon turned into a victory parade that led us back to the Carlisle campus. Between the victory over Harvard and the parade, this was one weekend that the Indian boys at Carlisle would long remember.

34

The conclusion of the 1911 football season was just the first phase of what would eventually become a very special year.

In December, Jim Thorpe and many of the other Indian ballplayers began to prepare for the 1912 winter indoor track season. The two stars on the Carlisle track team that season were Jim and Louis Tewanima, the Hopi Indian long-distance runner.

In the winter indoor track season, both Jim and Tewanima entered several meets and grabbed great victories in each of those meets. But these were merely tune-ups for the long and difficult outdoor season that lay ahead.

During the winter indoor track season, Jim had confined his efforts to the shot-put, high jump, broad jump and low hurdles. For the spring outdoor season, he added the pole vault, the javelin, the discus and the hammer throw.

Still, there was a difficult struggle to keep Jim's attention focused on track and the possibility of participating in the Olympic Games that would be held in Stockholm, Sweden, later that summer. Jim was more interested in playing baseball and hoped to be able to pursue a professional baseball career in the major leagues following the Olympic Games.

Whenever I tried to prod him to keep up his track workouts, Jim used to say, "What's the use in bothering with track? There's nothing in it."

But in the long run there was a lot of success waiting for him.

During the spring outdoor track season, Jim racked up the following victories:

1. The Boston Athletic Association Meet: Silver medal,

45-yard hurdles; bronze medal, the high jump; bronze medal, the shot-put.

    2. The Middle Athletic Association A.A.U. Meet: Gold medal, the shot-put (12 pounds); gold medal, the shot-put (16 pounds); gold medal, 25-yard dash; silver medal, the three standing jumps event.

    3. The Pittsburgh Athletic Association Meet: Gold medal, the shot-put (12 pounds); gold medal, 60-yard hurdles; gold medal, the high jump; gold medal, 60-yard dash.

    4. The Carnegie Meet: Gold medal, the shot-put; gold medal, the high jump; gold medal, the 220-yard hurdles; silver medal, the broad jump; silver medal, 120-yard hurdles; bronze medal, 100-yard dash.

Following a strong performance in these meets, I felt that Jim was poised to achieve great success in Stockholm.

35

There were no Olympic Trials in the spring of 1912 for the events which both Jim Thorpe and Louis Tewanima would be entering.

Without a doubt, Tewanima was the best long-distance runner in the country. He had set a new record with a victory in the 10-mile run on a wooden board track earlier that winter while competing in an indoor meet. This win brought him much notoriety and acclaim in newspapers across the country. He also won several other long-distance events during the winter and spring months of 1912. When it came time to pick the team that would be traveling to compete in the Olympic Games in Stockholm, Sweden, that summer, Tewanima was quickly chosen.

Jim also had received a lot of splashy headlines in the newspapers for his outstanding record in the winter indoor and spring outdoor meets. Because of Jim's all-around record, he was chosen to participate in the pentathlon and decathlon events on behalf of the U.S. Olympic Squad.

And since Jim and Tewanima were students at the Carlisle Indian School, and therefore wards of the government, I was asked by the school's superintendent, Moses Friedman, to accompany them on their trip to Stockholm for the 1912 Olympic Games.

An example of the great abilities of both Tewanima and Thorpe occurred in the late spring of 1912 in a track meet with Lafayette.

This dual track meet was quickly put together between Carlisle and Lafayette to celebrate Lafayette's Graduation Day exercises that weekend.

When we arrived by train in Lafayette, Pa., to participate in the meet, we were met by the Lafayette track coach.

"Where's your squad?" the Lafayette coach asked.

"Right here." I told him, while pointing to eight Indian boys who were getting off the train behind me.

The Lafayette coach was dismayed.

"You'd better call off the meet," he suggested. "We have a squad of 50. No sense in making a farce out of things."

I told him that we couldn't afford to bring an entire track team along for this meet, but "we'll compete in all the events except the pole vault and try to make a contest out of it."

That afternoon, Jim heaved the shot-put only once but his mark survived the attempts of a half dozen Lafayette contestants. The same thing occurred in the high jump and the discus events. Before the day was over, Jim had taken first place in six events.

In the 440-yard dash, or quarter-mile, event, I entered Jim, Tewanima and another Carlisle runner. They finished 1-2-3. Lafayette's lone first place win was in the pole-vault event which was uncontested by the Carlisle team. But this didn't matter because the final score was Carlisle 71, Lafayette 41.

Before the U.S. Olympic team sailed to Stockholm, an exhibition track meet was staged in Celtic Park in New York City. All of the U.S. Olympic track team members competed in this meet. One of its highlights was when Jim defeated both George Horine of Stanford and Alvah Richards of Brigham Young University, who were the best high-jumpers in the U.S. at the time.

The longest distance event on the program was the 5,000 meters run, so I entered Tewanima in this event to give him a good workout before the long journey across the ocean onboard the S.S. Finland. Normally, Tewanima would have participated in a much longer distance race.

James E. Sullivan, who was the Secretary of the A.A.U. and often considered "the Walter Camp of the track and field world," approached me at the track meet upon learning of Tewanima's intention to run in the 5,000 meter race against Tel Berna and George Bonhag, who were considered the U.S.'s top runners in this event.

Sullivan asked me: "Why do you run the boy in this event?"

He had figured that the little Indian wouldn't stand a chance in a race as short as 5,000 meters. (Editor's Note: This distance is approximately 3.3 miles.)

I had explained to him that "Tewanima needed the workout and

that even if he didn't win, the race would still be good for him."
Personally, I didn't think Tewanima had a chance of winning against
Berna or Bonhag either.

Berna was a famous Cornell distance runner who held the American outdoor two-mile record. Bonhag held practically all of the
American outdoor records from three to ten miles at the time.

In the 5,000 meters event, Tewanima trailed these two great
runners for most of the race. However in the final lap, when much
to my surprise and much to the consternation of Mr. Sullivan and
everybody else, Tewanima started a sprint for the finish line and beat
both Bonhag and Berna by several yards.

The race in New York was only a forerunner of his performance
in Stockholm in the Olympic Games, where he defeated both Berna
and Bonhag again and finished second to Hannes Kolehmainen, the
great Finnish long-distance runner, who was one of the sensations of
the 1912 Olympic Games.

In the marathon event at the Olympics, which was run on an
extremely warm day, Tewanima was up among the leaders until the
last five miles of the 26.2-mile race. Both the draining heat and the
fact that the race officials had not allowed water or juice to be served
to the runners during the race was enough to take their toll on
Tewanima and he was unable to stay with the race's leaders.

The marathon was also beyond Tewanima's traditional strength.
He most always ran his best at distances between 10 and fifteen miles.

Another factor which may have affected Tewanima's performance and kept him from winning both of these races was due to the
several bouts of "sea sickness" which he had while on the boat trip
during the trans-Atlantic trip to go to the Olympic Games. Having
been raised on the Western plains and never before having seen the
ocean's salt water, Tewanima was unable to cope with the S.S.
Finland's continual swaying while at sea.

Jim, however, proved to be the star of the American Olympic team.
He easily defeated the world's best all-around athletes in both the
pentathlon and the decathlon.

In the pentathlon, an event which was the Scandinavian athletes'
forte, Thorpe won four of the five events and established a new
Olympic record. In the decathlon, he captured four of the ten events

in the competition and scored 8,412.96 points out of a possible 10,000, which also established a new Olympic record. The runner-up in the decathlon was Hugo Wieslander, who trailed Thorpe by nearly 700 points with a score of 7,724.495. Thorpe's record in this event would last twenty years until it was broken by another American, James Bausch, in 1932.

When the meet was over, King Gustav V of Sweden placed a laurel wreath on the winners of the various events. After winning both the pentathlon and decathlon, King Gustav V said to Jim as he honored him with his laurel wreath and Olympic medals: "You, sir, are the greatest athlete in the world."

Jim, who in his own modest Indian way, simply acknowledged King Gustav's remarks by shaking his head and telling him, "Thanks, King." (Editor's Note: Thorpe also received a magnificent silver vase which was lined with gold and many precious jewels, shaped into the form of a Viking Ship, two feet in length by 18 inches in height and weight thirty pounds. It was a gift of the Czar of Russia. In addition, he received a life-size bronze bust of King Gustav V's likeness, measuring four feet high by 22 inches wide.)

All during the Olympic Games, Jim was the topic of most conversations. No one had ever seen an athlete with so much strength, speed, endurance and competitiveness. A familiar expression among the Europeans when discussing Jim's athletic feats was, "Isn't he a horse?"

Finally, when the Olympic Games were over, Jim and his teammates celebrated their success with a long night of revelry and great enjoyment by partying in many of the Stockholm hotels and bars.

Upon the team's late-evening return to their floating headquarters, the S.S. Finland, which was anchored in the Stockholm harbor during the duration of the Olympic Games, Jim — who was feeling quite jubilant and having had too much to drink — began to parade up and down the ship's decks, elbowing everyone out of the way and shouting: "Out of my way. I am a horse. I'm a horse!"

That evening, although a bit shocked and amused by such behavior, all of the ship's passengers stood aside and applauded as the great Indian athlete passed by in celebration.

36

Jim Thorpe and Louis Tewanima, the two marvels from the Carlisle Indian School, scored more points and won more medals than did the representatives of any other American college while competing in the 1912 Olympic Games.

Following the Olympic Games, Jim decided to remain in Europe to compete with several other members of the American Olympic track team in several special track meets. I, however, decided to return home to the U.S. with Tewanima. Along with my bags, I brought back the trophies from the Czar of Russia and King Gustav which Jim had won at the Olympic Games.

When all of the American team members had returned home to this county, a large parade was held for them in New York City. The U.S. Olympic team rode in a car caravan down Fifth Avenue as the excited New Yorkers showered massive doses of confetti down on top of them in appreciation of their great accomplishments at the Olympic Games.

Jim traveled alone in an open car in the parade and was a big crowd favorite. Behind him, in another automobile, were his trophies from the King of Sweden and the Czar of Russia.

Afterwards, the Olympic squad traveled to Philadelphia where a similar celebration and a banquet were held in their honor.

It was a wonderful sight to be able to see this great American Olympic team returning as conquering heroes.

Later, we returned to Carlisle where the students at the Indian School and the local townspeople had planned a great homecoming celebration. They put on a big parade in the town and later there was a large gathering at the Carlisle athletic field. Approximately 15,000 people were on hand and listened as prominent town leaders and the president of Gettysburg College, which was located nearby, spoke to the assembled crowd and heaped praise upon these two American heroes.

Finally, the crowd asked Jim to say a few words. He talked for a minute or two and the crowd responded by giving him a thunderous applause and a roar of loud cheers.

The crowd then began to cheer for Tewanima to speak. He got up from his chair, stepped forward and echoed Jim's comments by simply adding, "Me, too."

The Carlisle students and townspeople who were full of pride at this point, then let loose in a wild, deafening applause.

It was a day that I will always remember.

Jim later received letters of congratulations from President William Howard Taft, from the Commissioner of Indian Affairs and from the Congressman who represented the district in which Carlisle was located. The Carlisle town council also passed a resolution commending both Jim and Tewanima for their Olympic performances and the vast publicity which Carlisle had received from their successes.

Later that summer, Thorpe won the American all-around track championship and set a new American record in the decathlon, which broke the previous record held by Martin Sheridan.

In the fall of 1912, Thorpe was elected captain of the Carlisle football team. This season would be his last and best on the college gridiron.

One of our early games that season was against Washington & Jefferson College. It was played on a hot autumn afternoon and the Indian boys did not perform up to their usual abilities. The Carlisle squad had exceptional talent that season but the team's play-calling of fancy end runs and daring passes sapped them of their energy in the hot weather. As the Indian quarterback continued to call for end runs, these plays often resulted in numerous fumbles. The game eventually ended in a 0-0 score, although Carlisle should have won with little effort.

On the team's return trip to Carlisle, we were routed through Pittsburgh where we had a change of trains and a 3-hour wait. Jim, of course, was greatly disappointed over his performance and the team's outcome.

While waiting for the next train, one of the Indian boys inquired of his teammates, "Well, how about a glass of beer?"

To my later surprise, these players were next seen heading toward a saloon which was located down the street from the train station.

Before continuing my story, I should note that Jim would not stop at anything once he got started on performing a particular task — and that included beer drinking. He usually went the limit.

The result of Jim's merriment achieved full results an hour later. A report got back to me that Thorpe was now well tanked up — or drunk. After hearing this, I went down to the saloon and took him over to a hotel where he created a lot of excitement by his shouting and loud talking. There was little doubt that he was mad at me for breaking up his post-game party. A crowd of onlookers then gathered just outside the hotel to view what was happening inside.

Seeing that Thorpe was making an exhibition of this occurrence, I finally convinced him to go inside the hotel and quiet down — which he did.

When the train that would carry us on to Carlisle finally arrived at the Pittsburgh train station, I escorted Jim outside a back door of the hotel and then got him through the train station without much notice.

With little difficulty, we then boarded the awaiting train and continued our journey home.

In the next day's Pittsburgh newspapers, there was a story which detailed this embarrassing incident.

Unfortunately the newspaper story was somewhat fictional in its reporting. It had stated that Jim had gotten drunk and when I had tried to retrieve him from the saloon that the now juiced-up Indian and I were soon engaging in a free-for-all scrap. This, of course was completely wrong.

37

Upon our return to Carlisle following the Washington & Jefferson game and the ugly incident in Pittsburgh in which Jim Thorpe had violated the team's training rules, I felt it was my duty as a matter of discipline to drop Jim from the Carlisle football team unless he apologized to his teammates and promised to obey the rules in the future.

"Thorpe," I stated to him, "You've got to behave yourself. You owe it to the public as well as to your school. The Olympic Games have made you into a public figure and you've got to shoulder the responsibility."

I then gave him the example of the articles in the Pittsburgh newspapers and how I was credited erroneously with having knocked out the world famous Jim Thorpe in a street fight. His notoriety, of course, had gotten him this negative publicity.

Jim was very penitent after hearing my lecture to him. At the next team practice, he called all of his teammates together and apologized for his actions on that trip. From then until the end of the season, Jim stayed out of trouble and faithfully adhered to the team's training rules.

The 1912 version of the Carlisle Indians posted a record of twelve wins, one loss and one tie that season. But it was not quite as good as the 1911 team.

Against Penn, the game turned out to be a free-scoring contest with the Quakers winning, 34-26. One of the touchdowns which Penn scored was a long pass that was caught over the Indians' goal line. It had always been my opinion that Jim could have knocked down this pass if he had tried — but he didn't.

Following the game, I asked him about this and he said: "Oh, yes, sure, I could have knocked that (pass) down. I didn't think that the receiver could get it to him in time. I saw him running and the ball coming, but I didn't think it possible for him to reach the ball."

That incident showed the one weak trait in Jim's character, which is a dangerous trait in any football player. He was inclined to be careless. Instead of playing safe at all times, Jim was always a little too certain and consequently careless.

Later that season, Carlisle played the Springfield Y.M.C.A. Training School This game was also a free-scoring contest much like the Carlisle-Penn game. It featured a lot of the passing game, with the Y.M.C.A. team throwing on nearly every play. Fortunately, we were able to stay on top in this aerial battle and won, 30-24. (Editor's Note: The forward pass was still in its infancy at this time and would be made famous a year later in the 1913 Army-Notre Dame game.)

Next, we played the annual Thanksgiving Day game against Brown which would be played on their home field in Providence, R. I. Brown, who had beaten both Harvard and Yale that season, had yielded an unusually strong team to be reckoned with.

Percy Haughton, who was then the coach at Harvard, was a guest of mine on the sidelines during the game.

Early in the first half of the contest, Carlisle tried to execute a two-series play. In this effort, one of the Carlisle players on the play of the series would run behind with the ball to one side of the line and try to gain as much yardage as possible. Then, after being tackled, he would act as the team's center on the next play. After the remaining offensive team had lined up on one side of the ball — which was usually on the wider side of the playing field — he would toss the ball to a backfield runner who would run a sweep play behind his interference. This surprise play was called the "wing shift."

As it happened in the Brown game, this play was stopped for a loss. Haughton, who was standing next to me at the time, leaned over toward my direction and remarked, "These series plays are never worth a darn.

"If such plays do work," he maintained, "it is usually in the first attempt, because they are trick plays and surprise is the feature that usually makes them successful."

Later in the game, the same two-series plays were called again and this time a Carlisle back ran 65 yards for a touchdown. After seeing the two-series play perform successfully on the second attempt, Haughton begrudgingly admitted to me, "Well, it did work that time."

Another big game during the 1912 season was against Army, who was another rising Eastern football power. The game was played at their campus at West Point, N.Y. The Cadets had a fine team that season and several all-America players were on their roster.

Our Carlisle squad had entered this game with a new offensive weapon—an attack strategy which featured a formation in which one of the halfbacks was set up close to the line of scrimmage while also flanking the defensive tackle. It was a new and radical formation in 1912 but would become very popular much later. The new halfback position, which was located outside the lineman but still considered in the backfield, was called the "wingback."

The Cadets had never seen such a formation—or anything similar to it — and didn't quite know how to cope with it. And the Army defensive tackles were completely at sea. They were easily taken out of the play each time by our flanking halfback, or wingback. The final result of our surprise formation was that Carlisle gained ground easily on its wide plays and won the game, 27-6.

With nearly all of the big New York City sportswriters on hand to cover the game for their newspapers, Jim played one of his best games of the season that afternoon. The next day, they all wrote glowing stories on him in their newspaper columns.

At the end of the 1912 season, Jim was picked to be on Walter Camp's first team all-America squad.

Through the years, most football critics, sportswriters and historians have hailed Jim Thorpe as "the greatest football player of all time."

38

As Jim Thorpe entered the fall of 1912, he was a young man who was confronted with many opportunities.

Following his Olympic victories in the pentathlon and the decathlon, sports promoters of all types had begun to make their way to Carlisle, Pa., with their own personal version of exploiting Jim's new-found national popularity.

C.C. Pyle — whose initials were often referred to as "Cash and Carry" — was one of the first of these hustlers who appeared on the scene. Pyle, who would later transform Harold "Red" Grange, the "Galloping Ghost" from Illinois, into a pro football box office draw with his barnstorming football tours in the mid-1920's, approached Jim with a $10,000 payment to go on tour with his baseball team in a series of exhibition games.

Others wanted Jim to perform in track and field meets, pro football exhibitions, wrestling matches and one-on-one races against a thoroughbred racehorse.

Prior to the 1912 season, which already was going to be his final year at Carlisle, I pulled Jim aside and told him that with the anticipated large gate ticket sales at Carlisle football games for the season, along with a fine performance by him that season and his recent Olympic victories, there was little doubt that his market value would substantially increase by season's end.

Although he was a bit modest about his personal success, Jim finally agreed to my view of the situation. He also knew that he would have more leverage in commanding larger salaries and fees from promoters following another big football season against big-name opponents.

As the 1912 season marched forward, Jim was a promoter's dream.

He drew large crowds in the stands and a throng of newspaper writers. Everyone wanted to see the big Indian who had won the Olympics and was now leading a charge of gridiron warriors as they scalped one paleface football power after another en route to a 12-1-1 season.

Quickly, Jim became the favorite topic of most of the American sportswriters. And sports fans all across America were growing increasingly curious to learn more of this Indian gridiron wonder. Each week, newspapers and magazines were filled with stories on Jim Thorpe and the Carlisle football team. And with the big Indian's picture and name in the headlines this most always meant increased newspaper and magazine sales.

Then when life was juicy fat for Jim Thorpe, Fate decided to intervene.

In late January 1913, following Jim's victories in the Olympics and a memorable final college season at Carlisle, a newspaperman at *The Worcester Telegram*, in Worcester, Mass., wrote a story about Jim having played professional baseball in North Carolina.

An immediate investigation was launched and would eventually prove that the charges were true: Jim had, indeed, played on a semi-pro baseball team in a bush league in North Carolina after he had left Carlisle following the spring semester in 1909. This, of course, was news to everyone at Carlisle because we had thought that he had been at his home in Oklahoma during the period of late spring 1909 until he had returned to Carlisle in the fall of 1911.

This initial newspaper story on Jim's professional baseball career, along with the subsequent stories that followed, created great furor because, if true, they branded Jim as a professional athlete at the time when he had participated in the Olympic Game.

After hearing of these accusations, I went to see Jim and asked him if the story of his pro baseball career was accurate. Without hesitating, he told me: "Yes, Pop. It's true."

He then told me that he had played at Rocky Mount and Fayetteville of the Eastern Carolina League during the summers of 1909 and 1910. Jim told me of many other college athletes who had played in this league but they had been careful and wise enough to play under assumed names. Their identities were never revealed or exposed during the aftermath of Jim's adverse publicity.

Jim, of course, was a fellow who always laid his cards on the table face up. He explained to me that he had played in this league while using his real name because he had never considered that he would participate in any amateur sports after having left Carlisle in the spring of 1909.

In a way, the boys at the Indian School were very naive and did not understand the fine distinction between amateur sports and the professional sports leagues. Jim had seen no harm in playing baseball and earning a little honest money in the summer. After all, this was not the Philadelphia Athletics or the New York Yankees team that he would be playing for. He did not understand why that would prevent him from later being able to participate in the Olympic Games on the other side of the world.

The end-result of this revelation about Jim's pro baseball career was that his great collection of Olympic medals and trophies were returned to the International Olympic Committee and later awarded to the athletes who had placed second in the pentathlon and decathlon events in the 1912 Olympics in Stockholm, Sweden. Jim also returned the medals that he won at the other European track meets in which he had competed following the Olympics.

When it became known Jim had played professional baseball and that he was no longer considered an amateur, he suddenly began to attract the attention of many major league baseball teams. Several of these clubs wasted no time in sending representatives to Carlisle with contracts for Jim's signature.

These baseball executives figured that since Jim was a great athlete, he would also develop into a star baseball player. This opinion was greatly strengthened following the public disclosure of Jim's brief professional baseball career in the Carolina minor leagues.

Jim, of course, was rather unsophisticated in handling business matters, so he asked me to look out for his interests in dealing with the major league baseball people. I, of course, was glad to do so. Also, because of the loss of Jim's amateur standing, I felt that baseball was the only career in which he might succeed.

A week after the word had leaked out regarding Jim's loss of college eligibility, I wired all of the major league baseball clubs notifying them that the highest bid would get Jim's services.

He was set to sign with the Cincinnati Reds when my old friend, John McGraw, the manager of the New York Giants, telephoned to tell me that if Jim was going to play professional baseball, he was in the market to sign him. When I told McGraw that Cincinnati had been the highest bidder so far, in characteristic McGraw style he offered to double the Red's offer.

On hearing this, I told McGraw that he had a deal. The next day I took Jim to New York City, where he signed with the Giants.

This, of course, was a major public relations coup for the Giants. Jim's signing with the baseball club splashed headlines on all of the New York City, newspapers as well as most of those around the country.

As it turned out, Jim's major league baseball career was a washout. McGraw kept him on the Giants' bench for two seasons.

Finally, when Jim had gotten frustrated with his lack of playing time with the Giants and McGraw's handling of him, he asked, "When am I going to play, Mac?"

"I'm saving you," the Giants manager responded.

"For what?" Thorpe protested.

"I'll let you know when I'm ready for you," McGraw explained.

A year later, Jim was traded to the Cincinnati Reds. (Editor's Note: After playing briefly with the Reds in 1917, Thorpe returned to the Giants for nearly 3 seasons. In 1919, he finished his career with the Boston Braves.)

Looking back, it was a mistake for Jim to have gone directly into the major leagues without having spent some time while playing in the minor leagues. He was a competitive and extremely talented athlete, but sitting on the bench, both in New York and Boston, did not give him an opportunity to improve his baseball skills.

Had Jim joined a team where he could have been in there playing everyday, I think that he would have developed into a great baseball player. Unfortunately, his career in pro baseball was short-lived and disappointing.

After being cut by Boston, Jim did not take very good care of himself. Finally, he drifted down to the minor leagues and where he had first began — semi-pro baseball.

Although Jim did not enjoy great success as a baseball player, he later achieved stardom in professional football and for many years was an attraction on the gridiron wherever he performed.

Throughout his career, Jim was a very likeable chap and never changed. He was always popular with his teammates and the press, but his one great difficulty was in not being able to withstand the temptations which beset the path of all athletic heroes.

Still, it is my belief — and that of most sportswriters and historians — that Jim Thorpe will always be remembered as having been the greatest all-around athlete of all-time and the greatest Indian athlete in sports.

39

Carlisle had another good football team in 1913, while posting a record of ten wins, one loss and one tie.

One of our final games of the season was to be an outstanding one in what had been a very memorable year in college football.

Our opponent, Dartmouth, had a powerhouse team and was sporting an unbeaten record. Dartmouth was also in a tight race with Harvard, who was also unbeaten, for the Eastern championship.

Going into the game, which was to be played in Boston, Carlisle was picked as the underdog. However, the Indian teams always seemed to play their best in contests that they were supposed to lose. On this afternoon, they turned in a magnificent performance.

Prior to the game, I had gone overboard in my enthusiasm and wagered $300 that the Indians would win the game against Dartmouth. With the odds being 5-to-3 on the game, I figured to win $500 if Carlisle won.

But at halftime of the game, Dartmouth held a 10-7 lead.

While walking to the Carlisle locker room for intermission, I sized up the situation and decided that if I didn't want to lose $300 I definitely needed to give the Carlisle players a stronger incentive to win the game.

Once in the locker room, I gathered the entire Indian team up around me and told them, "If each of you wants to earn $5 apiece to have a little fun when we stop off in New York on the trip home, all you have to do is to win this game."

At this time, $5 was considered a lot of money. And my proposition to the players worked like a shot of adrenalin.

As the second half began, you couldn't hold back this redskin bunch. While using the double-wing formation, they ran all around and over Dartmouth in one of the greatest exhibitions of offensive football that I ever saw. Four times the Indians received the kickoff and carried the ball the full length of the field and scored. Carlisle ended up winning easily, 35-10.

This was the first time that Carlisle had played Dartmouth and the Indians used a lot of reverse plays which Dartmouth failed to stop.

I had developed the reverse play in 1912 from the old criss-cross play in which the entire backfield started to one side of the field. The player with the ball, after running a few steps in the direction of the rest of the backfield, then gave it to another back, who had reversed field and was quickly darting around the other side of the field by himself. This old criss-cross play had been used for years and often resulted in long gains. However, the play was a complete failure if the opposing end knew what was coming.

Realizing that good ends, while on defense, were seldom fooled by such plays, I conceived the idea of revamping the play and having a lineman go out and block him. This extra wrinkle, of course, usually put the end out of business.

Throughout the season, we had tried this play repeatedly in practice sessions against the scrubs at Carlisle. Knowing that we were working on the play and understanding just how it worked, the Indian boys were not easily fooled. As a matter of fact, the team did not think much of the play. Still, I insisted it was a sound offensive threat and tried to get the players to use it in several of our early games.

However, in spite of my faith in this play and my repeated instructions, our quarterbacks always managed to forget to use it in a game.

Every coach, of course, will tell you how his field generals invariably forget the plays in which they don't have much confidence. And this was the case here. But I kept them working on that play without a let up.

Although we had never used the play in a game, it remained in our offensive bag of tricks. Then in the Carlisle-Dartmouth game we pulled this play out of the bag.

Dartmouth had been stopping nearly every play that we attempted. Now frustrated, our Carlisle quarterback finally called his offensive players together to one side of the field and said: "They've stopped everything else we've run, so let's give Pop's reverse a try."

On the next play, they called the reverse play—the first time it had ever been used in a game.

The play gained 15 yards. Enjoying this unexpected success, the Carlisle quarterback immediately tried the reverse again on the next play to the other side of the field and it gained another 15 yards. The play was then used repeatedly during the remainder of the game, which Carlisle finally won, 35-10.

The Boston sportswriters in their post-game stories told of how the Dartmouth ends, while on defense, were completely fooled by the old criss-cross play. The truth, however, is that the sportswriters and the Harvard ends were both being fooled on the play by a lineman coming from his position.

After that, the reverse play became a great weapon for the Indians and they employed it with tremendous skill.

The reverse has since become one of the great offensive weapons of many college teams throughout the country. However, it is quite probable that if the reverse play had not worked that day against Dartmouth when it was first tried, then it would have been quickly discarded.

40

My last football season at the Carlisle Indian School, in 1914, proved to be a disastrous one. The Indians won only 5 games, lost nine and tied one.

There had previously been a change of administrations in Washington, D.C., in 1912, and this new revision of political power brought in many new opponents of the Carlisle Indian School. The school's principal opposition primarily came from the Senators and Congressmen who hailed from the West. They firmly believed that the money being spent on Indian education should only be spent on Indian schools which were located in those states in the western U.S. and where many of the Indian reservations were located.

An investigation was eventually started by this Washington crowd, which was apparently made with the idea of discrediting the superintendent at Carlisle. These were the same types who had also chased Major Pratt into retirement in 1904. And as you might expect, this kind of investigation put the Indian School in a rather demoralized condition. Many of the students began to leave and it was easy to see that the school might be closed in a few years unless these conditions changed.

After the Carlisle-Pittsburgh game during the 1914 season, the Pitt officials began to discuss with me the possibility of taking the head-coaching job at Pitt.

Realizing that the situation at Carlisle wasn't going to improve, I finally accepted the Pitt offer and took charge of their football program in the spring of 1915.

Through the years, I have often been asked what happened to the Carlisle Indian School following my departure. The school was eventually closed in 1918, with the Indian football team playing their final season in 1917. Their record that season was 2-7-0. During World War I, the campus was converted to a hospital for the wounded American soldiers. Later, it was converted into the Army War College.

Another question which I am often asked is "How did the Indian boys compare with the white boys in their adaptability to athletics?" Actually, there really is not much difference, but I think the Indians were able to learn blocking, tackling and running techniques much quicker than the white boys were able to. Having been trained for generations to be great observers, the Indian boys learned to do things by observing the performances of those who were more skilled in such athletic feats.

To illustrate this point, whenever I tried to teach an Indian boy the simple matter of falling on a fumbled football, I always seemed to run into a roadblock. An Indian boy who was a novice player would usually stand around and refuse to fall on a fumbled ball until he saw how the older players did it. He would then perform the action of falling on the ball and usually recovered it almost as well as a veteran.

As a rule, Indian boys were not fond of work, but they did like to play, and they always devoted a great deal of time learning to do things in the correct manner. During my coaching career, I found the Indian boys to be much more persevering than white boys. They would practice doing something for years, if necessary, in order to become experts, whereas white boys usually got discouraged unless results came rapidly.

I also found the Indian boys to be very sensitive and this trait could not be driven or abused. Above all, they hated to be ridiculed. To get results, I used to kid with them, pat them on the back and praise them when they did things well. I only criticized them in a friendly way when they made mistakes.

The Indians took great delight in beating their opponents in a football game. They were very clever in their ability to pull off a trick play — and nothing made the Carlisle players happier than being able to fool their white opponents. They would sooner show them up on a series of trick plays than win a game by a large score while playing *normal* football.

41

When I arrived at the University of Pittsburgh in 1915, it was the beginning of a special era for me.

Pitt, which had been formerly known as the Western University of Pennsylvania, had been around since 1886 and had been playing football since 1890, but the school had recently moved to a new campus and wanted a great football team to cheer for.

A.R. Hamilton, a wealthy Pitt alumnus, had been the primary leader in a group of ambitious alumni who had pushed for my hiring. These gentlemen wanted to see the Pitt program emerge from the shadows of obscurity and achieve a lofty place in the college football world.

The 1914 edition of the Pitt football team had won 8 of their nine games while being coached by Princeton grad Joe Duff. The Panthers only loss that season had been to Washington & Jefferson College, who was an Eastern powerhouse at that time and one of Pitt's biggest rivals.

My new team had many promising players who had been on the 1914 Pitt squad. The most talented were Robert Peck, James (Pat) Herron, Andy Hastings, Claude Thornhill, H.C. (Doc) Carlson and Jock Sutherland. Each of them would eventually be named to several all-America teams. What the Panther program needed most, however, was just a little bit of fine tuning to push them to new heights of success.

Prior to the opening of the 1915 season, I arranged to take the team to a training camp at Camp Hamilton, which was owned by the University's engineering school. It was located in Windber, Pa., and was approximately 75 miles southwest of Pittsburgh.

The training camp was a wild affair at the beginning. Most of the earlier Pitt teams had been trained in the rough and aggressive Princeton style of football which was the predominate brand of playing tactics being used in the East at the time. This trait of brutal football had not been lost on the current Pitt squad.

In the first few practices at the training camp, there must have been a dozen fist fights to break out and sometimes these would turn into a free-for-all.

Finally, after I had seen enough of this mayhem, I ordered the entire team into the camp's dining room and laid the law down. I explained to them my team rules and expressly stated that the first rule on this list was that there would be no more fighting in a practice or a game. A few of the players tried to test me on this subject afterwards, but I quickly set them straight on any confusion that they might have had regarding this rule.

Many of the members of the Pitt team enjoyed trying to sneak out of training camp in the evening after curfew so that they could visit the nightlife in the saloons, pool halls and hotels of the nearby towns. At the beginning of this late-night routine, I was quite successful in catching the guilty parties as they sneaked back into training camp. And I always made them pay dearly for their sins the next day at practice.

But some of these players began to wise up real quick. While returning from their nightly escapades out on the town, a few of them would stop on the outskirts of the training camp and if they heard my heavy snoring they figured it was probably safe to re-enter the camp. However if it was real quiet, then this was a sure sign that I was still awake and most likely would be on the lookout for any mischievous activity. Usually on these occasions, the players would turn around and go back to town for a bit more lively entertainment.

Realizing, of course, that these after-hours excursions were probably still continuing, I decided to play a trick on this wandering crew on one of the final nights of training camp. I pretended to be asleep and made some noise as if I was snoring. Then, as these thrillseekers returned to camp and walked past my tent, I let them know that I was still very much awake.

After a good chewing out that night, I held off punishing them at practice the next morning. My message, however, had been sent and was well received. These guys knew who was in charge of the Pitt team now.

A few days later, as we packed up our gear and left Camp Hamilton and the Western Pennsylvania hills to return to Pittsburgh and begin the 1915 season, I felt that the training camp had definitely served its purpose. Undoubtedly, we had the nucleus of a team who might achieve a lot of success.

The Panther squad that season included many notable players who would be long remembered in Pitt football history. Some of these players were James (Pat) Herron, Joe Matson and H. C. (Doc) Carlson at end, C.E. (Tiny) Thornhill at tackle, Jock Sutherland at guard, Bob Peck at center, and Guy (Chalky) Williamson, Jimmy DeHart, Andy Hastings, Ken Fry and George McLaren in the backfield.

My coaching staff consisted of two assistants who were both part-timers. One of them was an undertaker. And on the days that he had a funeral he usually missed, or was late for, practice. My other assistant was a doctor who specialized in obstetrics. On the days that he had baby-delivery duties to attend to, he always ducked practice. Often both would be unable to make it to practice, but fortunately they were usually always on the sidelines on gameday.

Pitt opened the 1915 season by blitzing Westminster College, 32-0. We then crushed Navy, 47-12, and ran over my former school, the Carlisle Indians, 45-0. Against Navy, Jimmy DeHart scored one touchdown by romping for 105 yards to reach paydirt.

Our next game was against Penn, who was on the Pitt schedule for the first time ever. I had scheduled this game with Penn because of the possibility of building a future cross-state rivalry with them, but, more importantly, I knew that a victory against the Quakers would significantly boost Pitt's standing as an up-and-coming power in the East.

Prior to the 1915 season, I had never forgotten those beatings which Penn gave to Cornell during my own playing days and later as a coach. With this knowledge, I began to ready my team for this game back in the summer when we were still in training at Camp Hamilton.

An interesting point that must be remembered about this game was that in the 1915 season we had decided to play freshmen in our varsity games. However, our contract with Penn had forbidden the use of these first-year players. As a result, three of our better players were unable to dress for the game.

The Penn scouting report against us stated: "Warner teaches his men to get the ball and hold on to it. Pitt has the best interferers (blockers) and tacklers in the game today."

When the game finally kicked off, Pitt was able to take the battle to Penn and gave them an excellent display of grind-it-out football. When it was over we had won, 14-7.

The Pitt offense used very little forward passing on this afternoon and, instead, went to an attack that was based on lateral passes and sweeping the ends on long runs.

Our offense finally began to rule the game when we started to wipe out the Penn defensive tackles and ends. This gave our speedy backs some wide running lanes. DeHart had a great day on offense for Pitt that afternoon.

Among the Penn players that we played against were Bert Bell, who would later become the Commissioner of the National Football League.

The news of our win over Penn gave the Pitt program tremendous recognition. All of the major newspapers between Chicago and the East Coast were writing stories whose headlines proclaimed that Pitt was now one of the new powers to be reckoned with in the East. Many of these newspapers even compared us as a challenger to Cornell whose program had finally stabilized and was now a big Eastern powerhouse.

The local press in Pittsburgh and the Pitt fans, however, were not content in the win over Penn. After having enjoyed the sweet taste of success, they now wanted wins over Penn State and Washington & Jefferson. Both of these schools had been established football powers in Western Pennsylvania and had often beaten Pitt through the years.

Against the Washington & Jefferson Presidents, Pitt handily disposed of them, 19-0, by scoring on long runs. We later romped over Carnegie Tech, 28-0, and Penn State, 20-0, in the final two games of the season.

In eight games, the magic of the Pitt Panthers had come to life as we went through the season undefeated and scored 247 points to our opponents' 26. Navy, Penn and Allegheny College were the only teams to score against the Panthers' great defensive wall.

At the conclusion of the season, the Pitt backfield was frequently toasted as the best in the country. They were led by Andy Hastings who had scored 11 touchdowns. Bob Peck, the five-foot, eight-inch 175-pound Pitt center, also received a great honor when he was picked as a member of Walter Camp's all-America first team that season.

Cornell, with whom we had been compared all season, also ended up finishing the season undefeated and was crowned as the mythical Eastern champion by the sportwriters of the major East Coast newspapers.

Following the last game of our regular season, I sent a telegram to their coach, Al Sharpe, challenging them to play in a post-season game at the site of their choice to determine who was the *real* powerhouse in the East, but this offer was quickly turned down.

42

No matter how memorable the 1915 season may have seemed to the Pitt alumni and fans, the 1916 season would prove to be much greater.

A. R. Hamilton and the other wealthy Pitt alums who had backed the build-up of the Panther football program were beaming with joy as they saw us begin to clip off victory after victory each week and capture the headlines of the sports pages of the East Coast daily newspapers.

As a result of this new-found success, Pitt began to attract large crowds wherever it played. The small stadiums of that era in which Panthers played were now being packed to capacity with "standing-room only" crowds, filling every available nook and cranny.

Without a doubt, the 1916 edition of the Pitt football program proved to be the best team in the East. They were also the best team in the country that season.

The primary cast on this squad was almost the same as the 1915 version, with our only major change being brought about by the graduation of quarterback Guy (Chalky) Williamson. Yet over the course of the 1916 season, this team grew closer together and proved to be much more wiser and stronger than the 1915 squad.

Jim Morrow stepped in and replaced Williamson at quarterback and Pitt ran through its eight opponents, while outscoring them 255 points to 25.

Bob Peck, who was our team captain, was again picked to Walter Camp's first team all-America at center and James (Pat) Herron was named as a second team all-America at end.

The Pitt defense had improved tremendously in 1916, which greatly aided our success that season.

Previously, my Carlisle teams were never noted for their defensive abilities because the Indian boys were much more interested in offense and scoring touchdowns. But once I got to Pitt, I put more emphasis on defense, and while we had been at our pre-season training camp at Camp Hamilton I worked the squad hard to build a strong forward wall.

Early in the season, we were lucky to get by Navy. The Pitt defense out-rushed and out-passed the Midshipmen, with Jimmy DeHart and Andy Hastings sweeping the ends for big yardage. But poor handling of several Navy punts that resulted in lost fumbles gave the Midshipmen excellent field position on each occasion. A late Pitt score finally allowed us to pull out a 20-19 win.

As the 1916 season began to shape up, it seemed that the road to an Eastern championship had two back-to-back obstacles which Pitt would need to overcome. Syracuse and Penn were those obstacles and they were the next two games on our schedule.

Syracuse was now being coached by a Penn disciple, Bill Hollenback.

The build-up for the Pitt-Syracuse game was enormous. Most of the major sportwriters of the era had been writing about this game in their newspaper columns for several weeks because the game would be an early-season test to gauge Pitt's superiority.

On gameday, all of the big East Coast newspapers sent their top writers to cover the game, which was being played in Syracuse. Walter Camp also made the trip to check on Pitt's all-America candidates. And even my father, who was 76 years old and was a great football fan, traveled by train from Springville, N.Y., to watch the game.

On the morning of the Pitt-Syracuse contest, I happened to run into a Penn assistant coach who was there to scout the game. He told me: "Pop, I'm going to get your stuff today. Penn is going to make up for last season's loss and beat you this season."

I smiled when I heard this. Without hesitation, I told him: "Why wait until the game. I'll show you all of our formations and explain them to you."

After a 45-minute tutoring session while sitting on a couch in the hotel lobby, where I had diagrammed all of the plays on a sheet of paper, I told the Penn assistant: "Now put this in your pocket. It'll save you a lot of trouble."

The Penn coach then walked away from our visit with a big smile on his face. He even wished us a bit of good luck against Syracuse, who was the heavy favorite in the game.

But that afternoon Pitt didn't need any extra help as it slaughtered Syracuse, 30-0. Behind George McLaren's powerful running, Pitt installed a new shift and out-gained Syracuse, 329 yards to 29.

The key to Pitt's victory, though, was our decision to attack at the great strength of the Syracuse defensive line.

On the first play of the game, Jimmy DeHart, who was calling signals for the Pitt offense, sent the Panther attack into the middle of the Orangemen defense. Pitt center Bob Peck bowled over Syracuse's Bebe White, a huge defensive lineman, and McLaren gained 6 yards.

The next play was directed at Syracuse's Chris Schlacter, a burly all-America lineman, and again McLaren ground out big yardage.

These two plays established the tempo for the contest and paved the way for victory.

Robert Maxwell, a former Swarthmore star and a referee in this Pitt-Syracuse battle, boasted of McLaren's greatness on the gridiron that afternoon when he wrote in his column in *The Philadelphia Evening Ledger*: "George McLaren, the Pitt fullback, played the greatest line-plunging game I have ever seen. This young man tore the Syracuse line into shreds, bent it and twisted it out of shape until he was able to gain as he pleased every time he took the ball. He was the hardest man to stop on the football field. When he hits the line he is going fast, but when he hits an opponent or is in the grasp of one, he puts on more steam and wriggles a couple yards further.

"I saw the best football team that ever stepped on a gridiron this afternoon," wrote Maxwell, "and I have been following the game for 20 years. I believe the University of Pittsburgh can beat any team in the country."

The next week, we took on Penn at Forbes Field in Pittsburgh. This ballpark also served as the home of the Pittsburgh Pirates baseball team and seated approximately 25,000. Every seat in the stadium had been sold for this game and several thousand standing-room passes were also sold. This game was one of the biggest sporting events to ever be held in Pittsburgh.

Before leaving the locker room for the game's opening kickoff, a Pitt fan stopped by and asked me: "Are we going to win?"

I told the gentleman, "Wait a minute while I go and find out how Bob Peck feels."

After going to check on Peck, I came back and told the Pitt fan, "Bob feels great. We'll win."

My efforts in this matter only heightened the Pitt fan's curiosity. He then asked, "What has Peck's health got to do with the outlook of the team?"

"Well, whenever Peck feels all right we win — easily. Yet when Bob is under the weather it has a depressing effect on the team."

Never in all my football career have I known a man who could inspire his teammates as Peck did. It is uncanny. He was to Pitt what Tom Shevlin was to Yale.

The game against Penn turned out to be a war. Pitt's football prowess, however, would rise to a new level of greatness this day.

Bob Peck played the game of his life while in the trenches against Lud Wray of Penn. Their personal duel became a bloody affair as the afternoon wore on with Peck often taking a beating.

But the Pitt defensive line played to their potential and wrecked the Quaker offense.

Then when Pitt had the ball, Andy Hastings led the Panthers' offensive attack. He scored a touchdown, booted a point-after kick and hit on two field goals as Pitt won, 20-0.

Following the game, Bob Folwell, the Penn coach, told the reporters: "Man for man, no team in the country can compare with Pitt."

Next, Pitt tangled with our cross-town rival Carnegie Tech, who was a feisty bunch. They were coached by Judge Wally Steffen, the former all-America back for Amos Alonzo Stagg at the University of Chicago who had led the Maroons in a memorable contest against my great Carlisle squad in 1907, which the Indians won, 18-4.

Steffen's defense shutdown our battering rams of DeHart and Hastings, whose offensive might had been running roughshod over

Pop Warner as a Cornell lineman in 1894.

The 1894 Cornell football squad. Warner (*second row, extreme left*) was the team's captain.

The 1895 Iowa State football squad, which was the first team that Warner (*third row, extreme left*) coached.

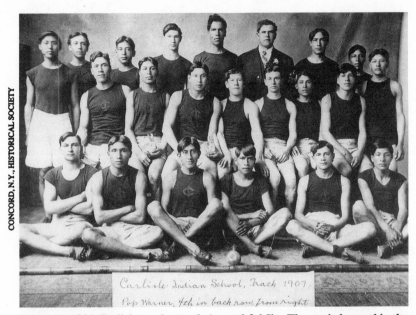

Warner's 1907 Carlisle track squad. A youthful Jim Thorpe is located in the middle of the second row.

Thorpe hurls the javelin during preparations for the 1912 Olympic Games.

The 1912 Carlisle backfield: *(left to right)* Arcasa, Powell, Welch and Thorpe.

Warner puts the finishing touch on his painting of the Stanford Stadium.

Warner poses with Ernie Nevers, the Stanford all-America fullback, who starred in the 1925 Rose Bowl against Notre Dame.

Warner with telegram from Stanford accepting his resignation there so that he could take the head coaching job at Temple in 1933.

Warner signs a contract to take the Temple job and thus begins his great football experiment. Looking on are Earl Yoemans, *at right*, Heine Miller and Charles G. Erny, *standing*, who brought Warner to Temple.

Warner illustrates the potent power of his famed single-wing offense.

Warner (*center*) is greeted by Al (Chief) Bender at a luncheon in Philadelphia while Rube Walberg of the Philadelphia Athletics looks on.

Warner after being made an honorary member of Jim Thorpe's Sac and Fox tribe.

Pitt's opponents for nearly two seasons. With the end sweep plays being shutdown, the Pitt offense switched to the inside power game to pull out a 14-6 victory.

After defeating Allegheny College, 46-0, Washington & Jefferson was our next foe. The Presidents were also being coached by a Penn grad, Sol Metzger, and were touted as a great passing team. But they were soundly defeated, 37-0.

In the final game of the season, the Pitt offense hit high gear again and blew out Penn State, 31-0. This was Bob Peck's final game for the Panthers and he celebrated the occasion by making 11 straight tackles during one stretch in the game.

Following the season, the Pitt administration rewarded me with a contract extension to carry me through the 1920 season, which I greatly appreciated.

Amongst this wild season of great glory and floods of newspaper headlines was a fact that most Pitt outsiders didn't realize, but the devout Panther faithful were perhaps most proudest — 32 of the thirty-five players on this memorable Pitt team had hailed from Western Pennsylvania.

During the past two seasons, my Pitt teams had now won 16 games in a row and lost none. The promise for the future at Pitt now shined brightly. And though we were losing some of our fine players, such as Peck, Tiny Thornhill and James (Pat) Herron, new waves of outstanding football talent had now heard of the Pitt success story and were wanting to come to play for the Panthers.

Still, I would never know another season as fine as this one.

43

The Pitt football machine continued to roll over the opposition during the World War I years of 1917 and 1918.

In 1917, the Panthers won all nine of their games against a rugged schedule that included West Virginia, Penn and Washington & Jefferson and outscored their opposition, 260 points to 31.

They also extended their winning streak to 25 games during my first three seasons at Pitt. And if the final two games of the 1914 season — which were against Carnegie Tech and Penn State during Joe Duff's tenure — are included, then this streak had actually continued for 27 straight games without a loss or a tie against an opponent.

The earlier success of the 1915 and 1916 seasons had brought much new talent to the Pitt campus and this allowed our offensive attack to broaden its potency with increased new power, speed and guile. But these much-welcomed new strengths to the Pitt team also brought several new concerns. This edition of the Panthers lacked experience in many areas and I wasn't sure what would happen over the next few months of the fall.

We opened the 1917 season by struggling to beat West Virginia, 14-9, and then blew out Bethany College, 40-0, and Lehigh, 41-0.

Then came the vaunted Orangemen of Syracuse. The game was to be played in our home territory, at Pittsburgh, which would be a much-welcomed benefit that we didn't have the previous season.

Syracuse was a highly-regarded foe who was coached by Buck O'Neill. The Orangemen's offensive attack was led by their great quarterback, Chick Meehan, who employed the "man-in-motion" formation with considerable success.

As expected, the Pitt-Syracuse game attracted a lot of attention due to the 30-0 blowout which we had dealt the Orangemen the year before. Most of the East Coast sportswriters, of course, believed that the 1916 game had been a fluke and were looking to the 1917 contest to be a truer measure of each team's abilities.

In the first quarter of the game, we witnessed the effectiveness of Syracuse's "man-in-motion" offensive strategy. On each occasion, Chick Meehan, the Orangeman quarterback, would start in motion, running parallel to the line of scrimmage and out beyond the defensive end, while signals were being called. Then, as the ball was snapped and the play began to develop, Meehan would turn back toward the line of scrimmage and attempt a "crack-back" block on the defensive end.

This strategy usually worked well for the Orangemen on end sweeps and counter plays.

But Pitt was able to slow down Syracuse's powerful offense by employing a great defense — the Pitt offense.

My theory on this was that if Pitt could control the ball for a long period of time while on offense, then this would significantly reduce Syracuse's opportunities of being able to run their "man-in-motion" attack.

And as it turned out, this strategy worked quite effectively and George McLaren picked up where he had begun the previous season against Syracuse. McLaren scored three touchdowns that afternoon, including a 91-yard romp that set a school record. Pitt showed its true strength and ability on this day and won, 28-0.

Robert Maxwell, a referee in the Pitt-Syracuse game, while recounting George McLaren's 91-yard touchdown run, in his post-game column in *The Philadelphia Evening Ledger* wrote: "McLaren took the ball and plunged through left guard. He was tackled, but the man was shaken off and the stocky fullback kept on going. Another player grasped him, but he, too, was shaken off. This gave McLaren a clear field and he surprised the multitude with a burst of speed that carried him down the field much like Hourglass (a famous thorough-bred racehorse of this era) did while running away from Omar Khayyam (another famous racehorse of this era)."

The next game on the Pitt schedule was against Penn and would be played in Philadelphia. Several of the East Coast sportswriters called this game a pivotal contest for the Pitt Panthers and began to pose questions in their newspaper columns such as "When is the bubble in the Panthers' winning streak going to burst?" or "Is Pitt going to break under the burden of their own success?"

On gameday, an overflow crowd and the cream of the crop of East coast sportswriters all gathered to see if Penn would be able to make amends for their 20-0 loss to the Panthers last season. Except for a small contingent of alumni and 800 Pitt students who had made the trip to Philadelphia by either taking the train or riding in the back of some trucks, the crowd was primarily cheering for the red-and-blue-clad Quakers.

Early in the game, Pitt took possession of the ball on their own 20-yard line following a missed field goal by Penn's Howard Berry.

Sensing a possible drop of morale on behalf of the Penn squad following this missed opportunity, I instructed our team to strike quickly with a pass play, which — if completed — might shake up the Quakers even more.

Lud Wray, the Penn linebacker, who had participated in the bloody battle with our all-America center, Bob Peck, in the 1916 game, earned a bit of revenge for the previous season's loss when he intercepted the intended Pitt pass. This steal allowed the Quakers to quickly score and take a 6-0 lead in the contest.

A few minutes later, however, Pitt began to bounce back. The Panthers moved downfield and scored on a long pass from halfback H.C. McCarter to Doc Carlson, an end.

Later, after blocking one of Berry's punts at the Penn 1-yard line, Pitt scored its second touchdown of the day to take a 14-6 lead, which proved to be the final score of the game.

Next, Pitt handed Westminster College a 25-0 licking.

A week later, we met up with our long-time rival, Washington & Jefferson. Our squad was unable to properly execute on offense, which caused us to struggle throughout the contest. Still, Pitt managed to win, 13-0.

We then finished our remaining schedule with an awesome display of offensive might by whipping Carnegie Tech, 27-0, and

Penn State, 28-6. We then whipped the Camp Lee military all-star team, 30-0.

At the end of the season, Pitt was crowned as the top team in the East by the big-city newspapers in Philadelphia, New York, Baltimore, Buffalo, Boston and Washington, D.C.

This clamoring of late November publicity soon led to a demand by the East Coast sportswriters for a post-season game which would feature the powerhouse schools from both the East and the South. As these newspaper stories continued to get a lot of attention and grab big headlines in the East, the possibility of such a game quickly picked up steam in the South.

Georgia Tech, who hadn't lost a game since 1914, was the sportswriters' choice to represent the South in such a gridiron duel. Their Golden Tornado squad, while employing a "jump shift" offense, had one of the most spectacular teams of the 1917 season and scored 491 points against their nine opponents, including a 41-0 walloping of Penn. They were coached by John Heisman, the Penn alumnus, who had previously coached at Auburn during the two seasons that I was at Georgia.

I very much welcomed the opportunity to settle this dispute of who was the best team in the country. (Editor's Note: College football was still considered by most sportswriters to be somewhat primitive while being played west of the Mississippi River. It was rarely written about in newspaper or magazine stories and the average football fan seldom knew the names of the schools or the players who competed in the West. However, this mind-set would quickly change in the next 5 or 6 years.)

In an attempt to work out the details for a Pitt-Georgia Tech post-season game, both Heisman and I exchanged several telephone calls and telegrams. But conflicts for both teams, which were caused by the end of the fall semester exams, prevented this game from being arranged. However, we did finally agree to settle the controversy in a regular-season game the next fall.

Pitt vs. Georgia Tech. It was a game that many would be waiting for.

44

In 1918, the country was heavily involved with World War I, which was being fought on the battlefields of Europe. Many thousands of college students, including athletes, were being drafted in the U.S. Army to fight in the War.

This incident alone would have affected the 1918 college football season. But a major flu epidemic also swept the country in the late summer and early fall. The heavy toll of illness that it spread brought reminders of the plagues which had hit Europe in the 1700's and 1800's.

Together, these two events contributed to force most schools to either abandon the 1918 season entirely, or, instead, play an abbreviated schedule.

Our original schedule for the 1918 season was canceled in late September after the initial impact of the flu epidemic had set in. However, by late October, the problem seemed to be under control and health officials were no longer concerned about the gathering of large crowds.

I then managed to pull together a new, abbreviated four-game schedule for the fall which consisted of the best teams that were on our original schedule.

With a new crop of talent that had arrived for the 1918 season, including Tom Davies and Herb Stein of Kiski Prep, we opened up by thrashing Washington & Jefferson, 34-0, and then crushed Penn, 37-0, which was the fourth season in a row that Pitt had beaten the mighty Quakers.

Afterwards, we met head-on with the great Georgia Tech team, whose impregnable defense had destroyed many powerhouse offenses in the past. Their Golden Tornado offense came into this contest averaging nearly 84 points per game, having already shutout Furman, 118-0, and scored 247 points in two other games.

It was a frigid, gray afternoon in late November at Forbes Field when the Pitt and Georgia Tech teams met in this long-awaited showdown. A crowd of over 39,000 — the largest to ever see a football game in Pennsylvania up to that time — had gathered to witness this bit of football history.

A strong, icy winter wind was blowing steadily across the already-muddy field that afternoon. As the chilled blast swept through the outfield area of Forbes Field, it began to pick up considerable speed. Upon reaching the infield area, these gusts created a loud, howling noise that at times seemed unbearable. A light snowfall also contributed to make the game's playing conditions much more miserable.

Deep in the bowels of Forbes Field, where the two teams' dressing rooms were located, both squads prepared for the contest which lay ahead of them.

Then, as the Pitt squad sat on their dressing room benches, waiting for me to make a few brief remarks before we departed for the game's opening kickoff, a strange happening occurred.

In the other dressing room, Tech coach John Heisman had begun to give his pre-game pep talk to his team. Heisman's style was both flowery and full of fire and brimstone — much like those that Knute Rockne would give.

Little did I realize that the wall between the two dressing rooms was so thinly divided.

As Heisman continued to address his squad, he got louder and more inspirational — and could now be clearly heard by the members of my Pitt team.

Suddenly, our dressing room grew very quiet as the Pitt team sat listening to Heisman's oratory. He was terrific! He told his Tech team — and mine — a story about the heroes of Ancient Greece. He eventually concluded his talk by telling them of the Greek soldier who had been killed while in battle and was later found while lying among the ruins of Pompeii.

This was great stuff. And as I looked around the Pitt dressing room, I noticed that my team was spellbound and gazing straight ahead at the bare red-brick wall that separated the Pitt and Georgia Tech dressing rooms.

Finally, when Heisman had concluded his talk, I decided to seize the moment and make it mine.

Walking over in front of the Pitt squad, I told them quietly, but with a big grin on my face: "O.K., boys. You heard the speech. Now let's go out and knock 'em off."

That afternoon the gridiron war of 1918 began.

Pitt's potent single-wing offensive attack of reverses and end sweeps, which had stunned its opponents for over three seasons, was suddenly brought to a screeching halt in the first half by Heisman's stingy Tech defense.

It was at this point that I reached into my past experience and instructed the Pitt quarterback to begin throwing the ball as often as possible.

Which we did. The Pitt offense even added a pass play off the reverse running play. Halfback Katy Easterday would hand the ball off to Tommy Davies, the wingback, who, instead of running the ball on the reverse play, would pass the ball downfield to a wide-open Easterday.

On defense, Pitt stopped Tech's great backs, Frank Flowers and Joe Guyon (the celebrated Indian halfback who had previously played for me at Carlisle), and destroyed Heisman's lightning "jump shift" offense.

The Panthers completed 6 of twelve passes for 126 yards that afternoon and collected 142 yards rushing and 126 yards on kick returns. Georgia Tech, however, didn't fare as well. The Golden Tornado managed only 87 yards rushing, didn't connect on any of its five passing attempts and had only 10 yards on kick returns.

The shivering crowd who was sitting in the stands at Forbes Field was shocked as they watched Pitt systematically dismantle the mighty Tech team.

"The vaunted jump shift that ripped the lines of smaller Southern colleges to splinters for the past several seasons and enabled the Georgians to pile up scores that caused the football world to wonder, was a dismal failure," *The New York Post* noted in their post-game story. "Throughout the game the Golden Tornado gained just four first downs, and just about enough ground to afford a comfortable grave for their football aspirations."

Davies, the young halfback from Kiski Prep, scored two touchdowns on punt returns of 50 and 55 yards and passed to Easterday for two more scores, connecting on passes of 20 and 35 yards.

"Davies brought the crowd thundering to its feet when he caught one of Joe Guyon's twisting, swirling, spiral punts and raced 55 yards to plant the ball behind the (goal) posts," *The New York Post* story stated. "In his journey he hurled off five would-be tacklers and crisscrossed the gridiron at least twice.

"Davies was a demon on defense; his great speed and tackling ability was responsible for breaking up Tech's sweeping end runs. The defense would spill the interference and then Davies would catapult that lithe frame of his into the runner and he would stop instantly — sometimes quicker than that. There may have been other backs in the past that have been better, but there is none who is his equal, much less his superior."

Davies also participated in a "triple pass" play that netted 36 yards and put the ball on the Tech 5-yard line. Two plays later, George McLaren carried it three yards for the final tally.

At the end of the blustery, late autumn afternoon, Pitt had pulled off a 32-0 victory that will be long remembered.

45

The blowout against Georgia Tech attracted national headlines for Pitt and the spotlight began to follow us as the 1918 season continued to unfold.

On Thanksgiving Day, which was only five days after the Pitt-Georgia game, the Panthers took on another long time foe, Penn State. This was to be the fourth and final contest in our quickly-patched-together schedule in this abbreviated season.

Penn State put up a brief struggle in this game but Pitt handily put 'em away to take the win, 28-6.

These were special days for Pitt.

Our growing prominence began to attract many offers by teams wanting to challenge us in a special post-season game. Scores of sportswriters around the country added fuel to this frenzy by suggesting in their columns the names of several worthy candidates who might be able to dethrone Pitt.

Finally, a telegram reached my desk from the Cleveland Naval Reserves, who had a team which was stocked with all-star players from colleges around the country. These players had been previously drafted to serve in the military in World War I but had not yet traveled to Europe.

An agreement was soon reached to play the Cleveland Naval Reserve All-Stars in early December at their home field in Cleveland, Ohio.

In the days that followed, the game was given a sensational publicity build-up — much like that given to the more recent New Year's Day bowl games.

From the beginning of the game, this contest was beset with problems.

One of the three referees who had been picked for the game didn't show up by kickoff, so a third official had to be hastily summoned to fill-in for him. This missing referee happened to be the one that I had personally selected to be on the officiating crew for this game. Cleveland, who had issued the challenge for this contest and would also be the home team, had selected the other two officials.

When the original third referee didn't arrive by kickoff, the Cleveland squad conveniently supplied a replacement referee who happened to be there to view the game.

A day or two later, I found out that the manager of the Cleveland Naval Reserve team had sent a telegram prior to the game to the original third referee — whom I had previously selected to officiate the game — and informed him that his services would not be needed at the Pitt-Cleveland Naval Reserve All-Stars game.

As the game began to develop, the harsh winter weather on the Cleveland lakefront started to make its presence known. The strong, bitter winds, which had been blown in after gathering force in Lake Erie, swirled across the field and quickly gave the hardened, grassy playing surface a glazened look.

A large crowd of sailors, townspeople and two trainloads of Pitt fans watched the Panther squad and the Cleveland Naval Reserve All-Stars furiously battle for yardage. There was a constant pounding along the line of scrimmage on each play. Both of these equally-talented teams continually prodded for a weakness among their opponent so they might exploit it and establish an advantage.

During the first half of the game, I noticed a very significant problem developing.

It seemed that the referees, either deliberately or a result of their incompetence, were repeatedly favoring the Cleveland team. And the game's clock was their primary tool.

The proof for this accusation can be found in studying the lengths of the four quarters in this game — none of them were the required length of fifteen minutes each. Instead, the lengths of the four quarters were 10 minutes in the first quarter, 9 minutes and 45 seconds in the second quarter, 10 minutes in the third quarter and 26 minutes in the fourth quarter.

While I was watching this sandbagging being conducted by the

Cleveland Naval Reserve All-Stars-picked referees, I began to remember the age-old practice that had been the vogue of the boxing clubs which I had visited as a young man while attending Cornell. These boxing managers would always bribe the timekeepers of a boxing match to either stretch or lessen the time of the boxing match according to the needs of their favored fighter. This way they could usually control the outcome of a fight and win big on the bets that were wagered on the fight's outcome.

Two blatant examples of sandbagging by the game's officials definitely affected the final outcome of this contest.

The first occurrence came in the closing moments of the second quarter. With Pitt on the Cleveland Naval Reserve All-Stars' 1-yard line and threatening to score, the referees declared the second quarter to be over. But more than five minutes were still remaining in the period.

Then in the fourth quarter a similar problem cropped up. At the end of the legal fifteen-minute period, Pitt was leading the contest, 9-3. Cleveland had just begun to move the ball, but it might be a good while before they were in scoring position, so the referees conveniently allowed the time in the game to continue to run.

Nearly ten minutes later, Cleveland finally scored to pull ahead in the game, 10-9.

Afterwards, one of the referees then fired his pistol into the air to signal that the game was over.

In the moments that followed, the heartache began to set it among both me and my Pitt team.

46

The next day's headlines for the Pitt-Cleveland Naval Reserve All-Stars game story in *The Philadelphia Evening Bulletin* stated: PITT WAS ROBBED.

Without a doubt, this headline clearly described the mutual feeling that was shared by all Pitt players, coaches and fans who were in Cleveland, Ohio, on that frigid day to witness this catastrophe.

Another headline, this one for the game story which appeared in one of the Pittsburgh newspapers, went even further and revealed that the Pitt loss was due to the game being rigged, or fixed. It read: PITT LOSES FIRST GAME IN 4 YEARS BY NAVAL TEAM'S CROOKED WORK.

The Pittsburgh newspaper story then went on to give one of the better editorials of the previous day's debacle.

> Pop Warner's Panthers were defeated by the Cleveland Naval Reserves here this afternoon, the final score standing, 10-9. The Panthers were really not defeated, they were robbed of what should have been a football game — for want of a better name we will have to let it be called that. The officials of the game, the players (on the Cleveland Naval Reserves All-Star team) — all of them ex-college stars — and the crowd were against the Pitt Panthers and they gave one of the greatest football teams in the country the rawest deal that was ever handed out to any visiting team in any city.
>
> The officials (for the game) were hand-picked by the Clevelanders. The contest's quarters, which were to have been 15 minutes each, were either cut too short — to 10 minutes or less — or allowed to run too long — to 26 minutes. When Pitt went onto the field this afternoon, the jury was

already in the box, with the outcome of the game having already been arranged for the Clevelanders. The jury had their verdict before they had ever heard the evidence.

To be perfectly blunt on this subject, I must tell you that we were robbed outright by the Cleveland officials. And to point the real blame, we were robbed by the people who oversaw the Cleveland Naval Reserve football program because they had issued the challenge to Pitt for this game, hired the game's referees and promoted the match.

I can take a beating when it is fairly administered, as well as anyone. But I never like to be cheated, and Pitt was certainly cheated at Cleveland. There was no attempt at fairness on the part of the officials. We didn't have a chance in the world.

The game's officials clearly didn't want to be fair in this game, and that charge is not difficult to prove. There were incidents at the Cleveland game that are impossible to describe in detail publicly. But there is plenty of evidence to show that it was a frame-up against us from the start.

For example, why did Mr. Ray — one of the referees — declare the second period to be over when my team was on the Cleveland Naval Reserve All-Stars' 1-yard line while more than 5 minutes were left remaining prior to halftime?

And why did he make the teams play 26 minutes in the final period? Perhaps the additional time was to allow the Cleveland Naval Reserve All-Stars enough time to score and win the game?

In the first half of the contest, the game's timekeeper, a Cleveland resident who was on the sidelines, claimed that his watch was broken. This was a convenient problem.

Personally, I think the whole thing looked too fishy. It had to be crooked!

The most blatant example that a fix was in on the game was the runaway duration of the final quarter. Everyone in the stands and on the field knew that we seemed to be playing in overtime just to give Cleveland an opportunity to score and win the game. It was a disgrace to watch!

Then, after the game's final gun was sounded a few minutes later, the fix became final. The Cleveland Naval Reserves All-Star squad had won, 10-9.

Unfortunately, one of the by-products of this fix was that Pitt's 31-game winning streak — including 29 straight games during my tenure — had come to an end.

After returning to Pittsburgh, I spent much of the next 2-3 days trying to arrange a return match with the Cleveland team. This time, however, the game's officials were to be chosen by Walter Camp and the contest would be played at Forbes Field in Pittsburgh. But the Clevelanders flatly refused our offer.

For the remainder of my coaching days this contest would remain a bitter memory.

47

As the 1919 season rolled around, the Pitt football program should have been at its peak. World War I was now over and Jimmy DeHart and Andy Hastings, the great Panther halfbacks, were returning from military service, along with Jim Morrow, the quarterback from our 1916 squad. Herb Stein had already proven to be the best center in the East and an overabundance of football talent was now finding its way to Pittsburgh to play on our great teams.

Still, something wasn't quite right.

Following the 10-9 robbery of our game against the Cleveland Naval Reserves All-Star team at the end of the 1918 season, the returning Pitt team seemed to have lost its air of invincibility. Their 29-game win streak (which was actually a 31-game win streak if the final 2 wins of the 1914 season under Joe Duff's tutelage were included) had been halted. And when the sportwriters now wrote stories in the newspapers about them, or football fans spoke of them, the once-glowing mystique and awe of the Pitt Panthers seemed to be missing.

In essence, our long and enjoyable honeymoon was finally over. Reality and a rapidly-changing world of football was setting in and Pitt would soon have to adapt to these changes in order to stay on top.

I first noticed these changes early in the 1919 season. After smashing Geneva, 32-2, and West Virginia, 26-0, we then met up with Syracuse. The game was played on their home field and the Orangemen played like they were repaying us for the 30-0 and 28-0 whippings in 1916 and 1917 that Pitt had applied to them — which, in hindsight, I guess they were doing.

It was in this game that I realized that this Pitt edition simply didn't have the ability to bounce back and swiftly counter the opposition's downfield onslaught. Our offensive fire power was lacking and our defensive line proved to be rather porous.

On the offensive first play for Pitt, Tom Davies swept around end on a reverse and fumbled after being hit. Afterwards, Syracuse quickly moved the ball into position and a few plays later converted on a field goal.

Willard Ackley, the pint-size Syracuse quarterback, who had kicked the field goal, ended up scoring 18 points that afternoon as the Orangemen won, 24-3.

The next game, Pitt tangled with John Heisman's Georgia Tech squad, who had returned to Pittsburgh to avenge their unexpected 32-0 thrashing from the year before.

This time, Tech was at their pre-war strength, with Buck Flowers, Red Barron and Judy Harland in the backfield. But Pitt scored twice in the first quarter and held on for the remainder of the game.

Without a great line to clear the path for our talented backs, I instructed our offense to throw the ball on every possible occasion. Our first touchdown came on a through-the-air strike from Davies to Jimmy DeHart. The second touchdown was set up by one of my famous gadget plays. Andy Hastings faked a dive play into the line and then flipped the ball back to Davies, who raced 50 yards around end before being pulled down at the Tech 7-yard line.

The final score was 16-6 and a much-needed victory for Pitt.

The next two weeks, the Panthers struggled against their opposition. They narrowly defeated Lehigh, 14-0, and Washington & Jefferson, 7-6.

Then came the annual showdown with Penn. The Quakers had lost four straight games to Pitt and only scored 13 points against the Panthers defense during this same period. With the game being played in Philadelphia and knowing of Penn's great pride in their glowing past gridiron history, I should have been ready for the trap that we were walking into.

Overall, the game was a defensive struggle. Both squads scored early in the contest, with Bert Bell, the future owner of the Philadelphia Eagles and later the Commissioner of the N.F.L, booting a 32-yard drop-kick that put Penn ahead, 3-0.

Shortly thereafter, Hastings hit on a 37-yard field goal which evened the score at 3-3.

Both sides hurled endless offensive assaults at the other's opposing defense, but neither team managed to move the ball deeply into unfriendly territory, except on one occasion when Pitt got to the Penn 1-yard line and the Quakers held them back on a memorable defensive stand.

The game finished on a 3-3 tie, which in some ways was a moral victory for the Quakers.

A week later, Pitt came back and defeated our cross-town rival, Carnegie Tech, 17-7. This victory helped a lot with our waning confidence.

We then took on our long-time traditional foe, Penn State, in the final game of the 1919 season. The Nittany Lions were coached by Hugo Bezdek, who had been a star halfback on Amos Alonzo Stagg's 1905 Western Conference championship squad at the University of Chicago .

Bezdek and I had been feuding for several years because of the Penn State coach's tactics. Before every game, he was noted for moving his team's bench up next to the sidelines. So when a Penn State player went to the sidelines to get some water during a game, he always had to stop in front of Bezdek where the water bucket was conveniently located. As the player bent over to retrieve a ladle full of water, Bezdek would counsel his player on strategy that should be used in the upcoming plays. At this time, the counseling of players from the sidelines during a game was illegal.

With the 1919 contest scheduled to be played in Pittsburgh, I decided to employ a little home-field advantage and make it a bit more difficult for Bezdek to pull any more of his shenanigans. Primarily, this meant preventing Bezdek from getting his favorite seat along the sidelines.

On the night before the Pitt-Penn State game, I went over to Forbes Field where I was joined by five of my seniors. There, we nailed Penn State's benches to the big six-foot posts which were located in front of the Stadium's bleacher seats — which were located nearly 20 yards from the sidelines. To insure our effort, we used heavy nails so that the Penn State benches could not be removed from the posts without tearing them apart.

Still, Pitt lost the game, 20-0.

A few days before the contest, we were dealt a major setback when Jimmy DeHart and Jimmy Morrow were both suspended from the team due to academic eligibility problems. This caused a great weakness in what little offensive spark that Pitt had been able to muster during the season.

Also, Bezdek was able to get back at me for my sideline tricks when in the first quarter of the game, with Penn State backed up to its goal line, the Nittany Lions' punter Harold Hess faked a punt and, instead, passed to Bob Higgins, an All-America end, who caught the ball on his 25-yard line and raced untouched for a touchdown.

Although we didn't win the game against Penn State, I must state that I did get a lot of pleasure out of seeing Bezdek squirm on the sidelines bench — way away from the action of the game.

Pitt finished up the 1919 season with a record of six wins, two losses and one tie. While compared to the previous four seasons at Pitt and the shining glories that had been earned, this campaign was much more dismal. The school's officials, however, were quite upbeat about the football program's prospects. They even offered me an extension on my contract which would go through the 1923 season.

Realizing that Pitt was now beginning to outgrow Forbes Field, I told the school officials that I would accept their offer on the condition that they would begin making plans to build a new stadium for Pitt to play in. Forbes Field, which had a seating capacity of only 32,000, was now too small for Pitt's growing alumni, student body and the draw of local fans, who were causing sellouts at almost every home game. These overflow crowds, of course, were interested in one thing — they wanted to watch the great Panther teams play football.

After presenting my case, the Pitt officials quickly agreed with my assessment of the need for a new stadium and promised to begin making plans for one to be built. With this understanding, I accepted their offer for a contract extension.

Eventually, Pitt Stadium would be built in 1924 and the Panthers played their first game in the new arena on September 1, 1925, against

Washington & Jefferson. The stadium was originally built to hold 69,400 and could be expanded to include an additional 30,000 seats with double-decks, if necessary.

Unfortunately, I would not be there to coach the Panthers when this glorious occasion rolled around.

48

The 1920's signalled a new beginning in college football. Larger stadiums would be built and increased travel by bigger, faster trains created big intersectional match-ups by schools from different areas of the country. Also, new forms of communication would bring the game of football along with other forms of entertainment into many more living rooms for Americans to enjoy.

In 1921, the Pitt-West Virginia contest was the first game to ever be broadcast on a new "music playing box" called the radio. KDKA in Pittsburgh, the first radio station in the country, which had signed on the air waves in November 1920, broadcast the Pitt-West Virginia game that afternoon with Harold Arlin serving as the contest's play-by-play announcer.

Arlin didn't have a fancy broadcast booth much like the ones which would be used in the 1930's and 1940's. Instead, he sat in the stands at Forbes Field, while talking into a makeshift microphone which was lined with felt to filter out the noises of the field. Most of the radio sets at that time — and there weren't many of them — were simple, handbuilt crystal radios that had been fashioned from a Mother's Oats box with galena wire wrapped around it.

Pitt went on to win this contest, 21-14.

Later that season, Arlin and KDKA would make a second attempt in broadcasting a football game to be aired on radio. This game was the Pitt-Nebraska contest at Forbes Field, which the Cornhuskers would eventually win, 10-0. However, the game's broadcast became more notable because it was marked by an oddly-timed technical glitch when Arlin's voice suddenly went off the air after he had announced: "Nebraska is over for the touchdown!"

The broadcast then went dead silent. Undoubtedly, many listeners must have attempted to find out what had been the problem by shaking their ear phones and tinkering with their crystal radio sets. Finally, after approximately five minutes of silence — and as mysteriously as it had stopped — Arlin's play-by-play of the game began to sputter across the air waves again.

The invention of the radio and the public's fascination with it soon inspired more college games to be broadcast over the air waves. By the mid-1920's, most major games were being picked up by radio stations which were scattered across the country. Farmers, store-keepers, clergy, businessmen and neighborhood taverns all listened in to this magical phenomenon.

Later in the 1920's, "talking" movies would further open up the college game to an even larger American audience as newsreels, which showed highlights of the previous Saturday's big-game contests along with short, personality film clips on the college's star players and coaches, were shown in movie theaters each week during the fall. These newsreels allowed college football fans an opportunity to keep up with their heroes in weekly action and created a national following for certain schools.

The 1920's were also part of a postwar business boom in this country that was much different than any previous economic boom that the United States had previously experienced. Suddenly, life seemed to be juicy fat and Americans everywhere had a greater availability of extra spending money. They then began to look for more enjoyable avenues in which to spend it.

The great Prohibition Era of liquor, of course, was also on the law books during these unruly times. This led to the opening of speakeasy saloons, backroom gambling parlors and brothels which could be found in most cities and towns.

Bookmaking and wagering on sporting events and horse racing, fancy clothes, dazzling women, brassy automobiles, riveting music and head-spinning tunes such as *Rhapsody in Blue, Stardust* and *Someone To Watch Over Me* and the Charleston dance were all the vogue of this era. It was a time for Charlie Chaplin, F. Scott Fitzgerald and Will Rogers.

College football and other sports during the 1920's grew tremendously in acceptance as larger and larger crowds began to flock to these events. Yankee Stadium in the Bronx, just outside the borough of Manhattan in New York City, the Los Angeles Memorial Coliseum and Soldier Field in Chicago — three of the largest stadiums in the country and the sites of many memorable sporting events — were built during this period.

In the 1920's, small schools with no direct links to the Big Three of the East powers — Harvard, Yale and Princeton — would quickly rise up to become big college powerhouses and began to attract large followings of fans.

There were several of these new kids on the block.

In the South, Alabama, who was coached by Wallace Wade, leaped to the forefront of would-be contenders and started to overshadow Georgia Tech who had previously ruled the Southern game while under John Heisman.

In the Midwest, Notre Dame — who was led by that pied piper of the gridiron, Knute Rockne — became the darling of American football as Rockne's Fighting Irish football squad traveled from coast to coast and almost always demolished their competition. (Editor's Note: Many newspapermen often joked about the large following of subway Notre Dame fans, including priests, parishioners and sinners alike, who would snuggle up close to their radios on autumn Saturdays to pull for the Fighting Irish, whom they had usually bet heavily on.)

In the West, the schools there had begun to cancel their short-lived (10-15 years) fascination and experiment with rugby and were now playing college football again. But all of these teams in the West were dwarfed while in comparison to Andy Smith's "Wonder Teams" at the University of California (in Berkeley, Calif.), which dominated the Pacific Coast scene.

Overnight, it almost seemed, crowds of 50,000 and 70,000 at college football games were commonplace. Soldier Field on several occasions attracted gatherings of over 100,000 to see Notre Dame play U.S.C. or Navy. And Yankee Stadium and the Los Angeles Memorial Coliseum frequently pulled in crowds of 70,000, or more, to watch Army, Notre Dame, U.S.C., Fordham and others do battle.

It was in this crazy milieu of fast times and fast money that some of America's greatest sports giants also came to life: Knute Rockne,

Red Grange and the Four Horsemen in football; Babe Ruth and Ty Cobb in baseball; Jack Dempsey in boxing; Johnny Weismuller in swimming; Bobby Jones in golf; and big Bill Tilden in tennis.

And it was America's great newspaper writers who fed the unquenchable thirst of the public's fascination with sports and their heroes. Newspaper owners also noticed this unquenchable fascination. Knowing that they could both sell more newspapers and increase their advertising rates, newspapers soon began to devote more coverage to sports in an attempt to satisfy their readers' demands. This commitment soon led to more scintillating writing, longer feature stories and a new breed of journalism. Men like Damon Runyon, Ring Lardner, Westbrook Pegler, Arch Ward and Grantland Rice were the ranking members of this literary fraternity and they wove the tales which created the myths and mystique of these great sports teams and heroes.

The 1920 season at Pitt would yield my last undefeated team there. The Panthers would post six wins and two ties that autumn, with memorable victories over Georgia Tech, 10-3, and Penn, 27-21. The two blemishes on that record were both ties: one was a 7-7 standstill against Syracuse and the other was a 0-0 whitewash against Penn State.

Penn was now being coached by my old rival, John Heisman, who had returned to guide the football fortunes of his alma mater. On that afternoon the Quakers filled the air with the footballs, but Pitt still managed to pull out a win. Tom Davies, our star halfback, contributed heavily in this effort as he returned a kickoff 96 yards for a touchdown and later intercepted a forward pass and scampered 65 yards for a second touchdown.

Along the way, Pitt also defeated cross-state rival Lafayette, 14-0, who was now being coached by one of my former pupils, Jock Sutherland. Sutherland had gone to Lafayette in 1919 and in a five-year tenure there would build a fine powerhouse. His 1921 squad would be crowned as champions in the East.

The final game of the 1920 season for Pitt was against Penn State. The Nittany Lions were picked as heavy favorites in this contest, which was to be played at Forbes Field. The Panthers, however, held

Penn State in check for the entire game and it ended just as the contest had begun, 0-0.

Afterwards, many of the Penn State fans, while trying to pin blame on their unexpected tie, accused me of soaking the playing field prior to the game in an effort to slow down their speedy backfield. But their complaints were really nothing but sour grapes.

49

The 1921 season at Pitt was a pivotal one for me.

The Panthers put together a record of five wins, three losses and one tie that fall, with their defeats coming at the hands of Jock Sutherland's exciting Lafayette squad, 6-0; then to Nebraska, 10-0, and finally to Washington & Jefferson, 7-0. The Presidents were a stellar group that season and would later play to a scoreless tie against Andy Smith's California Bears in the Rose Bowl on New Year's Day 1922. Our lone tie was a 0-0 lackluster contest with Penn State.

However as the 1921 season progressed, the winds of change were blowing in all directions on the Pitt campus.

My Panther teams were on the verge of breaking out as a national powerhouse, but at the same time they were also being forced to keep up with Knute Rockne's emerging football factory at Notre Dame and Army's talent-laden war chest. And the Pitt shakers and movers, who had originally lured me to their beautiful campus in 1915 with a mandate to take them to the big time of college football, were now mired in school politics.

The primary sticking points involved in the debate were:

1. How important it is to build a new football stadium for Pitt and discontinue playing their games at Forbes Field?

2. If a new football stadium is to be built, then what size should it be?

3. More importantly, how big of a college football power does Pitt want to become?

These three questions caused tremendous soul-searching among

Pitt administrators, alumni and fans.

Meanwhile, most of the players who had previously been recruited during the peak of the Panther's meteoric rise to power, from 1915 through 1918, either had already graduated or were now nearing graduation. This left the Pitt football program at a crossroads: Was it going to renew and strengthen their commitment to being a major football power as they had originally planned in 1914, or were they going to lower their sights a bit and, instead, field a winning football program, yet one that would no longer be running with the elite of the college crowd?

While Pitt grappled over their plans for the future, I had begun to receive telegrams and letters from some prominent alumni of Stanford University in Palo Alto, Calif., who were dead-set in building a football powerhouse so that they could silence their neighboring rival, the University of California, whose "Wonder Teams" under the tutelage of Coach Andy Smith were the kingpin of Pacific Coast football.

With the booming euphoria of college football that was now sweeping the country, the Stanford folks saw this as an opportunity to achieve their share of the glory.

Previously, Stanford had been a revolving door for football coaches. In a three-year period between 1919 and 1921, there had been three different head coaches who had produced a combined record of 12 wins, eight losses and two ties. During the 1918 season, Stanford did not field a football team due to the height of World War I and the flu epidemic, which was hitting most of the country that fall. Between 1906 and 1917, Stanford had abandoned football entirely and only competed in rugby.

Leland Cutler, who was a member of Stanford University's Board of Athletic Control, and had been responsible for bringing the 1915 World's Fair to San Francisco, was the person that Stanford had tapped to lure me away from Pitt and build a big-time program at Stanford. Cutler was a persuasive sort who, if he believed in something, could sell it to anyone.

I was now 50 years old and had planned on staying at Pitt for a long time. I had been raised in the East, attended college there and had coached there for most of my career in football.

During the seven years that I had been coaching at Pitt, I had received many offers to leave and build another school's football program. But I usually dismissed these offers rather quickly. However in the fall of 1921, with the Pitt folks wavering on the direction in which their football program was headed, I started to listen to Cutler's overtures.

Little did I realize it then, but this was the beginning of a strange set of events that were soon to go in motion.

After I had received several telephone calls and telegrams from Cutler, I called and told him that I had liked what I had been hearing from him regarding the Stanford situation and requested that he come to visit with me in the East so that we could discuss the details of Stanford's offer.

A week later, when Cutler arrived in Pittsburgh we met for dinner at The Pittsburgh Athletic Club. There, he laid out for me the elements of Stanford's financial package as well as the type of commitment that they were willing to make to the school's football program a winner. Clearly, the Stanford folks were serious with their offer and it was an impressive one.

But the key point that sold me on their proposal was when Cutler began to tell me of the school's founder, railroad magnate Leland Stanford, and his original vision of building a great university — which had since occurred. Cutler then told me that the hopes and dreams of Stanford alumni and fans was to also have a great football team.

Being a bit overtaken with emotion by Cutler's very inspiring message, I told him that I would be honored to take the Stanford job.

However, before wrapping up our meeting, I told Cutler that there might be a hitch in the deal that would have to be first resolved. I revealed to him that my original contract at Pitt had earlier been extended through the 1923 season and that I felt honor-bound to keep my word to the Pitt officials and football fans who had been so supportive of my teams.

Cutler didn't sweat one bit at my predicament. He told me that if Pitt didn't want me to leave until after my contract had been fulfilled following the 1923 season, then perhaps we could still go forward with the deal in such a way that would benefit all parties involved.

When he said this to me, I became a bit confused.

Cutler went on to suggest that if Pitt insisted on me staying for the next two seasons, I should go along with their request. He also stated that perhaps I could send in my place two of my best assistants to Stanford for the 1922 and 1923 seasons. They, in turn, would be able to teach the Stanford team my coaching philosophies and system of blocking, tackling and the single-wing and double-wing offenses.

He then added, "After the 1923 season you can join them and pull the whole program together."

Upon hearing Cutler's plan, I was stunned. Undoubtedly, it was one of the strangest proposals that I had ever heard of in a long time. As a matter of fact, it was almost as strange a setup as my earlier dual-coaching assignments at Iowa State and Georgia, Cornell and Carlisle in the mid- and late 1890's. However as the winter evening grew on, I began to warm up to Cutler's plan and became convinced that it could probably work.

Finally at the end of the evening, we shook hands on the deal.

Afterwards, one of the most memorable moments in my entire sports career occurred.

It was getting late as we stepped outside of The Pittsburgh Athletic Club and into the wind-chilled, snowy evening. As we said our good-byes and Leland Cutler was climbing into the back of the taxi which would deliver him to his hotel, I couldn't help but notice that he was wearing the biggest, cheshire smile that I had ever seen.

Perhaps it was the champagne that we had just toasted on, or the excitement of the moment, but before the cab had an opportunity to drive away, Cutler leaned out of the car's window and yelled to me: "Don't you worry, Pop. Everything is going to work out. I know it will."

On that evening, Leland Cutler was probably the greatest salesman in the world.

50

It was during the course of the next few days that the reality of my new commitment to Stanford University began to set in.

When the word of my decision started to leak out into the public and the Pitt folks heard the news, they really got riled up.

Specifically, there were two items that fueled their anger. One, the Pitt administration and key alumni were upset because they were not aware that I might be contemplating a change of schools and, if I was, then I should have given them an opportunity to better the offer which Stanford had made. Second, they were shocked that I would make a deal to coach another team two years later and still want to stay at Pitt during the interim as a lame-duck coach and try to conduct a winning program.

Finally, when the press got a hold of this story the public outcry at such news was tremendous. Some factions of the Pitt following wanted to see me fired, while others felt that I should back out of the newly-arranged deal with Stanford.

I tried to explain to the Pitt officials and alumni my reasons for taking the Stanford offer, but they felt betrayed by my actions and didn't want to listen. The Pitt folks felt that my decision to send two of my assistants to Stanford for the next two seasons to coach the team until my arrival after the 1923 season was stripping the Panthers football program of some of its best assets. They also believed that over the next two seasons I would be forced to spend my time trying to serve two masters — Pitt and Stanford — and this was not a good situation for either school.

Now, many years later, as I look back at all of this, I must agree that Pitt was treated unfairly. The right thing to have done in this situation would have been for me to either turn down the Stanford offer outright and remain at Pitt, or I should have asked the Pitt officials to release me so that I could have taken the Stanford coaching job beginning in the fall of 1922.

As it turned out, the deal went through almost like Leland Cutler had envisioned it might. One of my Pitt assistants, Andy Kerr, who coached the freshman squad, and Claude (Tiny) Thornhill, who had been a star tackle for me at Pitt in 1915-16 and was now coaching at Centre College, were my picks to go westward to Stanford to install my system of football. Kerr had been on my staff since I first arrived at Pitt in 1915 and he would serve as the Stanford head football coach until I arrived there.

In addition, Wallace Denny, the Pitt trainer, who was a full-blooded Indian and had been with me since my coaching days at Carlisle, went with Kerr and Thornhill to Stanford in 1922. Denny's job was to get the Stanford players in top playing condition.

These three guys knew my system and style of coaching well. With full confidence, I knew that they would get the job done at Stanford.

Despite the uproar that I had created in Pittsburgh during the winter months of 1922, the fall football season arrived with much fanfare. This edition of the Panthers program was blessed with loads of young talent and several seniors who had arrived at Pitt after that memorable 1918 season and our knockout win over John Heisman's Georgia Tech Golden Tornado squad.

After losing a pair of back-to-back games early in the season, to Jock Sutherland's Lafayette team, 7-0, and West Virginia, 9-6, Pitt then bowled through the remainder of the schedule and had a record of seven wins and two losses with one final game remaining to be played.

This contest was to be against Stanford and it would be played in their home stadium in Palo Alto, Calif. Stanford had posted four wins and four losses up to this time.

I had previously made a trip to Stanford during the spring to see the Cardinal team perform in spring practice drills. I now hoped that this return trip would allow me to gauge first-hand the talent level at Stanford as well as their progress under the tutelage of both Kerr and Thornhill.

However for the Pitt team and its fans, the trip to Stanford meant much more. It was an opportunity to take out a lot of pent-up frustration and resentment on the Cardinal football program for having stolen both their coach and perhaps their future.

During the Pitt-Stanford game, I was awestruck at the budding talent that the Stanford squad possessed. They had improved noticeably since my earlier visit there. Both Kerr and Thornhill had done an excellent job in preparing them fundamentally.

Still, when the final whistle blew, Pitt had pulled off a 16-7 win, which boosted their season record to eight wins and two losses. It also made the long train ride back to Pittsburgh a happy one.

The following spring of 1923, the Pitt officials began to finally get serious about their football program's future and started to make plans for the much-talked-about new stadium. They acquired nine acres of land from the Bailey estate, which was located next to some property that the University of Pittsburgh had already owned.

Afterwards, they began to have architectural plans drawn up for the new stadium. It was to be a mammoth and beautiful facility with the school's basketball arena, the Stadium Pavilion, being built beneath one side of the stadium which would seat 4,500 for basketball games.

That fall, my Pitt Panthers and I faced our final season together. Andy Gustafson, a talented sophomore fullback (who would later become a top offensive assistant to Red Blaik at Army and would also be instrumental in developing a pair of Heisman Memorial Trophy winners, Doc Blanchard and Glenn Davis) led our attack that season.

We had a youthful but talented squad and it showed as Pitt continued to progress through its schedule.

The Panthers only won five games that season while losing four. Still, we finished strong with a 20-3 win over our traditional season-ending foe, Penn State.

A few weeks later, Pitt officials huddled together and announced that they were going to hire my former pupil, Jock Sutherland, who had been enjoying great success at Lafayette during the past five seasons, to be my replacement.

Sutherland was a phenomenal coach, who would guide the Pitt

program to the next level of greatness that I knew could be achieved there. Over the next 15 years that followed, Sutherland would compile a brilliant 111-20-12 record while at the helm of the Panthers. They would also have four undefeated seasons, play in four Rose Bowl games and be recognized as national champions five times.

In the long run, perhaps my decision to leave Pitt and take the job at Stanford may have spurred the University's officials to make the much-needed decisions to insure that the Panthers' football future was secure. I can only speculate what part, if any, my actions may have played in this unfolding athletic drama.

Still, I do know that Pitt built a magnificent facility in the new Pitt Stadium that was opened in 1925. And their hiring of Jock Sutherland would keep the Panthers among the elite of college football for a long, long time.

51

As my train headed westward following the 1923 season at Pitt and toward the wondrous mountains and expansive valleys of Northern California, I began to experience a rush of adrenaline as my thoughts began to shift focus to the new world which awaited me at Stanford University.

After having made this bold move and surviving the tremendous amount of controversy and negative press that it had caused during the past two seasons, I now had an extreme calmness about having taken the Stanford offer.

Many of my critics had chastised me in their newspaper columns for what they had termed "a high-wire balancing act of trying to serve two masters: Pitt and Stanford."

Yet, Pitt was poised to achieve greatness with Jock Sutherland at the helm and Stanford was quite simply a reservoir of untapped potential still waiting for someone to open it up and unveil its greatness.

Having already seen the promising talent on Stanford's squad during my spring training visits in 1922 and 1923 and then watching Pitt pull off their memorable 16-7 victory against the Cardinals on their home turf in late December 1922, I was eager to arrive there and take charge of the Stanford program.

My two assistants, Andy Kerr and Claude (Tiny) Thornhill, had laid the foundation for me and painstakenly emphasized the fundamentals of my system to the Stanford players during the past two seasons, while awaiting my arrival. Now, I had to apply the master's touch and weave this squad's various strengths and weaknesses together so that it yielded a slashing, hard-hitting outfit that could unleash at will the much-noted explosive firepower of my single-wing and double-wing offenses.

Without a doubt, California was the place to be in the 1920's. Each week, hundreds of families were migrating there from the Midwest and East so that they could be part of the exciting boom times and awaiting opportunities that were being widely reported in newspapers and magazines around the country.

In a way, I, too, had become a member of that thrillseeking group who were now traveling west to seek their measure of fame, fortune and glory.

Much like those settlers, who three generations earlier had originally traveled this route during the fabled California Gold Rush of 1848 to stake their claims and share in those highly-publicized rivers of gold, we wanted to tackle the challenge of taming what lay in front of us and, of course, receiving the rewards that went with achieving this task.

It was during this time in California that the game of football was receiving a tremendous amount of publicity. The sport had become the vogue of the newly-settled Californians, who had been nurtured on it while growing up and having lived in the Midwest and East. To them, football's quick-striking aerial game and adventurous end sweeps and reverses were in tune with the Californian's new spirit and lifestyle.

Previously, the game had been sidelined and almost entirely abandoned from 1905 to 1917 by California high schools and colleges who had taken up the sport of rugby following the rising number of injuries and deaths in football in 1905, which led President Theodore Roosevelt to prod the ruling fathers in college football to overhaul the game and make it much safer and more wide open.

Andy Smith, who had been a great fullback at Penn in 1903 and 1904, had led the revival of interest in college football, both in California and the entire West Coast, with his Wonder Teams at the University of California.

Prior to my arrival at Stanford, Smith's Golden Bears, who were also the Cardinals' arch-rival, had gone undefeated during the past four seasons, from 1920 to 1923. During this period, they won 36 games and posted only two ties. En route they had won the 1921 Rose

Bowl game against Ohio State and returned the following season in the 1922 Rose Bowl and tied Washington & Jefferson. And to make matters worse, Stanford had not defeated the University of California in a football game since 1905.

Undoubtedly, Andy Smith's Golden Bears were the gridiron kingpins of the Pacific Coast. My job, of course, as the new Stanford head football coach was to make sure that they were dethroned.

52

My first season at Stanford was one that I will long remember.

The lengthy public relations build-up prior to my arrival had detracted a lot from the original reason that I had taken this job, which was the challenge of turning Stanford into the West Coast powerhouse that Leland Cutler, the Stanford administration and alumni had desired.

My first team there was loaded with talent; men who in the next two or three seasons would end up writing some of the greatest chapters in the history of Stanford football.

The key players on that squad were Jim Lawson, an end, who would be Stanford's first all-America selection following the 1924 season, and Ted Shipkey, who would win all-America honors in 1926 while starting at the other end. Harry Shipkey and Chuck Johnston were at the tackles; Fred Swan and Bill Neill were the guards; and George Baker was the center. In the Cardinal backfield was Ernie Nevers, the talented fullback who was injured most of the season but would be picked as an all-America in 1925; Howard (Mugs) Mitchell at quarterback; Norman Cleaveland and Murray Cuddeback at the halfbacks; and Cliff Hey and George Bogue alternating in for Nevers at fullback.

But the 1924 season did not get off to a good start.

Prior to our first game with Occidental College, Ernie Nevers broke his left ankle in a pre-season scrimmage between Stanford and a local Navy team and would be sidelined for six weeks.

Finally, the season got underway and we managed to sweep by Occidental, 20-6. Our offense piled up 455 yards in the contest while holding Occidental to only 48 yards.

The next week we took on the talented Olympic Club of San

Franciso team and their all-star squad of former college players put up a gallant effort. Eventually, we squeaked by with a 7-0 victory.

Afterwards, we tangled with Oregon in our first conference game of the season. The Webfeet scored first in the contest with an 80-yard gallop for a touchdown, but Stanford bounced back and scored four touchdowns with Norm Cleaveland leading the effort for the Cardinals. Cleaveland, a speedy and cagey halfback, would end up that afternoon with 129 yards rushing on ten carries. Oregon scored once more on a long pass in the fourth quarter. However, Stanford had it sewed up by then, 28-13.

We then traveled to Portland, Ore., the next week to play the University of Idaho. Multnomah Stadium's playing field had been reduced to a sea of mud when a terrible rain storm had settled in on the Portland area that afternoon.

Earlier in the morning, before the contest, I was told that Idaho had arrived for the game with only their red jerseys packed among their traveling gear. We were supposed to wear our customary red jerseys in this game, but after my earlier experience against Penn in 1898 I had my equipment manager always pack both our red and white sets of jerseys. Upon hearing of the mixup by the Idaho team, I sent word over to their locker room that we would accommodate this situation by wearing our white jerseys in the game and they could wear their red jerseys.

Once the contest got started, the steady downpour began to hamper the Stanford attack. Our single-wing and double-wing offense couldn't run its reverses, end-arounds and sweeps due to the slippery and muddy field.

Fortunately, the Cardinals managed to survive an Idaho assault in the first half when the Vandals fumbled inside the Stanford 1-yard line. In the second half, the Cardinals' Chuck Johnston blocked an Idaho punt that was recovered by Cliff Hey on the Idaho 26. Cuddeback later booted a field goal to give Stanford a 3-0 lead and the eventual victory.

Against Santa Clara a week later, I kept the Stanford first team on the bench the entire game so that they would be fresh for the U.S.C. game the following week. Still, we posted a 20-0 win.

However, my actions in the Santa Clara contest — in which I held out my starters — proved to have been wasted. To fully understand my reasoning on this, I should also explain a parallel incident which would quickly impact the upcoming Stanford-U.S.C. game.

On the same Saturday that we had blown out Santa Clara, 20-0, our arch-rival, the University of California, had played host to U.S.C. in a full house of over 75,000 in their new Memorial Stadium and had pulled out a 7-0 win.

But in the weeks leading up to the U.S.C.-Cal game, both schools had been feuding over certain eligibility rules that affected a U.S.C. player. The U.S.C. player ended up being disqualified before the U.S.C.-Cal game, but at the beginning of the next week — this would be the week of the Stanford-U.S.C. game — the U.S.C. student body voted to cancel their upcoming game against Stanford and to break off all athletic relations with the University of California.

This action put us in a difficult position.

Many Stanford alumni groups had already chartered trains for the trip to Los Angeles to see the Stanford-U.S.C. game and large blocks of hotel rooms had also been reserved. A banquet for 2,000 people, with both the Stanford and U.S.C. squads being in attendance, along with an elaborate schedule of events had also been planned for the game. Reluctantly, all of these had to be scrapped at the last moment.

After being notified of U.S.C.'s cancellation of the Stanford-U.S.C. game, our graduate manager of athletics, Paul Davis, scrambled around to find an opponent to fill in on our new open date on the Cardinal schedule. He made a dozen or more telephone calls to check and see if certain schools would be interested in playing a game on such short notice. Finally, after a *sweetened* financial offer, the University of Utah agreed to play.

Both schools had initially agreed to play the game at our home field in Palo Alto, but we soon realized there would be a conflict with the already-scheduled Stanford-Cal freshman game on Saturday afternoon — and there was no way that our student body was going to allow that game to be moved or rescheduled. After another round of telephone calls, Utah agreed to meet us at Cal's Memorial Stadium.

Then on Saturday afternoon, a Stanford squad, who had been highly motivated by the flurry of events which had gone on during the week, went out and crushed Utah, 30-0. Except for the large financial guarantee that Utah had received for playing the game, they probably wished that they had stayed home in Salt Lake City and not made this trip.

Our next game was against Montana, who was a member of the Pacific Coast Conference. This contest marked Ernie Nevers return to action in the Stanford lineup, but unfortunately it was a brief one.

Nevers played less than three minutes in the game before he had severely injured his other ankle, the right one, in a pileup at the end of a play. On the following play, Stanford was forced to punt, which was Nevers' assignment. As he booted the ball downfield, the right ankle bone snapped due to the pressure of kicking the ball and he had to be carried to the sidelines.

And though the Cardinals went on to win, 41-3, the game had exacted a heavy toll, especially with the much-awaited game with Cal being next up on our schedule.

At this point in the season, Stanford, who was unbeaten in eight games, was the top-ranked team in the Pacific Coast Conference. Cal was ranked second in the league, having previously tied Washington, 7-7.

Then two days prior to the Stanford-California game, Cal officials brought up the fact that Norm Cleaveland had played two minutes against Nevada in 1921 when he was a sophomore. Although this was only a brief appearance, it officially counted as a year's eligibility. This meant that Cleaveland's three years of eligibility had ended in 1923 and that he was ineligible for the 1924 season.

The controversy quickly grew. Stanford alumni, administrators and my assistant coaches loudly protested Cal's eleventh hour decision to bring this matter up. They had been sitting on such information for several weeks, but had waited until the week of the Stanford-Cal game to hopefully throw Stanford off-balance by creating a controversy.

However, controversies before big games usually are great gate-boosters. When Cal had previously tried a similar stunt against U.S.C. at mid-season in regards to a Trojan player's questioned eligibility, that controversy created enough hoopla and interest that it brought in a packed house at Cal's Memorial Stadium on gameday. And the Golden Bears won that one, 7-0.

With our game also scheduled to be played at Memorial Stadium, I quickly saw through Andy Smith's tactics. After all, he was just playing a bit of gamesmanship with us, trying to create enough controversy to draw a big crowd for Saturday afternoon's match and at the same time cause our squad to worry more about our own problems rather than focus on them (Cal).

The newspapers loved such coaches' shenanigans because these controversies always seemed to bring out the best in their writers, who usually ended up writing rather passionate stories on the subject. It also usually yielded larger sales of the newspaper at the newsstands.

By midweek, the matter was settled when our school administration announced that Cleaveland would not be playing in the game against Cal. They also offered to forfeit the other Pacific Coast Conference games that we had won, but the other member schools declined to accept this offer.

I had protested this solution because Cal had waited beyond the legal date to file an eligibility claim on the matter, however, my supervisors on the academic side of the school overruled me.

Now with my two best backs out of the Stanford lineup — Nevers and Cleaveland — I moved decisively to reorganize my offensive stable.

Jim Kelly, who was a big back with powerful strides but lacked the speed and shiftiness of Cleaveland, stepped in to the right halfback spot. Murray Cuddeback remained at the left halfback spot, with Cliff Hey at fullback and Howard (Mugs) Mitchell was the quarterback. Remarkably, our front line remained in tact. Six of these linemen would end up playing the entire 60 minutes against Cal.

The Stanford-Cal game was one of the greatest and most memorable gridiron classics that occurred in the 1920's and 30's. Walter Camp, who had coached at Stanford in 1892, had traveled across the country by train to view this spectacle so that he might include one or two of the key Stanford or Cal players on his all-America squad.

At game time, Camp observed the action as a guest on Cal's bench.

The Stanford-Cal game was the first big football extravaganza for the West Coast football fans to really rally behind. A sellout crowd of 77,000 who had paid $5 a ticket packed the stands in Memorial Stadium. Another 20,000 or more who hadn't paid watched from the grassy area atop Tightwad Hill. (Editor's Note: The price of a $5 ticket for the 1924 Stanford-Cal game is equivalent to paying $30 for a ticket in today's era.)

Their curiosity and their passion would soon be rewarded.

After a scoreless tug of war, Stanford broke rank in the action with a Cliff Hey to Ted Shipkey pass for 20 yards. The Cardinal offense then grinded out the yardage until it reached the Cal 7-yard line. There, Cuddeback booted a field goal to break the ice and give Stanford a 3-0 lead.

On the next series, Cal's offense tried to put their vaunted firepower to good use, but after crossing into Stanford's territory an errant pass was picked off by Cuddeback at the Cardinal 27.

My Stanford bunch then began to clip off yardage as we drove downfield but the drive stalled at the Cal 3-yard line when we failed to punch the ball in for the score.

Now, deep in their own territory, Cal punted the ball safely out to midfield.

With the final seconds of the first half ticking away, the Cardinal offense attempted to push the ball upfield. Then just before the gun sounded, Cuddeback connected on a 43-yard field goal which split the uprights and gave Stanford a 6-0 lead.

In the stands, the crowd roared in amazement over such a long kick.

Cal, however, didn't put much stock in the halftime score. In the third quarter, they bounced back and amassed an 81-yard drive, which included a 47-yard romp by the swifty Tut Imlay that put Cal out front, 7-6.

Later in the third quarter, the Golden Bears began a drive from the Stanford 42, which led to a score early in the fourth period when Jim Dixon connected on a pass to Imlay. The extra-point conversion boosted Cal's lead to 14-6.

Andy Smith's squad then added to the tally a few minutes later when they scored in four plays following a recovery of a Stanford fumble at their own 29. Glenn Carlson, who had made the two previous extra-point kicks for the Golden Bears, failed to connect on this attempt. Cal now led, 20-6.

The game seemed to be safely in Cal's hands at this point.

Andy Smith must have agreed with my assessment because he pulled his two best players, both Imlay and Dixon, from the game.

Then moments later, I watched while across the field as Walter Camp got up from his seat on the Cal bench and walked over to congratulate Andy Smith on such a terrific — and apparent — victory.

This sight quickly fueled the fire that burned inside of me. The eligibility controversy with Cal earlier in the week regarding Norm Cleaveland was one thing which I could have lived with, but the sight of seeing my good friend, Walter Camp, congratulating my opponent well before the game had concluded was something else.

I had just sent in Ed Walker, a sub halfback who was, perhaps, the most unlikely of heroes on the Stanford squad. Several times during the season, I had been criticized for playing him because of his noted clumsiness and lack of size or speed. Still, Walker was a game lad whose spirit always seemed to lift the others on the Stanford squad.

With 10½ minutes remaining in the contest, Stanford soon found itself on the Cal 35-yard line following a 15-yard pass from Walker to Fred Solomon. Three plays later, after the Cardinals had lost three yards on two running attempts, Walker then connected with Ted Shipkey on a 38-yard, arching pass in the Cal end zone for a touchdown. Shipkey had masterfully outmaneuvered a pair of Cal defenders on the play and this had led to the score. After Cuddeback booted the point-after kick, it was now 20-13, with Cal still leading.

The clock on the end zone scoreboard continued to run and I knew when Cal got the ball, they would try to score once more.

Unfortunately for the Golden Bears, their efforts were hampered because Andy Smith had already removed their best offensive threats, Imlay and Dixon, earlier in the fourth quarter. And the rules during this era prevented a player from being re-inserted back into action in the same quarter.

The Golden Bears then mounted a drive which carried them to the Cardinal 19-yard line, but the Stanford forward wall stiffened and halted the Cal advance.

Now with the ball resting 81 yards from the Cal goal line and time running out, Stanford attempted to pull together another scoring drive.

Moments earlier, Cuddeback had crashed into a movie camera which was too close to the sidelines. The movie camera, its tripod and the cameraman had all gone spilling along the sidelines when Cuddeback fell on them after the play. Cuddeback, although temporarily knocked woozy during the mishap, had elected to continue to stay in the game.

Ed Walker opened Stanford's drive by hitting the still-dazed Cuddeback on a 20-yard toss downfield, and by some sort of miracle Cuddeback evaded the Cal defender and raced the remaining distance for a touchdown. This reduced Cal's lead to 20-19.

Cuddeback then booted the point-after kick with great accuracy, which evened up the game at 20-20.

Moments later, the official's gun signalled that the game was now over.

And for both Cal and Stanford fans, it was a thrilling contest.

For nearly two hours following the game, the crowd hung around the Memorial Stadium recounting the marvelously-thrilling contest which they had just witnessed. And those who had left the game early, including some frustrated Stanford fans who had gone to pay off what they thought were losing bets on Stanford, all returned to hear of the exploits that they had missed.

This game would be talked about and debated for many years to come. Most importantly, it served notice that Stanford would no longer be another patsy for Cal to continue pushing around.

53

With the tie against Cal, Stanford was ranked as the top team in the Pacific Coast Conference with eight wins, no losses and only a single tie to blemish their record. Cal, however, remained the second best team in the Conference with seven wins, no defeats and two ties in the 1924 season.

Because of our status as the number one team in the Conference, Stanford was to be the representative of the West in the upcoming Rose Bowl.

However, a considerable amount of political backroom maneuvering was going on by U.S.C. supporters so that they would be picked instead. But Les Henry, the chairman of the Tournament of Roses Football Committee rejected their pitch and noted that the Trojans had already been beaten by Cal, 7-0, and St. Mary's, 14-10, earlier in the season. He also mentioned that U.S.C. had cancelled its game with Stanford during the 1924 season and that if U.S.C. had won this game it may have settled their claim as to who the rightful West Coast representative should have been.

During this era, the rules of the Rose Bowl allowed the West Coast representative to pick their opponent for the game.

Knowing that Knute Rockne's powerhouse Notre Dame squad was undefeated in 1924 and were led by a great senior backfield that had been christened the "The Four Horsemen" by *New York Herald Tribune* sportswriter Grantland Rice earlier in the season, I quickly suggested them as our opponent.

The game would be a promoter's match made in heaven. Rockne's Notre Dame box offense against my single-wing and double-wing offense. Undoubtedly, it would be an offensive fireworks display.

The capacity of the Rose Bowl at that time was 53,000. After the two teams for the game had been announced, all of the tickets were sold out within two weeks. The tickets sold at prices of $1.50, $3.00, $5.00 and $6.00 for a box seat. And the requests for tickets were such that we could easily have sold over 100,000 for this contest.

Ten days before the Rose Bowl game, the doctors gave us an early Christmas present when they removed Ernie Nevers' cast. He was instructed to walk with the aid of his crutches for another five days before attempting to run.

Nevers, however, was determined to play against Notre Dame. The day after his cast was removed, he came up to me during practice and asked for permission to practice with the team as soon as the doctor had cleared him to begin his running exercises.

I kinda laughed under my breath at his request, but I liked his spirit and told him that he needed to be able to protect himself because the Rose Bowl game would be a hard-fought battle.

Over the next few days the orthopedic doctors tried to build a brace inside his shoe that would give his right ankle both stability and protection, as well as some mobility. Yet with each attempt they fell short of what Nevers needed.

Finally, I asked him to come over to my house one evening. And in my garage workshop, I tinkered around and eventually constructed a device which was made of aluminum that would fit inside his shoe and a rubber inner tube that was heavily strapped along the back of his injured leg, from his upper calf to the bottom arch of his foot. Then, I taped both of his ankles thoroughly with adhesive tape to provide support.

This device seemed to be helpful to Nevers and he agreed to try it out at practice. After a bit more tinkering over the next few days we found the right mix and Nevers felt confident enough to use it in the game against Rockne's Fighting Irish squad.

Little did I realize that he would be playing the biggest game of his career in the Rose Bowl contest.

When New Year's Day and the big game arrived, I walked onto the Rose Bowl sod and surveyed the massive crowd that had packed out the place. The press had built the game up to frenzied proportions and called it "the game to decide the college national championship." The local bookies did pretty well on the game, too. They branched out into all of the saloons and bars in Pasadena, Beverly Hills and Hollywood and their business was brisk.

Prior to the game, I had often laughed whenever I read of the sportswriters' claims of this being a national championship game and how it pitted the two best teams in America against one another, because I didn't believe that any game could have topped our recent thriller against Cal.

But I was wrong.

Notre Dame opened the game by using their "shock troops," who were their second-team players. This group was used to pound and soften up the opposition. Afterwards, the Fighting Irish's first team would be inserted.

Stanford struck first in the contest when Chuck Johnston, a tackle, recovered Notre Dame halfback Don Miller's fumble deep in the Fighting Irish's territory. Cuddeback booted a 17-yard field goal shortly thereafter and Stanford took a 3-0 lead early in the game.

On the next series, Notre Dame began to show its real prowess. The Fighting Irish took over the ball on their own 20-yard line following the kickoff and quickly put their magical offense in motion. Jimmy Crowley, the Notre Dame halfback, got loose on a 27-yard romp behind the blocking of Miller and Elmer Layden, the Notre Dame fullback, and the march was on.

Notre Dame wasted no time in traveling to the Cardinal 10-yard line before Nevers and the Stanford defense rose up to stop their penetration.

When Stanford could only manage a short punt a few plays later, which went out of bounds at the Cardinal 32, the Fighting Irish were once again back in business. They moved upfield in short bursts of yardage and finally reached the Cardinal 7-yard line as the second quarter began. Moments later, Layden slammed in from the 3-yard line for a touchdown. Fred Swan blocked the point-after conversion but Notre Dame now led, 6-3.

Later in the second quarter, after Layden had boomed a 72-yard punt over the Cardinal goal line, Stanford took over at its 20 and drove to the Irish 31. Jim Lawson greatly aided on this drive with a 14-yard end-around carry. However, Nevers did most of the gritty work en route.

While facing a critical fourth down and needing six yards, Nevers attempted a pass to Ted Shipkey in the flats, but his pass never reached the intended Shipkey. Instead, Elmer Layden, who was in the Irish defensive secondary, had sensed the play developing and stepped into the path of the aerial and temporarily bobbled it into the air while in full stride. He finally got a firm grasp on it and set sail for a 75-yard scamper down the sidelines.

Nevers made a valiant attempt to catch Layden before he crossed the Cardinal goal line but the Irish back had too much of a head start for Nevers to stop him. Following the point-after kick, Notre Dame assumed a 13-3 lead.

It was at this juncture that I realized that a change of game strategy was needed to turn the tide in this contest. Notre Dame's defense was set for a straight-ahead power attack, which was the strength of my Stanford offense. I then changed our strategy to emphasize the outside running game.

While using a mixture of sweeps, reverses, end-arounds and passes, Stanford began to make their move on the Irish squad. And as the remaining minutes in the second quarter clicked away, the Cardinal offense marched to the Irish 10-yard line and were in excellent scoring position, but a fumble halted this effort and Notre Dame took over at their own 17.

In the second half, Stanford continued to cover lots of real estate and journeyed into Notre Dame's territory twice but missed on two Cuddeback field-goal attempts of 36 and 45 yards each.

Following the second missed field goal, Notre Dame was unable to move the ball and had to punt. Layden then booted a terrific 50-yard kick which Fred Solomon, a Cardinal back, seemed to have lost in the sun and fumbled. Solomon made two futile attempts to recover the ball, but Ed Huntsinger, an Irish end, scooped it up and ran 20 yards for a touchdown. The Irish then made the point-after kick and led, 20-3.

At a time when most teams would have given up, my game

Stanford boys dug in and played their hearts out.

Nevers got things going when he intercepted a pass from Notre Dame quarterback Harry Stuhldreher and returned it to the Irish 29. Nevers then pounded the line on three straight plays to advance the ball to the Irish 16. He followed this with three more assaults into the middle of the Notre Dame defense which brought the ball up to the Irish 7-yard line.

It was now fourth and 1-yard remaining for a first down. With the Irish gathered in tightly together to stop another line plunge by Nevers, the Cardinals reached into their bag of tricks and, instead, called on Ed Walker, who had previously sparked the fourth quarter rally against Cal, to pass to Ted Shipkey for the much-needed touchdown. Afterwards, Cuddeback's extra-point kick narrowed Notre Dame's lead to 20-10 as the third quarter came to a close.

The Cardinals then got back into the action shortly thereafter when George Baker, a linebacker, intercepted a Notre Dame pass and returned it to the Irish 31.

Once again, Stanford was in position to score.

Shipkey circled the backfield on an end-around play and gained five yards, then Nevers blasted through the Irish forward wall for eight yards, while carrying what seemed to be most of the Notre Dame team hanging onto him. This put the ball at the Irish 18.

Shipkey gained five more yards on an end-around, but two line-plunges by both Nevers and Cuddeback failed to pick up any yardage. Then on fourth down, Nevers pounded into the line for seven yards and a first down.

With the ball now at the Irish 6-yard line, Nevers, the swifty Swede, once more battered into the middle of the Irish defense on three straight tries and moved the pigskin to inside the Irish 1-yard line.

It was now fourth and goal.

The two lines then met in a terrific smashing of beef, muscle and pads as Nevers blasted straight ahead again and seemed to have crossed the goal line for the touchdown before being thrown back into the massive pileup.

All of the Stanford players and fans thought this to be the case, including the head linesman, Walter Eckersall, who had raised his arms to signal a touchdown.

But the Notre Dame players strongly disagreed with this decision.

Referee Ed Thorp, who had the final voice in the matter, also agreed with the Irish's viewpoint and overruled Eckersall's touchdown call and awarded the ball to the Irish, just inches from their goal line.

To this day, I firmly believe that we got cheated on this call. And a touchdown at that point in the game would have made a big difference.

Still, the Cardinals refused to quit. When we got the ball on offense once again, Nevers let loose on some magnificent running and, with two good passes to Shipkey and Larson, Stanford was at the Irish 35 and knocking on the door again. However, Jim Crowley, the swift Notre Dame halfback, stole a touchdown pass out of Larson's arms at the Irish 10-yard line to turn back the Cardinals' advance.

Then with just 25 seconds remaining in the contest, Nevers attempted a pass to Shipkey in the flats, but the ever-present Layden again turned up at the right moment, intercepted the ball and raced 70 yards for the game's final touchdown. This put Notre Dame ahead, 27-10.

Moments later, the final gun sounded and the Rose Bowl game was over.

It had been an afternoon packed with much drama and emotion.

A total of 14 Stanford players saw action in the Rose Bowl game as compared to 28 players for Notre Dame.

Nevers, Cuddeback and six other Stanford players played the entire 60 minutes in the contest. Nevers set a Rose Bowl record by carrying the ball 34 times while gaining 114 yards. The entire Four Horsemen backfield of Layden, Crowley, Miller and Stuhldreyer only gained 127 yards that afternoon.

Nevers also passed for a touchdown in the game, had a 42-yard punting average, was in on 75 percent of all of the tackles on defense and also intercepted a pass which set up a touchdown.

Rarely have I ever seen such a magnificent display of athletic talent as I saw Nevers put forth on that day. And his feat was made more special when one must realize that he was still recovering from two recently broken ankles.

A review of the statistics for the Rose Bowl game will show how conclusively the Cardinals had outplayed Notre Dame, but the breaks in the game had greatly benefitted the Irish. Stanford had 18 first downs to only seven for Notre Dame. The Cardinals netted 172 yards rushing in comparison to only 127 for the Irish. In the passing department, Stanford had racked up 126 yards to 53 for Notre Dame. Overall, the Cardinal had 298 yards on offense and the Irish had 179.

In the years that followed, I don't think I ever saw a greater game than that one.

54

Ernie Nevers was, without a doubt, the greatest football player that I ever coached or ever saw play.

In an era of great ones — Red Grange of Illinois, George Gipp and the Four Horsemen from Notre Dame, Elmer Oliphant and Chris (Red) Cagle of Army, or even Jim Thorpe of Carlisle — Nevers always stood a bit taller when trying to compare others to him.

Single-handedly, he almost brought Stanford back to defeat Notre Dame in the 1925 Rose Bowl. Ernie Nevers had that rare kind of courage and special ability that you see only once in a lifetime.

But the great Stanford fullback wasn't always the star that he was with the Cardinals.

Nevers began his days in football as a tackling dummy on the local high school team in Superior, Wis.

"I didn't even know a football from a squash when I reported for the Superior High School team in 1917," Nevers would later explain.

"I was so lousy that I didn't even get a uniform during my freshman year. So Ira Tubbs, the school's football coach, used me for live bait in tackling drills.

"I used to stand in a sawdust pit and let the other players tackle and block me. And I wasn't allowed to move. The only difference between me and a regular dummy was that I could talk and didn't have a rope around my neck."

Nevers eventually got out of the tackling pit and began to play at both the tackle and end positions for the Superior High School team.

On the school's basketball team, Nevers was a starting guard and helped them to win a state championship one season and was the runner-up for the title the next season.

Then following his junior year of high school, Nevers' family moved west where his father bought a ranch in Santa Rosa, Calif. It was here that Nevers became a fullback and started his journey to greatness.

"They didn't have a football team at Santa Rosa High until the year I got there," Nevers once shared with me. "Vic Hodge was the coach of our team and he had never before played football. Everything that he knew about the game he had learned from books.

"I taught him the offense which we had used at Superior High, where our team had won the sectional high school championship. Then when the season began, Coach Hodge asked me what position I had played. Without hesitating, I told him *fullback.*

"You see, I wanted a chance to carry the ball and kick."

As a high school senior, Nevers had filled out to where he weighed 190 pounds and could pass and kick the football with great accuracy.

He led the Santa Rosa High School football and basketball teams to winning seasons that year, but before Santa Rosa's basketball season was over Nevers disappeared and returned to Superior, Wis. There, he led the Superior High School basketball team to a third-place finish in the state championship.

By then, Nevers had intended to enroll at the University of Wisconsin. But his father had other plans. "We live out here now," the elder Nevers wrote to his son that spring. "So you had better go to some California college."

After completing the spring semester at Superior High School, Nevers returned to the West Coast.

He had wanted to enroll at Stanford in the fall, but was short a half-unit of credits to get in. Feeling a bit dejected, Nevers then packed his suitcase and went to Berkeley to enroll at Cal.

It was at this point that Fate intervened. Before Nevers had an opportunity to register for classes, some Stanford alums found him. They then hid him out until Cal had started classes.

It was then that Nevers decided to enroll at Santa Rosa Junior College for the fall semester. And though there had never been a football team at Santa Rosa Junior College, Nevers formed a team with just 13 players. He also arranged a schedule for that season, coached the squad and played fullback. His brilliant play that season attracted a lot of publicity as well as the attention of every college football coach on the Pacific Coast.

I was still at Pitt at the time, but Andy Kerr and Claude Thornhill were keeping an eye on Nevers' progress.

And, of course, the University of California was also keenly interested in Nevers and wanted him to be a part of their Wonder Teams.

"Cal had started to work on me," Nevers once told a newspaper reporter. "They had seen me play. And 'Brick' Mueller (an all-America end for the Golden Bears in 1920, '21 and '22) had been an idol of mine, and I got to know him. But I knew Pop Warner was coming to Stanford and that sold me."

Despite all of the recruiting hullabaloo, Nevers remained strongly interested in attending Stanford. And after he had finished the fall semester at Santa Rosa Junior college and earned the necessary half-unit credit to get into Stanford, Nevers transferred there in the winter of 1923.

Several months later, while on my visit to the Palo Alto campus to watch Andy Kerr and Claude Thornhill put the Cardinals through spring training drills, I met Nevers for the first time.

After having seen his dazzling punting and passing abilities in practice, I went up to him, introduced myself and told him, "You're gonna be a great fullback for the Cardinals."

He just smiled and didn't say much at the time.

But later on, we were both glad that this prophecy came true.

Nevers was selected as a first-team all-America fullback by Grantland Rice, the legendary sportswriter for *The New York Herald Tribune* who picked the *Collier's* all-America squad, for 1925.

After completing his career at Stanford, Nevers played for the Duluth (Minn.) Eskimos and the Chicago Cardinals of the National Football League.

He was also a pitcher for the St. Louis Browns baseball team in the American League. When Babe Ruth of the New York Yankees hit his record 60 home runs in 1927, two of these were hit off Nevers' pitches.

55

The arrival of the 1925 season brought on a period of rebuilding for the Stanford Cardinals. Many of the players who had been developed by Andy Kerr and Claude Thornhill in 1922 and 1923, prior to my arrival, were now graduating and thus their positions needed to be filled by a new crop of youngsters.

Among our returning starters were Ernie Nevers, Fred Solomon and George Bogue in the backfield, with Ted Shipkey, an end, and Fred Swan, a guard, in the line.

Those missing due to graduation were George Baker, the center; William Neill at guard, Harry Shipkey and Chuck Johnston at the tackles; and Jim Lawson, our all-American end.

Although this was an experienced lot, their youthful replacements stepped into their vacant spots and achieved much greatness.

We opened up the 1925 season by playing a lot of our young players while experimenting to find the right combination that would help us to win.

Against our cross-town rivals, the Olympic Club all-star team, in the season opener, we used 22 players and lost, 9-0. Then the following week we tried 25 players in the game against Santa Clara and pulled off a 20-3 victory. Nevers, in a great performance, averaged nearly five yards per carry in this contest.

The next week, Stanford finally began to shake things up a bit as we unloaded on Occidental and won, 28-0, with Nevers and Solomon both scoring twice that afternoon. Mike Murphy, a sophomore halfback, turned in the most memorable play of the game when he set up the Cardinals' first score on a 50-yard romp.

Nevers also turned in a stellar showing. Besides his two touchdowns, he wound up with 100 yards rushing in 19 carries. Stanford managed to dominate the action in the game by chalking up 21 first downs to just two for Occidental.

This victory set the stage for our match against Southern California, who was now being coached by Howard Jones, the former coach at the University of Iowa and Duke University.

There had been a big build-up of publicity for the 1925 Stanford-U.S.C. game due to the tumultuous uproar which had been created during the previous season when U.S.C. had debated with Cal over the eligibility of a certain Trojan player and then, following their loss to Cal, sought out revenge by cancelling the game with Stanford just five days before it was to be played.

With the 1925 contest being played in the Los Angeles Memorial Coliseum, it turned out to be a thriller because most of the game's scoring was determined by big plays.

The Cardinals' first score was set up when Ted Shipkey recovered a fumbled punt on the Trojan 12-yard line. From there, Nevers, our powerful fullback, smashed into the U.S.C. line on several carries and eventually scored to give Stanford a 6-0 lead. Nevers, however, was unable to convert the point-after kick.

Before the halftime gun was sounded, the Cardinals struck back once again when Mike Murphy, a stocky back with quick moves, fielded a punt and raced 55 yards through the grasping arms of most of the U.S.C. squad and on to paydirt. Nevers' extra-point kick was good this time and Stanford's lead was now boosted to 13-0.

In the third quarter, U.S.C. came roaring back with a strong passing attack and quickly drove down the field to score a touchdown. Following their conversion kick, which was successful, the Trojans narrowed the Stanford lead to 13-7.

Afterwards, U.S.C. continued to keep the heat on the Cardinals when they stopped a Stanford drive deep in our territory and forced us to punt. With Nevers back deep to handle the kicking duties, Brice Taylor, a U.S.C. guard, broke through on the play and blocked Nevers' intended punt.

The ball then bounced crazily over the Stanford goal line. Nevers, who saw this happening, also saw Taylor, the U.S.C. player who had blocked the kick and was now hotly pursuing the ball to make a recovery which would have given the Trojans another touchdown.

Realizing that he could not reach the ball ahead of Taylor, Nevers, instead, managed to block Taylor from getting to the ball. This allowed Stanford teammate Don Hill to arrive at the ball and fall on it, thus causing a safety and yielding only two points to U.S.C.

Stanford's defense then rose to the occasion and held off the Trojans' additional advances to take a 13-9 victory.

Next, we tangled with Oregon Agricultural College, which is now known as Oregon State University and is a Pacific Coast Conference foe.

The Aggies — who are now called the Beavers — opened the scoring first with a field goal to take a 3-0 lead. But the Cardinals bounced back with Nevers leading the offensive advance downfield by completing passes to both Hill and Dick Hyland. Hill then hit for a 16-yard run to put Stanford deep in the Aggies' territory. A few plays later, Nevers carried it over on a short line-plunge to give Stanford a 7-3 lead.

Ted Shipkey added the Cardinals' second touchdown on a memorable end-around run which caught the Aggie defense flat-footed and put Stanford ahead, 14-3.

The Aggies came back in the third quarter and on an end-around touchdown run of their own kept the score close at 14-10.

Ward Palmer, a junior tackle, who had been ill for several days prior to the game and had orders from the doctor not to play, entered the contest when the game got tight and soon afterwards intercepted an Aggies' pass and returned it to their 19-yard line. Nevers took the Cardinals in for the score two plays later.

I then pulled Nevers from the game and replaced him with a sophomore, Ernie Patchett. That afternoon, Nevers, the Cardinals' stellar fullback, had turned in a splendid performance with 126 yards rushing on 24 carries.

Afterwards, Patchett drove the Cardinals in for the final score and a 26-10 victory.

The following week against the University of Oregon, we held a slim 14-13 lead at halftime and scored three touchdowns to easily win, 35-13.

Dick Hyland, who had acquired the nickname of "Tricky Dick"

from the newspaper sportswriters because of his swift running style, was the big spark in this contest when he returned the third-quarter's opening kickoff 70 yards to set up a touchdown which was later scored by Patchett.

Next, we traveled to Seattle to play the University of Washington in a game that would be a showdown to decide the Pacific Coast Conference title.

The playing field in Seattle was a muddy and sloppy surface with little grass.

The Huskies' great backs, George Wilson and Elmer Tesreau, ganged up on Nevers all day long. Knowing that the field's horrible conditions prohibited the mounting of a passing attack, the Huskies famed duo plugged up the middle of the Washington defense and continually pounded on Nevers as he and the Cardinal offense tried in vein to establish running lanes in the middle of the line.

Stanford did manage to get inside of the Huskies' 10-yard line once, but the drive was stopped on the Huskies' 4 when the Cardinals couldn't punch it in.

Washington won the game handily, 13-0.

Afterwards, we took on the University of California-Southern Branch, or U.C.S.B., which has since become the University of California at Los Angeles, or U.C.L.A. This was their first appearance on the Stanford schedule.

The Bruins were a member of the Southern California Conference at the time and a weaker version of its big brother, Cal. However, the Bruins were intent on cracking into the level at which the West Coast's big-time football played.

While using mostly reserve players, Stanford crushed the Bruins, 82-0.

Unfortunately, I was not there to enjoys such a wonderful victory. Instead, I had taken most of the Cardinals' first-team players with me to scout the Cal-Washington contest that was being played on the same afternoon. My assistants, Andy Kerr and Claude Thornhill, were left in charge to coach the Cardinals against the Bruins and ended up using the entire Stanford bench.

The game against Cal proved to be a major emotional turning point for the Cardinals, who had long played in the shadows of the great Cal teams.

In the first quarter, Nevers recovered a Cal fumble on their 30-yard line. In three plays, the Cardinals, while on strong bursts by Bogue, Nevers and Murphy, took the ball in for a touchdown, with Nevers making the final plunge for the score.

Later in the first period, the Cardinals drove 78 yards for another touchdown, with Bogue scoring on a dazzling double reverse from the 11-yard line to boost Stanford's lead to 13-0.

In the second quarter, one of our drives stalled on the Cal 4-yard line, but after a Cal punt which only went to their 29, the Cardinals hit quickly and Nevers scored on a 5-yard plunge into the line. Murphy converted his second point-after kick and this gave us a 20-0 lead.

Cal later scored in the fourth quarter to narrow the gap to 20-7. However on the next possession, Ed Walker blocked a Cal punt and recovered the loose ball on the Bears' 2-yard line. Nevers then punched the ball in for the score to make it 26-7.

Cal scored once more in the final quarter, but it was too late. The scoreboard now read 26-14 and the Cardinals owned the lead.

Those valiant Bears from Berkeley, however, would not quit. They staged another drive that went to the Cardinal 3-yard line before Nevers and a stingy Stanford defense held them off in a great goal-line stand.

Soon afterwards, the final gun went off and the Cardinals had at last achieved the impossible by defeating Cal. The celebration by the Stanford alumni and fans that followed the game went late into the evening.

Yes, there was much to celebrate. For the first time since 1905, Stanford had managed to achieve a victory over Cal (in American football).

And although it was long in the making, this victory was quite sweet to enjoy.

56

The 1925 season had allowed Stanford to turn the corner and escape its past.

During the course of a single season, the Cardinals had defeated two of their oldest rivals, U.S.C. and Cal. This was the first time that the Cardinals had beaten both schools in American football since 1905. The fact that we had defeated both of them in the same season made our success even more spectacular.

The only major regret of this memorable season was the fact that we would be losing Ernie Nevers, our great fullback who was also the best ballplayer on the Stanford squad, due to graduation. Yet during the 1925 season, two other promising backs, Dick Hyland and Biff Hoffman, had been discovered who might be able to fill the void following Nevers' departure.

Both were former rugby players whose horseplay often kept my blood pressure near a boiling point, yet in a football game they were spectacular sights to behold. Hyland was a magnificent runner whose elusive moves and glowing speed gave him the rare ability to single-handedly be a gamebreaker. Hoffman, the other part of this duo, ran with great power and was always a potent passing threat.

Hyland and Hoffman were among the talented and youthful crop of players that gave me much optimism for the 1926 season. However, the Cardinal program did have to overcome a significant setback when Andy Kerr, who had been one of my assistants at Pitt and later served as the interim head coach at Stanford in 1922 and 1923 prior to my arrival and then assisted me there in 1924 and 1925, resigned his position to accept the head-coaching job at Washington & Jefferson.

Following Kerr's departure, I brought in Chuck Winterburn, who had played for me at Pitt in 1921 and 1922.

The 1926 season opened with a crazy innovation that I had long wanted to see tried — a doubleheader against Fresno State and Cal Tech. The games were to be played just 10 days after the beginning of fall practice, yet it would give me an opportunity to see a lot of young players in action. In all, 51 players would see playing time that day, with many of them playing for at least a portion of both games.

The Cardinals routed Fresno State, 44-7, in the first game of the doubleheader, but the contest against Cal Tech proved to be much more difficult.

I had started my reserve squad against the Engineers, but the feisty Cal Tech team scored first. The reserves then managed to come back and tie the game, 6-6. Afterwards, I put my first team into the game and they moved quickly to add another score and point-after kick to land a 13-6 lead. The Cardinal defense then stiffened and held on to preserve the victory.

Against Occidental the following week, the young Cardinals struggled early in the contest but finally broke the ice in the second period when Biff Hoffman punched it in for a touchdown.

In the third quarter, Occidental came dangerously close to even up the score when they drove to the Cardinal 13-yard line. But the stubborn Stanford defense put the brakes on this advance and eventually got the ball when Occidental failed to make a first down.

Stanford then responded by marching 87 yards with Ed Walker taking the ball in for Stanford's second score of the afternoon.

Our final points in the contest were contributed by an unlikely star, Tom Work, a lanky, high-jump star on the Stanford track team, who had entered the game in the fourth quarter. With only five minutes left in the game and Occidental again deep in Stanford territory and threatening to score, Work intercepted an Occidental pass and sprinted 95 yards through open field for a touchdown.

The game ended a few minutes later with Stanford on top, 19-0.

Tom Work's fame, however, was short-lived. A few days later, he quit the Stanford football team and returned to the Cardinal track squad, where he became a full-time high jumper.

The next week, Stanford took on cross-town rival, the Olympic

Club, who once again was stocked with former Stanford players. Feeling that we could easily handle the opposition, I left the team in the capable hands of my assistants, Claude Thornhill and Chuck Winterburn, to coach the Cardinals while I traveled to Los Angeles to scout the U.S.C.-Washington State game.

As it turned out, Stanford had its hands full that afternoon. The Olympic Club led, 3-0, after booting a field goal in the second quarter and held on for most of the game.

Finally, with two minutes remaining in the fourth quarter, Hoffman, Mike Murphy and Bob Sims began to rally the Cardinal squad. Murphy scampered the final 20 yards of the Stanford drive for a touchdown, with Sims adding the point-after kick to give the Cardinals a 7-3 come-from-behind victory.

My Stanford squad seemed to enjoy flirting with near defeat and then pull out a victory in the last few minutes of a game. In their next two games, the Cardinals were behind in both contests and had to mount second-half comebacks in order to win.

Against Nevada, the Cardinals were trailing, 9-0, but caught fire in the second half and scored 33 unanswered points to land a 33-9 win. Then in the game with Oregon, the Cardinals were once again in the uncomfortable losing position. This time, they were behind, 12-9. A second-half rally produced three touchdowns and enough redemption to give Stanford a 29-12 victory.

With six victories now under our belt, Stanford's path to the Rose Bowl had only one serious hurdle still in its path — U.S.C. The Trojans, while under Howard Jones' tutelage, had been undergoing a renaissance of sorts and were rapidly becoming a West Coast contender.

In the first half of this contest U.S.C. opened up with an impressive showing. During the first quarter, they pounded the Cardinal forward wall for big yardage, with their talented backs, Mort Kaer and Manuel Laraneta, leading the charge, and drove to the Stanford 17-yard line before being stopped. Later in the same period, they set off on another drive that would take them to the Cardinal 1-yard line, but the first quarter ended before they could make an assault on the Stanford end zone.

On the first play of the second quarter, the Trojans managed to achieve their objective and scored as Kaer smashed up the middle to cross the goal line. After a failed conversion attempt, U.S.C. led, 6-0.

Then as the scoreboard clock was nearing halftime, U.S.C.'s Lloyd Thomas grabbed a Hoffman mid-air fumble and raced 48 yards to give the Trojans their second touchdown in the contest and a 12-0 lead.

Following Don Hill's kickoff return to midfield, a determined Cardinal squad with Hoffman at the helm of the Stanford offense began to mix-up their attack with a series of well-timed fakes, passes and single and double reverses.

George Bogue, who had been previously injured, replaced Hill in the Cardinal backfield and he seemed to supply the necessary spark to get the Stanford offense moving.

Hoffman connected on a 20-yard pass to Ted Shipkey and then sent Bogue on a double reverse for 16 more yards.

When the Cardinal advance reached the Trojan 2-yard line, Hoffman took it in for the touchdown. Bogue, however, missed on the point-after kick and U.S.C.'s lead was reduced to 12-6.

In the third quarter, Kaer of U.S.C. fumbled and the ball was recovered by the Cardinals' Chris Freeman on the Trojan 36. The Cardinals then punched the ball closer toward the U.S.C. goal line but an attempted field goal by Bogue missed its mark.

After the Trojans couldn't get their vaunted passing attack unfurled, they were forced to punt. This put the Cardinals in great field position at midfield. Hoffman quickly hit Hyland on a pass downfield at the Trojan 15 and the Stanford speedster sprinted into the end zone untouched. Bogue was able to make good on his conversion kick this time and this boosted Stanford into a 13-12 lead.

Although both schools made serious advances in the final quarter, neither was able to score again and Stanford took the victory.

Against Santa Clara, I rested all of my starters except for Hoffman, who was my field general. Bob Sims, the halfback; Lawrence Lewis, who was a quarterback; and Ernie Patchett, the fullback, all contributed greatly to a 33-14 win over the Broncos.

Len Cassanova, who would later be a famous coach at both Santa

Clara and the University of Oregon, led the Santa Clara attack as he passed for one Bronco touchdown and caught a pass for the other.

Adam Walsh, who had played center on the Notre Dame team that had beaten my Stanford squad in the 1925 Rose Bowl, was the coach of the Santa Clara squad and their offense was a replica of the one that Knute Rockne had been running. And though we had successfully defensed them in this contest, we would not always be so lucky in future meetings.

Our next opponent was against Washington. With the score tied, 10-10, in the third quarter, the Cardinal offense broke loose and scored three touchdowns in an 11-minute span to defeat the Huskies, 29-10, and settle a bit of revenge for our 13-0 loss from the previous season. Hoffman, Shipkey, Hill and Bogue were the stars for the Cardinals that afternoon as they overshadowed Louis Tesreau and George Guttormsen, the Huskies' captain, who turned in magnificent performances for Washington.

A week later, Stanford traveled to Berkeley to take on Cal in the Big Game. A crowd of over 90,000, including some 15,000 perched up on Tightwad Hill, saw the Cardinal offense at its best.

On the first play that Stanford had the ball, which was on the Bear's 48-yard line following a Cal punt, Hyland circled the backfield on a reverse around right end and then sprinted past three Cal defenders and on toward the end zone and a touchdown. His breakaway speed and deceptive moves were an amazing sight to behold.

From there, the game turned into a rout as Hyland, Bogue and Shipkey let loose a mighty offensive fireworks display and began to grind up large chunks of Cal real estate.

To describe how awesome the Cardinal attack had become that afternoon, perhaps the following story will give you some insight:

> Bert Schwartz, who was a sophomore guard and would later become an all-America player, was a strong, quick and overzealous type.
>
> In an attempt to exploit his zeal, I had previously installed a fullback smash play in which Dick Hyland, the Cardinal left wingback, would trap Schwartz from the blind side and then roll away from him to go downfield to block

another Cal player.

As I had figured, Schwartz didn't know who was blocking him on this play. And apparently neither did the other Cal
defensive players. We probably used this play five or six
times during the game and picked up good yardage each time
it was run.

However after our fourth time of successfully executing
this play, a dejected Schwartz who had been knocked to the
ground by Hyland's block, rose slowly to his knees, raised his
hands high, looked upward, and before a jammed-packed
crowd of more than 90,000 in Memorial Stadium screamed:
"God Almighty, please tell me where they are coming from."

This sight was indeed a memorable moment.

We ended up blasting Cal, 41-6, that afternoon to earn our first win
in Memorial Stadium.

My good friend, Andy Smith, who had coached the great Cal
teams, had passed away following the 1925 season and had been
replaced by Clarence (Nibs) Price, so I didn't mind running up the
score a bit.

With two back-to-back wins against Cal now under our belt, we
were hopeful that their string of dominance was now over.

57

Stanford's crushing victory over Cal gave the Cardinals an undefeated season with 10 straight victories. It also gave us the Pacific Coast Conference title over U.S.C. and the automatic selection as the West Coast representative in the Rose Bowl.

U.S.C., who had lost to Stanford, 13-12, had beaten all of their other opponents during the 1926 season except for Knute Rockne's Fighting Irish. Notre Dame had narrowly defeated them by the same score of 13-12. As a result, the Trojans finished as the runner-up team in the Conference.

The University of Alabama, which had defeated Washington, 20-19, in a thriller in the 1926 Rose Bowl, was selected to be our opponent. Wallace Wade's Crimson Tide squad was sporting a 20-game winning streak that stretched back to the 1924 season.

As the game unfolded, it turned out to be a great chess match.

My Stanford squad was dressed in cream-colored, silk pants, which drew a lot of wisecracks and catcalls from the Southern visitors, but they quickly found out that the Cardinals weren't a bunch of sissies.

Instead, this was a gamely Cardinal squad, who was blessed with great speed, power, passing ability and the daring to pull off the big play. Knowing of these attributes, I had earlier planned for a bit of hocus-pocus to be used in the game with Alabama.

All during the season, the Cardinal attack had been keyed around our great end, Ted Shipkey, and Dick Hyland, the speedy Stanford wingback. I knew that Wallace Wade had probably drilled his Alabama defense to keep a close eye on these two players. But the Tide defense would probably pay little attention to Ed Walker, our right end who hadn't been thrown a pass during the entire season.

For our opening offensive play in the game, I had instructed both Hyland and Walker to trade positions. Alabama's safety — as I had predicted he would — then moved over to cover Walker, while thinking that he was covering Hyland. In the meantime, the real Hyland broke fast from the line of scrimmage and soon was all alone on the Tide 15-yard line. While running downfield and looking over his shoulder, Hyland saw that the pass was going to be a bit short, so he abruptly turned and raced toward the ball, catching it on the Tide 27-yard line for a 45-yard gain.

Hoffman then hit Hyland on another pass to the Tide 8. The Cardinal's advance was eventually stopped when a field goal attempt went wide.

On our next possession, the Cardinals' offensive drive was stopped after entering Alabama's territory on a lost fumble.

But shortly thereafter, the Cardinals began to show their true talents.

After Hyland made a fair catch of an Alabama punt at the Cardinal 37, Stanford's offense began to move downfield on a mixture of reverses, line plunges and passes which carried them to the Tide 18.

With Alabama now confused about Hyland's true identity and whereabouts on the field and the supposed emergence of Walker (or whom they thought was Walker) as the Cardinals' key pass receiver, George Bogue then opted to throw to the real Walker, who had been heavily covered while playing in Hyland's wingback position for most of the first quarter but was now open. Walker gathered in the pass with great ease and darted into the end zone. Bogue's point-after kick gave Stanford a 7-0 lead.

In the second quarter, I almost swallowed my cigarette while watching one of Hyland's crowd-pleasing antics. He fielded a punt on the Cardinal 5-yard line and then started to his left but was hemmed in and couldn't find any running room, so he promptly reversed his field. In an attempt to find more space to maneuver in, Hyland circled deep into the Cardinal end zone and, whether by design or by sheer luck, one of Alabama's pursuers who was hot after him ran into the goal post, thus knocking him unconscious. Hyland quickly turned upfield and raced toward the other end zone, but he was forced out of bounds at the Cardinal 20 by a lone Tide defender.

Both the Alabama players and I were almost spent after that splendorous performance.

The game, however, continued to be a contest of near-misses for Stanford. Several of our drives were either halted by lost fumbles or a stingy Crimson Tide defense.

In the fourth quarter, with the Cardinals holding onto a slim 7-0 lead and the clock winding down, Alabama got a lucky break.

Frank Wilton, who had replaced Hyland, was back to punt while at Stanford's 47. Wilton's punt, however, was blocked by Clark Pearce, the Tide's great center, and the ball bounced off his chest with such force that it rolled all the way to the Stanford 14-yard line.

Wasting no time, Alabama pounded the Cardinal forward wall for five consecutive plays and penetrated it for the touchdown. Jimmy Johnson, a Tide back who had been injured during most of the season, along with Lou Winslett, the Tide's all-America halfback, carried the load on this abbreviated drive.

With the score now at 7-6 and Stanford leading, Alabama would need a conversion kick to even the score. And my counterpart, Wallace Wade, was ready for this eventuality. He had set up a play which was designed to relieve the game's tension on the man who would be kicking the point-after conversion. And in this situation, it was Herschel Caldwell.

As Alabama lined up to attempt the conversion kick, with Winslett kneeling on one knee to hold the ball for Caldwell's placement, an ever-ready Stanford defense was tensed for the charge to block the kick.

At that point, Junie Barnes, the Tide captain and quarterback, yelled out: "Signal's over."

Suddenly, the Stanford players began to relax. Yet, it was at this same time that the Alabama center snapped the ball to Winslett who spotted the ball and Barnes booted a perfect kick to add the extra point to make it a tie game at 7-7.

A minute later, when the final gun sounded, the Stanford players walked off the field highly embarrassed.

In reviewing the statistics, it is quite evident that Stanford easily dominated the contest. The Cardinals had amassed 350 yards rushing in comparison to Alabama's 117 yards. The Cardinals also had 12 first downs and the Tide had six. In the passing column, Stanford completed 11 of 16 passes for 133 yards while Alabama only completed 1 of 7 attempts for nine yards.

Ted Shipkey, our all-America end, had another big Rose Bowl performance. He caught five passes, recovered two fumbles and made 23 yards on an end-around run. He was also our best player on defense that afternoon.

Afterwards, Stanford was awarded the Rissman National Trophy, which was one of the national championship awards given in the 1920's and 1930's prior to both the Associated Press and United Press beginning their football polls. This trophy was given to the top football team in the country at the end of the season.

Finally, the Stanford program had reached the big time of college football that they had long wanted. They were indeed among the very best in the country.

But as I had previously found out at Pitt, the initial road to the mountaintop of the college football world was both challenging and very rewarding. However, staying there would prove to be much more difficult. The headaches and frustrations were always much greater. And suddenly, you were placed in the difficult position of constantly having to defend yourself against schools who envied your success and who would soon be seeking to dethrone you.

Still, in comparison to where the Cardinal football program had been prior to my arrival, the Stanford alumni and fans considered themselves fortunate to have these kinds of problems.

58

After a record of 24 wins, three losses, two ties and two Rose Bowl appearances in the past three seasons, along with two straight seasons of defeating both of our biggest rivals, U.S.C. and Cal, and winning a national championship in 1926, our growing success had greatly instilled a lot of confidence in the Stanford football faithful.

Our single-wing and double-wing offense was now the vogue of the country and usually seen more often than any other offense. And that includes the famed Notre Dame box offense, which had been made popular by my good friend, Knute Rockne.

But football is a game of constant change and I knew that in order to maintain a successful program at Stanford we were going to have to keep ahead of the competition. I therefore re-directed our offensive attack for the 1927 season to change from a heavy, line-plunging style with big, powerful backs to one which utilized a lighter, deceptive and quick-striking unit.

Once again, we opened up the season with a doubleheader, with our opponents being Fresno State and the Olympic Club.

I played our reserves in the first contest which was against Fresno State and they slaughtered the Bulldogs, 33-0.

However, the second game turned into a real donnybrook. I started my sophomores against the all-stars from the Olympic Club. Both squads battled furiously but neither team was able to score on the other in the first half.

Then in the third quarter, the Olympic Club broke the ice when one of their players blocked Biff Hoffman's punt, which bounced backwards into our end zone. The same Olympic Club player recovered the ball there and this gave them the touchdown and a 6-0 lead.

George Bogue, who had previously starred for the Cardinals, was now one of the starting halfbacks on the Olympic Club all-star team. He booted the point-after kick, but fortunately for us it sailed wide of its mark.

At the beginning of the second half, I had installed my veterans and they responded to the Olympic Club's challenge. The Cardinal offense, while mixing up an array of reverses, passes and counter plays, proceeded to march downfield on a 75-yard drive for a touchdown with the tally coming on a six-yard reverse play. Hoffman then added the conversion kick which put the Cardinals ahead, 7-6.

In the closing minutes of the game, Bob Sims, our halfback, attempted a field goal from the Olympic Club's 12-yard line, but his kick was blocked and Russell Sweet recovered the ball for the opposition and started running toward the Cardinal goal line with it. Fortunately, Sims ran Sweet down and stopped him from scoring, thus preserving the narrow 7-6 victory for us.

The second game of the season-opening doubleheader proved to be much closer than I had originally anticipated, yet it served its purpose because 31 Cardinal players played in the Fresno State contest and 26 played for us in the Olympic Club scrapper.

The next week, we took on St. Mary's College, which was a Catholic school that fielded a small, but determined team.

In an attempt to shake some life into my older players, whom I didn't feel were giving their best performances, I demoted the veterans to the second and third teams. Frank Wilton moved up to the first team and replaced Dick Hyland at wingback, while Ralph (Lud) Fentrup and Sims alternated at Don Hill's halfback position and Chuck Smalling filled in for Hoffman at fullback.

These moves, however, didn't provide the necessary spark that I was hoping to achieve. St. Mary's capitalized on 16 Cardinal fumbles to take a 16-0 victory, with both of the Gaels' touchdowns resulting from fumble recoveries. Larry Bettencourt, who was later named an all-America tackle, scooped up one of the fumbles in the first quarter and darted 15 yards for the Gaels' first touchdown. Then Homer Hicks grabbed Sims' second quarter fumble and breezed in the final 15 yards for the opposition's second score. This put St. Mary's ahead, 16-0, and the score remained there until the final gun had been sounded.

The game with St. Mary's was one of the most brutal contests that I had ever seen played. It was even worse than the first game that I had ever coached — the Iowa State-Butte Athletic Club match in 1895. The St. Mary's players employed several roughhouse tactics, including late hits, spearing, forearm chops and out-of-bounds gouging. Besides this, they were extremely foul-mouthed.

The following week, we rebounded and blew away Nevada, 20-2. I missed seeing this contest because I had, instead, gone to scout the U.S.C.-Oregon State game which was played the same afternoon.

U.S.C. was by now a formidable football team.

With Cal in the midst of a transition following the death of their great coach, Andy Smith, Howard Jones had become the rising new star in the West Coast football picture.

Undoubtedly, the upcoming Stanford-U.S.C. game was going to be a dogfight.

Knowing this, I switched back to my original backfield of Larry Lewis at quarterback; Hill at halfback; Hyland at the wingback slot; and Hoffman at fullback.

And when the Stanford-U.S.C. game finally arrived, my prediction came true. For nearly three quarters, both teams attempted to penetrate the opposition's forward defensive wall, but neither squad was able to wrestle away enough momentum to take the upper hand.

In the first quarter, the Trojans made two drives into Stanford's territory, but was stopped on both occasions by the Cardinal defense. Then in the closing minutes of this period, tragedy struck when Frank Wilton, our reserve wingback, fumbled at the Cardinal 27 and Russ Saunders of U.S.C. scooped up the loose ball and dashed to the Stanford end zone for a touchdown. The point-after conversion that followed was successful and this gave the Trojans a 7-0 lead.

As the second quarter began, Stanford's offensive machine went into gear and drove from our 20-yard line to the Trojan 11. But after four unsuccessful attempts to score, we were forced to give up the ball.

U.S.C. took possession of the ball and proceeded to march almost the entire length of the field. When the Trojans reached the Cardinal

10-yard line, our defense dug in and halted their advance.

We then took over. And in a dash of bravado, the Cardinal offense began to stage a lightning-quick offensive strike. First, Bob Sims ripped 16 yards on a running play. Next, Hoffman took to the air lanes and flung a perfect pass to Wilton, who was 30 yards downfield. Without breaking stride, Wilton gathered the ball in his arms and set sail for the Trojan goal line — some 44 yards away — which he soon found. In all, the aerial play covered 74 yards for the touchdown.

Hoffman added the extra-point kick, which evened the score up at 7-7.

In the third quarter, we weren't able to penetrate beyond the midfield stripe and into the Trojans' territory. But in an odd twist of fate, following a U.S.C. punt which had rolled into our end zone, a referee called a holding penalty against one of our players and rewarded the Trojans by giving them the ball on the Cardinal 9-yard line.

Morley Drury, who was having a great day for the Trojans that afternoon, then proceeded in the next two plays to punch the ball in for the touchdown. On the extra-point attempt, Hyland, who also played in the defensive backfield for us, crashed through the U.S.C. line and blocked the kick. U.S.C.'s lead now stood at 13-7.

Slowly the game seemed to be moving in U.S.C.'s favor.

But after one Stanford drive failed early in the fourth quarter, the Cardinals were presented with another opportunity when U.S.C.'s Drury fumbled the ball and it was recovered by Wilton.

Quickly, Hoffman took to the air lanes once again.

With a mighty effort, he unleashed a long, arching pass that landed among a group of U.S.C. and Stanford players, who all jumped into the air to grab the pass. In midair, they all seemed to have bobbled the ball temporarily while it bounced off the hands and helmets of several players. The pass finally landed in the hands of Roland Sellman, a Cardinal end, who gathered it in and ran with it to the Trojan 30.

Hoffman followed this with an 8-yard completion to Louis Vincenti, another Cardinal end.

It was at this point that I made a rather daring move.

With two minutes remaining in the contest, I called on Herb

Fleishhacker, a reserve fullback who until then had been mostly known for his large size rather than his football prowess, to replace Hoffman in the backfield. I also instructed him to pass the ball to Vincenti, who would probably be open in the end zone.

Fleishhacker was so excited to be in the game that upon checking with the referee — which was a rule during this era — the big fullback blurted out to the official: "Fleishhacker for Hoffman — throw the pass to Vincenti."

Now many years later, I'm still amazed that U.S.C. didn't pick up on what Fleishhacker had said, because nearly everyone else on the playing field heard his proclamation.

Fleishhacker must have realized his mistake, too, because he led Stanford on a ground attack for six straight plays that advanced the ball up to the Trojan 3-yard line.

I then sent in Lud Frentrup, who was another big runner, to replace Don Hill. This move would bolster the Stanford backfield with more power. U.S.C. apparently interpreted this move to mean that the Cardinals intended to blast their way into the end zone. But, instead, Fleishhacker lofted an awkward pass to Vincenti, the 155-pound Stanford speedster, who had found an opening in the U.S.C. secondary. His reception gave Stanford the touchdown and tied up the score at 13-13.

There were now only 20 seconds left in the game.

We then took a time-out to discuss our strategy for the extra-point kick, which would give us the lead and a probable victory.

In the confusion of the moment, Larry Lewis, our usual holder on extra-point kicks, didn't get into the game and this required Fleishhacker to step in and assume a task that he had never before attempted. The bulky youngster, upon receiving the center's snap, planted the ball into the ground with such a firm grip that Mike Murphy, the Cardinal kicker, was barely able to get the ball into the air and it failed to make it through the goal post's uprights.

When I later questioned Murphy how he had missed the extra-point try which would have put us ahead, 14-13, he explained, "The only way I could have made it was to kick both the ball and Herb Fleishhacker over the crossbar."

Fate it seems had other plans for us on this day. A few moments later, the referee's gun sounded and the scoreboard in the end zone reflected that the game had ended in a draw: Stanford 13, U.S.C. 13.

Undoubtedly, this was one of the greatest gridiron battles ever played on the West Coast. Both squads won on this day. There were no losers.

Morley Drury turned in an outstanding performance for U.S.C. He carried the ball 40 times for 161 yards and intercepted several Cardinal passes which halted many of our advances.

Remarkably, the game with U.S.C. had not drained us of our emotional energy. Usually, a big game like that either saps you of your confidence and strength or, instead, propels you on to greatness.

In our case, the Cardinals received a much-needed boost of confidence after the hard-fought contest.

In the next three games, Stanford rushed for 228 yard and swamped Oregon State, 20-6, on a field of sand and sawdust following a heavy rainstorm; blasted Oregon, 19-0; and knocked off Washington, 13-7, on a wet, slippery field that saw the Huskies lose five fumbles to the Cardinals.

Feeling a bit confident of our recent successes and with a record of seven wins and one loss and the Big Game against Cal just two weeks away, I decided to let my assistants lead the team in our upcoming game with Santa Clara while I, instead, went to scout the Cal-Washington game. Both of these contests were scheduled for the same afternoon.

I had not considered Adam Walsh's Santa Clara squad to be much of a threat and felt that my presence on the Stanford sidelines was not necessary for us to achieve victory. In a short period of time, I was to be proven wrong about that conclusion.

My Cardinals turned in a flat, unemotional performance that afternoon and the Broncos took advantage of this opportunity. Their hustle and fine execution enabled them to pull off a 13-6 win and left us with much embarrassment.

While I was leaving the Cal-Washington game I was told of the Stanford-Santa Clara score by a sportswriter who had heard the scores being announced in the stadium's press box by the telegram operator. Quickly I took my frustrations out on a nearby garbage can.

Afterwards, I told myself that there was no way I could allow us to lose the upcoming game against Cal. Because if we did lose, then my efforts in missing the Santa Clara contest to instead view Cal in action against Washington would have been wasted.

At the beginning of our game with Cal, the Cardinals opened the scoring early. Hoffman, Hill, Murphy and Hyland each ripped through the Bears' line for nice gains. Hyland took it over for the opening score, with only five minutes having elapsed in the contest. Hoffman then added the extra-point kick and Stanford led, 7-0.

After our early bit of success, the Cardinals were unable to get on the scoreboard again in the first half as the Cal defense stiffened up considerably.

In the third quarter, Cal's offense finally came to life and drove the ball to the Cardinal 1-yard line but was unable to cross the goal line.

With the ball deep in our own territory, we then tried to punch it upfield.

However, our offense couldn't gather enough steam and was soon forced into a punting situation. As we attempted to kick, the Bears poured through the Cardinal line and blocked it. One of their players quickly scooped up the loose, bouncing ball and dashed 15 yards to paydirt in the Stanford end zone. Fortunately for us, Cal's extra-point attempt was unsuccessful and we still held the lead, 7-6.

Later, Wilton returned a punt 37 yards to the Bears' 45-yard line and the Cardinal offense got cranked up. Hoffman ran for 23 yards on one play. He then directed Sims around left end for eight yards on a Statue of Liberty play.

Realizing that a big play was needed to continue the drive, Hoffman reached into the Cardinals' bag of tricks and pulled out a special play that I had made up as a follow-up to a successfully-run Statue of Liberty play.

On this play, Hoffman sent Sims circling behind him in the backfield, just as he had previously done on the Statue of Liberty play, except that this time Hoffman pulled the ball down from his passing stance and, instead of handing the ball to Sims, who would sweep to the outside of the left end's block, Hoffman put the ball behind his back and slipped around the other end, unseen by the defense. Then he scampered down the sidelines untouched to score. The Bears' defense was completely fooled.

This was the first time that the bootleg play was ever run — and thankfully for us it worked magnificently.

The Cardinals were unable to convert the point-after kick, but the 13-6 lead was enough to insure a Stanford victory.

Afterwards, Ed R. Hughes of *The San Francisco Chronicle* called this game the greatest game of Biff Hoffman's career and even compared him to Ernie Nevers.

With seven wins, two losses and one tie under our belt, we were tied with U.S.C. at the top of the standings in the Pacific Coast Conference. Both schools had identical 4-0-1 records in the Conference. The Trojans' lone loss for the season was to Notre Dame, 7-6, while my Stanford squad had been beaten by both St. Mary's and Santa Clara.

The Rose Bowl officials had the final word in this matter and they wanted a big match for the New Year's Day game. Knowing that Stanford would be a bigger drawing card than U.S.C., we were chosen to represent the Pacific Coast Conference.

59

After Stanford was finally chosen to be the West Coast representative in the 1928 Rose Bowl, all of the sportswriters wanted an answer to the same question: "Who will be your opponent on January 2nd?"

A half-dozen or more schools from the East and the South were given consideration for this spot, but the final decision went to the University of Pittsburgh.

Pitt was being coached at the time by one of my former players, Jock Sutherland, who had succeeded me following the 1923 season. In his four seasons while at the helm of the Blue & Gold juggernaut, Sutherland had built Pitt into a solid contender in the East. His 1927 edition of the Panthers were undefeated that season, except for a scoreless tie to Andy Kerr's Washington & Jefferson squad.

The newspaper writers tried to make a big deal about the "Old Master" and the "Young Pupil" coaching against one another in the Rose Bowl game. But I knew Sutherland was one of the most talented young and upcoming coaches in the country and his 26-6-4 record at the time spoke prominently of his abilities. So I didn't buy into the psychological trap that was being set for me.

The Rose Bowl Stadium, which had been expanded by 15,000 seats to a new capacity of 72,000, was definitely a great setting for the Stanford-Pitt battle. Yet for Pitt fans, there remained a lot of pent-up frustrations. Many still felt betrayed because I had left Pitt to go West to take the Stanford job. The added controversy and circumstances under which I had left Pitt just added to their emotions.

Because of this family feud, the Rose Bowl contest got a mountain of publicity. And for weeks the country awaited its outcome with great curiosity.

Prior to the game, I decided to add a bit of *insurance* to help us win the game. I installed three special plays which could be run off the Statue of Liberty formation and undoubtedly throw Pitt off-balance. One play had Biff Hoffman handing off to Dick Hyland, our wingback, on a reverse. On a similar play, while using the same action, Hoffman could hit our left end on a pass. Our third insurance special was a line-buck (or trap) with Hoffman hitting behind the guard position. (Editor's Note: This third play proved to be quite effective since the Pitt defensive guard — or noseman — spent most of the afternoon pulling out of the line and backing up whenever he saw Hoffman release his arm to pass.)

Going into the Rose Bowl contest, Pitt was the favorite of the odds-makers. But once the opening kick was made, my Cardinals dominated the action. The big difference in the game was that the Stanford linemen were able to control the line of scrimmage for most of the game. Hal McCreery, Seraphim Post, Don Rubesky, Roland (Tiny) Sellman, Chris Freeman and Walt Heinecke were the main-stays on the Cardinal line that day.

In the first half, both squads fought furiously and neither team was able to score. My Cardinals had managed to reach the Pitt 7-yard line in the first quarter and the Pitt 1-yard line in the second period, but was unable to penetrate the Panther forward wall and reach the goal line on either occasion.

However, in the third quarter, the action in the game really began to heat up.

Our defense got the theatrics started when they put the brakes on Pitt's long drive at the Cardinal 20. Then on the first play of the new offensive series, Stanford halfback Frank Wilton fumbled while sweeping around end. Pitt's Jimmy Hagan, who was nearby, saw the ball bouncing loosely and quickly scooped it up at the Cardinal 17 and raced in for a touchdown. This score gave the Panthers a 6-0 lead.

For Wilton, this event was another case of bad luck. In the 1927 Rose Bowl, his punt had been blocked by an Alabama player which set the Crimson Tide up for a touchdown and an eventual 7-7 tie. It was also Wilton's fumble in the recent Stanford-U.S.C. contest that resulted in a touchdown for the Trojans.

With all of this frenzied action going on, Walt Heinecke, a five-foot, six-inch, 174-pound sophomore center on the Stanford line, was sent in to replace Chris Freeman, our big bruising tackle. On Pitt's extra-point attempt, Heinecke broke through the Panther offensive line and blocked the kick, which later proved to be a pivotal point in the game.

For on this afternoon, Lady Luck must have been on the side of both Wilton and the Cardinals.

On Pitt's kickoff, Stanford carried the ball out to the Cardinal 37 and immediately began to make things happen. Hoffman connected on two passes that moved them down to the Pitt 31. Hoffman then went for 11 yards on a spinner play and traveled three more yards on another spinner on the next play. Wilton added four yards while hitting up the middle and Seraphim Post shook things up some more when he ran a guard-around play for five yards to advance the ball to the Pitt 8-yard line.

Then came the moment of Wilton's redemption. Hoffman hit Bob Sims on a pass in the flats, but a Pitt tackler jarred the ball loose. Wilton, who happened to be in the area, moved quickly toward the bouncing ball, snatched it away from the grasp of three Pitt defenders and ran it in for the touchdown. After Hoffman booted the extra-point kick, Stanford moved ahead, 7-6.

For the remainder of the contest, we proceeded to protect our lead.

Finally, when the official's gun had sounded to end the game and our Rose Bowl victory had become official, I paused to look up at the scoreboard and saw those magical numbers: "Stanford 7, Pittsburgh 6."

This wondrous sight would forever remain etched in my memory.

60

The 1928 season was a time of significant changes for both Stanford and college football on the West Coast. To get a better understanding of this statement, it is perhaps best to back up and review a brief history of the college football scene on the West Coast and some of the key events leading up to the 1928 season.

In 1916, Andy Smith had left Purdue University and made the original excursion westward to take the job for Cal. There, he lifted the Bears into the lofty status as the best football power on the West Coast. A record of 74-16-7 and two trips to the Rose Bowl, while under Smith's tutelage, solidified this powerhouse aura.

Then in 1924, I finally was able to complete my contract with Pitt and moved westward to take the job at Stanford.

The next season, other West Coast schools also began to look to the East and the Midwest for coaches who could come to their schools, work similar magical spells and quickly turn their lowly football programs into dazzling, stadium-packed, gridiron power-houses.

This exodus began in 1925 when Howard Jones left Duke to take over at U.S.C. and Bill Spaulding departed Minnesota to lead the U.C.L.A. Bruins. Soon afterwards, others began to be swayed by big salaries, wonderful lush weather and the adventure of building a big-time football squad from what had once been a meager program. Jimmy Phelan left Purdue to take the coaching job at Washington, Dr. Clarence Spears departed from Minnesota to lead Oregon and Paul Schissler went from Lombard College to Oregon State. This new coaching roundtable became complete in 1931 when Bill Ingram left Navy to replace Clarence (Nibs) Price at Cal.

Of course, it was both Cal's and Stanford's early success which contributed to the creation of this football monster. From this point forward, these new pretenders to our already-established dominion would attempt to nip away at our heels and steal our thunder.

At the Stanford campus in Palo Alto, we tried to adapt to these changes. Prior to the 1927 season, we had changed our backfield from one which boasted of big powerful backs to one which was based on smaller players who possessed speed, quickness and shiftiness. In 1928, I modified our offensive attack to take advantage of both our talent and the college football rules book, which always seemed to be revised each year to hinder the more successful schools.

Then before the season began, I installed a new "Formation B" attack which featured two fullbacks in the Stanford backfield, Biff Hoffman and Chuck Smalling. In this new formation, the two fullbacks were placed at different distances behind the linemen and they, of course, had different responsibilities. The deep fullback was located six yards behind the center and was usually your best athlete, possessing both good speed and keen passing kicking skills. The other fullback was located three yards behind the line and to the right of the deep fullback. He needed to be a good line-plunger and adept at handling the ball on reverses.

This new offense worked well when it was perfectly executed, but my 1928 squad was a very inconsistent one. On some days, they performed magnificently, while on other days they struggled against weaker teams. Many of these weaker teams usually ended up winning these games, too.

In our season opener, we played another of my doubleheader games, and when it was over I regretted that I had even thought up such a stupid idea of playing two games on one afternoon.

In the first game of the doubleheader against Y.M.I., an all-star squad, we lost 7-0, as Ed Storm, a former Santa Clara player, intercepted Harlow Rothert's pass in the closing minutes of the game and ran 86 yards for a touchdown.

Then in the second game, we took out our frustrations on the West Coast Army team and won, 21-8. Hoffman scored two touchdowns that afternoon and Frank Wilton added the third.

Next, we lost to the Olympic Club, 12-6. Mort Kaer, the former U.S.C. star halfback, shined brightly for the Olympic Club in this contest as he passed for one touchdown and returned a punt 68 yards for their second score.

After a rather frustrating up and down early season, the Cardinals suddenly seemed to find themselves. With Biff Hoffman turning in a brilliant performance as field general, Stanford proceeded to romp over their next four opponents. They throttled past Oregon, 26-12, on a road game in Eugene, Ore. Then in our first meeting with U.C.L.A. since the 82-0 shellacking that was administered in 1925, the Cardinals blasted the Bruins, 45-7. Next, Idaho was routed, 47-0, in a game that was played in the fog at Kezar Stadium in San Francisco. And while I rested my starting team for the upcoming U.S.C. game, the Cardinal reserves whipped Fresno State, 47-0. Harlow Rothert scored four touchdowns in leading the way to victory that afternoon.

But a week later in the U.S.C. game, the Cardinals off-again, on-again playing style met with disaster. We completely outplayed the Trojans that afternoon, while out-gaining them by more than 100 yards in total offense. The Stanford offense also picked up 10 first downs on the ground while the Trojans were unable to muster even one. Yet when the Cardinal offense got inside the Trojan 5-yard line, we either fumbled, threw an intercepted pass or got a penalty which set us back.

Being unable to penetrate into the Trojan end zone, Stanford ended up losing the contest to U.S.C., 10-0. It was the first time that we had lost to them since I had arrived at Stanford in 1924. It was also the first time that one of my teams had ever lost to a Howard Jones-coached team.

Following the contest, the U.S.C. fans remained in the stands of the Los Angeles Memorial Coliseum for a long time while savoring their great victory.

The next opponent on our schedule was Santa Clara, who had been a spoiler against the Cardinals in 1927 when I was absent from the sidelines while scouting our upcoming opponents, both Cal and Washington, in the California-Washington game.

I decided to discard the "Formation B" attack for this contest and reverted back to our "Formation A" attack, which was the basic single-wing offense. With President-elect Herbert Hoover in the stands viewing the game, Stanford gained revenge and defeated the Broncos, 31-0.

Against Washington, Bob Sims hit Don Muller for two touchdown passes to lead the Cardinals to a 12-0 victory.

Now, with a bit of momentum under our belt, we were ready for the Big Game with Cal.

The Bears, who were having their best season under Nibs Price's tutelage, entered the Stanford-Cal contest with only a loss to the Olympic Club, 12-0, and a scoreless tie with U.S.C. marring their record. Offensively, Cal had scored 121 points while holding their opponents to only 22 points. (Editor's Note: A touchdown by Santa Clara, a field goal by Washington and the Olympic Club's 12 points were the only points scored against Cal defenders in the 1928 season.)

The 1928 edition of the Bears reminded me a lot of the 1924 Cal squad which Andy Smith had coached. They hit hard, had good execution and played with a special kind of intensity that is needed to field a winning team.

The Stanford-Cal match got off to a slow start for the Cardinals. Most of our first-half advances were halted by pass interceptions by the Bears. As a result, the Stanford defense was called upon to rise up and defend against several threatening Cal penetrations into Cardinal territory.

In the second quarter, Stanford drove to the Cal 22-yard line, but an aerial attempt was deflected and unexpectedly fell into the arms of a Cal defensive tackle who, after being surprised with having possession of the ball, then raced 76 yards for a touchdown. When the Bears converted the extra-point kick, they assumed a 7-0 lead.

In the closing minutes of the first half, Cal halfback Bennie Lom tossed a 38-yard pass to Russ Avery for a second touchdown which increased Cal's lead to 13-0. But the Bears' point-after kick failed to make it through the goal post's uprights.

At halftime, I opted to bench several of my veterans in the Cardinal backfield and, instead, go with a younger squad who might breathe new life into our sputtering attack. Lud Frentrup, a Berkeley native, took over for Frank Wilton and Bill Simkins replaced Biff Hoffman.

Early in the third quarter, Frentrup and Simkins began to shake things up. Frentrup fielded a Cal punt near midfield and darted 19 yards to the Cal 28. Simkins then connected with Frentrup on a 10-yard pass, and both Frentrup and Simkins hit into the Bears' defensive line to grind out a first down at the Cal 4-yard line. Two plays later, Simkins blasted through the Bear forward wall and scored. Spud Lewis then added the extra point kick to narrow Cal's lead to 13-7.

Stanford would make three more threatening marches before finding the Cal end zone once again. The first two attempts were halted by pass interceptions. But with only three minutes left in the contest, the Cardinals made a final bid. Starting at the Stanford 34, my youthful offense drove to the Cal 10-yard line behind a mixture of end-arounds and passes.

Simkins then found Frentrup open in the corner of the Cal end zone and tossed a perfect strike to him that tied up the score at 13-13. Our point-after attempt, however, proved to be unsuccessful.

Shortly thereafter the contest ended in a 13-13 draw.

The Cardinals' final game of the season was a cross-country trip to New York City to play against Army in Yankee Stadium on December 1st.

It would be the first time that I had brought my Stanford team back to the East since I had originally arrived at the Palo Alto campus in 1924. And at this point, I didn't quite know which squad of mine would be playing against Army — either the swift, quick-hitting version of the Cardinals or the crew that got bogged down in their own mistakes and mediocrity.

To add to my concerns, Army was probably the best team in the East. Powered by Chris (Red) Cagle and with strong support from Art Meehan and Blondy Saunders, two players who later would become heroes in World War II, the vaunted Cadets had won eight of nine games already that season. Their lone loss came at the hands of Knute Rockne's Notre Dame squad, 12-6, just weeks earlier in Yankee Stadium. (Editor's Note: This is the same Notre Dame-Army game in which Rockne made his famous "Win One for the Gipper" halftime speech that had inspired a demoralized Fighting Irish squad to go out in the second half and win the game in honor of

George Gipp, a Notre Dame star halfback who had died in 1920 due to pneumonia. According to Rockne, Gipp had requested from his deathbed that one day in a big game against Army, in which Notre Dame was losing, Rockne should tell the team that Gipp wanted them to "Go out there and win one for the Gipper." In the 1928 Army contest, Rockne found his squad in such a jam. He then proceeded to conjure up the ghost of Gipp. The result was a 12-6 victory against a great Army team. This story has since become a part of American folklore.)

Prior to the Stanford-Army contest, most of the country's big-city newspapers and radios along with that new rage of America cinema — the "talking movie" newsreels — attempted to sensationalize this match. Damon Runyon of *The New York American* and Grantland Rice of *The New York Herald Tribune*, who were the deans of American sportswriters, were among the ringleaders in whipping up this frenzy with the sporting public. Along the taverns and saloons on First and Second Avenue, the bookies made Army the game's favorite. Taxi drivers, shoeshine boys, businessmen, restaurateurs and members of the Broadway establishments — all of them had wagered that the Cadets would reek havoc against the West Coast upstarts from Stanford.

So it was into this sea of hysteria that I took my squad of Cardinals. Strangely, I felt that disaster awaited us there and that my return to the East, after five long, eventful seasons on the West Coast, would prove to be an embarrassing flop.

But once the ball got kicked off in Yankee Stadium in front of 86,000 ticket-holders, plus several thousand more who had standing-room-only passes, my jitters began to subside.

While using an impressive array of reverses, end-arounds, double reverses, delayed line-bucks and passes, the single-wing and double-wing attack began to unfold its magic.

On our first two drives, the Cardinal offense marched to the Cadet 1-yard line and the Cadet 10, but failed to score on either occasion. However on the third drive, Hoffman, Fleishhacker, Wilton and Sims led the Cardinal attack downfield and Hoffman carried it over for the score.

Army then made a serious foray into Cardinal territory and reached the Stanford 10-yard line before being finally stopped.

Later, Hoffman led a 56-yard drive that gave the Cardinals a second touchdown for the afternoon.

Early in the fourth quarter, Cagle attempted to get the Cadets moving again when he picked off an errant Stanford pass near the Army goal line. The West Point squad, however, was quickly stopped by the Cardinals' Walt Heinecke who recovered a bouncing fumble at the Cadet 13. Frentrup then went for eight yards and Sims pounded the remaining five yards for a touchdown to increase the Cardinals' lead.

Our final score came when Frentrup fumbled a bad snap from center, but the quick-handed back soon put a handle on the ball and scampered through the Cadet defense for 65 yards and a touchdown.

At the end of the game the scoreboard read: Stanford 26, Army 0.

Never before had Biff Jones' Cadets been beaten so handily. Stanford amassed 322 yards of offense to Army's 113 yards and the Cardinals made 26 first downs as compared to only eight for the Cadets.

Suddenly, the Stanford Cardinals were the toast of Broadway.

But our success was largely due to the splendorous play of two Cardinal players — Biff Hoffman on offense and Bob Sims on defense. Sims kept Army's Chris Cagle from breaking loose all afternoon on any of the long and exciting runs that he was known for.

The next day as we began our long journey home to California, I read with great pleasure the many wonderful stories and commentaries on the Stanford-Army match. It was during this momentous occasion, while scanning through the various headlines of the sports sections of *The New York Times, The New York Sun, The New York Daily News* and several other Gotham dailies that I came across one headline that stood out boldly. It read: "STANFORD ROUTS ARMY, 26-0, AS CARDINAL OFFENSE LETS LOOSE IN YANKEE STADIUM."

This was the day which I had long awaited. My Stanford team had come back to the East and conquered the best that the East had to offer. Now, I knew that the Cardinal program had truly arrived and deserved to be considered among the elite of college football.

61

Prior to the 1928 season, Stanford had joined both Washington and Cal in voting to not accept an invitation to the Rose Bowl game. Collectively, we had some complaints on how the bowl's officials were administering the contest and protested so that a stronger set of rules and procedures might be implemented.

However toward the end of the 1928 season, and after much lobbying, Cal, who had posted a record of 6 wins, 1 loss and 2 ties, reversed their earlier stance and agreed to accept an invitation to play William Alexander's Georgia Tech squad in the Rose Bowl. Nonetheless, Cal's greediness was to become their downfall. In a hardfought contest, the Yellow Jackets beat Cal, 8-7.

The 1928 season was to be remembered for several quite memorable moments, but it also possessed many depressing low points. I especially recall the 1928 season because it marked the final year for seven of the best football players to ever wear a Stanford uniform — Biff Hoffman, the stellar fullback; Don Robesky and Seraphim Post, who were undoubtedly the two best guards that I ever saw play; Bob Sims and Frank Wilton at halfback; Tiny Sellman, at tackle; and Spud Lewis, who played both quarterback and halfback.

Following our fine victory over Army, 26-0, at the conclusion of the 1928 season, I looked forward to the 1929 season and a returning cast of a dozen or more exceptional players with much optimism.

And after a strong start and five straight victories to kickoff the 1929 season, my spirits were soaring. But the next week, I quickly got a dose of reality when my Cardinals lost a heartbreaker to U.S.C., 7-0, in Stanford Stadium.

We then rebounded with two big wins as the Cardinals ripped Cal Tech, 39-0, and narrowly defeated Washington, 6-0, in a thriller which was played in a rainstorm in Seattle.

A week later, an underdog Santa Clara squad caught us looking ahead to the Big Game with Cal. Playing with great heart, the Broncos defeated us, 13-7.

This unexpected loss to Santa Clara bruised a lot of egos on the Cardinal squad, and thankfully, it properly focused our attention on the upcoming Big Game with Cal.

And rightly so. The Golden Bears were undefeated and the odds-makers' favorite in the contest. The Big Game was to be played at the Stanford Stadium and it attracted a sellout throng of 89,000. Tickets for the game were in such demand that I even heard of one Cal player trading six tickets — which were located on the 40-yard line — for a 1925 Lincoln touring car.

The build-up for the game in the newspapers added a lot of emotional fire for both rivals.

Realizing that Cal was getting perhaps too much attention for this game, I decided to pull out an emotional booster for my Cardinal squad.

Before kickoff, I presented them with a new set of uniforms — white jerseys with red stripes on the sleeves and red pants with a white stripe, which ran down the back of each leg. We looked like a million dollars!

And once we hit the field, the inspired Cardinals quickly flexed their muscles.

Following Don Muller's recovery of a fumble in Cal's territory, the Cardinal offense took over and marched to a touchdown in just six plays with Lud Frentrup scoring on a reverse play. Harlow Rothert contributed the point-after kick which put Stanford in the lead, 7-0.

At this point, only five minutes had elapsed in the game.

Later in the first quarter, the Bears recovered Frentrup's fumble at the Cardinal 30 and in five plays Cal had scored, with Benny Lom passing to Ellis Thornton for the touchdown. The Bears missed the point-after attempt, which kept Stanford still in the lead, 7-6.

The Cardinals then proceeded to close down the Golden Bears' much-feared running and passing attack.

After a Stanford drive failed to score and died on the Cal 1-yard line, Muller, who was playing the greatest game of his career as a Cardinal player, blocked a Cal punt at the Bears' 25, scooped it up and raced in for a touchdown. Phil Moffatt made the point-after conversion and Stanford now led, 14-6.

In the third quarter, Stanford was able to put the icing on the cake.

But there were to be several eventful moments before the Cardinals reached this apex. The most memorable of these was when the Cardinals were penalized 37 yards — this was half the distance to the goal line — after Corwin Artman, a rather large Stanford tackle, took a swing at the Bears' Ted Brackett, who had tackled him following Artman's interception of a Cal pass. To make matters worse, in addition to the 37-yard penalty, the referee also threw Artman out of the game.

This fireworks display proceeded to fuel the Cardinals' intensity to a new level. We then drove 65 yards downfield for a touchdown, with Moffatt twisting his way over left tackle for 7 yards to get the tally. The extra-point attempt proved to be successful and this increased the Cardinals' lead to 21-6, which also turned out to be the final score of the contest.

Without a doubt, this was a great upset victory for us and, perhaps, the biggest that we ever enjoyed over Cal during my tenure at Stanford.

Our season-ending victory over Cal produced a three-way tie for the Pacific Coast Conference title, because Cal had already beaten U.S.C., 15-7, and U.S.C. had defeated our Cardinal squad, 7-0.

In a vote of the Tournament of Roses officials, U.S.C. was picked to be the West Coast representative that season for the 1930 Rose Bowl game. This allowed us to go ahead with a tentatively-arranged game with Army on December 28th, which was to be a return match of our memorable contest that had been played a year earlier in Yankee Stadium.

A crowd of more than 70,000 was in attendance to view the Stanford-Army game in Stanford Stadium. Chris Cagle, the Cadets' all-America halfback, played valiantly all afternoon, but the Cardinal defense contained his efforts for most of the game. Cagle would end up with only 48 yards rushing on 11 carries. Chuck Smalling, the

Cardinal fullback, was to be the big star of the day as he romped for 113 yards on 26 carries and three touchdowns to lead Stanford to a 34-13 win.

For Army, this was a crushing defeat.

After their unexpected loss to the Cardinals in 1928, the Cadets had traveled westward for the 1929 matchup with high hopes of redeeming themselves. They had even moved into one of our college dorms, which was vacant due to the Christmas holidays, for a few days and set up a command post to prepare for the game. During their pre-game stay, the Cadets ate by themselves, wouldn't speak to the press and held their own secret football practices — but still to no avail.

Following the game, I met with Biff Jones, the great Army coach, and he told me that General Douglas MacArthur, the former superintendent of West Point, and famed Army commander — who was also a strong supporter of Cadet football — had given him explicit orders to win this contest and that he didn't look forward to having to explain this loss to MacArthur.

(Editor's Note: The next season, in 1930, Biff Jones left Army to take the head-coaching job at Louisiana State University. He would later return to West Point in the 1940's as director of athletics. His 1940 Nebraska squad lost to Stanford, 21-13, in the 1940 Rose Bowl.)

62

The 1930 season was a time of renewal for the Stanford football program.

The Cardinals carved out a record of nine wins, one loss and one tie that season, but U.S.C. pulled off a third straight victory over us, and Minnesota, who was being coached by a youngster named Fritz Crisler, managed to hold us to a scoreless tie. Crisler would later have great success at the University of Michigan in the late 1930's and 1940's.

My backfield was loaded with an abundance of athletic talent. Harlow Rothert, Bill Simpkins, Phil Moffatt, Guido Caglieri, Henry Hillman, Bill Clark and two promising youngsters, Ernie Caddel and Rudy Rintala, were among those who had stepped forward to fill the vacancies in the Cardinal lineup which were created by the graduation of Lud Frentrup, Herb Fleishhacker and Chuck Smalling.

In our first five games of the season, the Cardinals won four of the five games, with the only blot on our record being the scoreless tie with Minnesota. Along the way, Stanford outscored its opponents, 83 points to 7. Oregon State was the only team who managed to get a touchdown against us. This occurred in a 13-7 victory over of the Beavers just prior to the Stanford-U.S.C. contest.

The next week, the Trojans were a 3-point favorite against the Cardinals. In an attempt to get my squad relaxed and focused to play against U.S.C., I even took them off-campus to a hotel in San Mateo on the night before the game. Still, this didn't work.

The next afternoon, U.S.C. ran wild against us. Phil Moffatt hauled in two passes to give us a pair of touchdowns but this wasn't enough. The Trojans plastered us, 41-12.

When U.S.C. returned to Los Angeles after the game, Howard Jones, the Trojans' coach, got thrown in the Pacific Ocean by his squad, who had decided to cash-in on a long-standing offer by Jones to get drenched in the Pacific by his U.S.C. team if they ever beat Stanford by three touchdowns.

Well, this ill-fated day had finally arrived. We lost by a margin of five touchdowns that day.

Later, when I had been told of Jones' unplanned, mid-autumn ocean swim, I was glad to see that my coaching rival had to at least had to pay a small price for the Trojans' victory.

We then took on U.C.L.A. in the Los Angeles Memorial Coliseum. It was the first night game that Stanford had ever played and the Cardinal players all had trouble seeing the damp football, except for Rothert. The rugged Stanford fullback, who was playing in front of a hometown crowd, rushed for 118 yards and averaged 44 yards on his punting in this contest. Rothert also scored two touchdowns that evening on runs of 65 and 40 yards in the third period.

The final score was Stanford 20, U.C.L.A. 0.

The Cardinals then got on a roll and beat Washington, 25-7; whipped Cal Tech, 57-7; and destroyed Cal in the Big Game, 41-0.

The game with Cal was a lot closer in the first half with a 6-0 score at halftime. But after a good chewing out during the intermission, the Cardinals exploded in the second half behind Rothert's leadership and rolled off 35 more points.

We then took on Dartmouth, who was an East Coast powerhouse. The Green Indians from New Hampshire were undefeated that season and had scored five shutouts before making the trip to the West Coast.

Phil Moffatt, who was our leading ballcarrier in the game with 96 yards on 16 carries, helped us to overcome the Easterners' challenge and the Cardinals won, 14-7.

During the late portion of the 1930 season, the Stanford student executive committee voted to adopt the "Indians" as the official symbol and logo of the University and the nickname for its athletic teams. But this wasn't an earth-shaking move. For several years, newspaper cartoonists and sportswriters had been referring to Stanford as the "Red Indians."

In a way, I guess this was another step in Leland Cutler's grand design to build a football powerhouse at Stanford.

63

In an attempt to reverse our recent string of bad luck against U.S.C., which consisted of three consecutive losses and included a pair of shutouts, I tinkered throughout the spring and summer of 1931 with a new defense that might stop the Trojans. This new defense was rather radical in both its design and actual implementation.

The key to my defense was to halt, or at least, slowdown U.S.C.'s highly successful running game, which had been the cause for most of our problems. We simply were unable to contain them.

Realizing this, I set up a defense which had the defensive ends being set 15 yards outside of the defensive tackles. The defensive ends were then supposed to begin running parallel to the line of scrimmage as the offensive signal-caller barked out the signals before the play began. Their goal was to crash in and break up the Trojans' offensive play before it could get underway.

Unfortunately, when the U.S.C. game came around this tactic didn't work out as I had planned. U.S.C., at that time, was using a shift in which the center came up to the line of scrimmage, while the other linemen were located a yard behind the line and with their hands on knees. From this position, they then shifted forward into either a balanced or an unbalanced formation.

My plan, of course intended for the defensive ends to go in motion once the Trojan line was set. However, Howard Jones, the U.S.C. coach, crossed up my plan when he told his quarterbacks to adjust their signal-calling at times so that the Stanford defensive ends would be caught offsides.

U.S.C. ended up winning the game, 19-0, and continued the Trojans' 4-year domination of this series. It was also their third shutout in four years against Stanford.

And to make matters worse, one of my best players, Phil Moffatt, a running back, was seriously injured while being tackled near the sidelines on a lengthy return of the game's opening kickoff at the Stanford 34.

This key injury severely limited our passing attack. But I don't mean to take anything away from the Trojans, who were a great team that season. They went on to show their majesty on the playing field that afternoon as Gus Shaver and Irv Mohler, who were two of their star players, led U.S.C. to victory.

Prior to the Stanford-U.S.C. contest, we had two scoreless ties against the Olympic Club and Washington. But there were also five victories that the Indians — yes, that's our new nickname — picked up en route, including three shutouts. Stanford soundly whipped the West Coast Army, 46-0; knocked off Santa Clara, 6-0, and Minnesota, 13-0; walloped Oregon State, 25-7; and held off a feisty U.C.L.A. bunch, 12-6.

We then went on to defeat Nevada, 26-0, before our annual encounter with Cal in the Big Game.

The Golden Bears were under the new tutelage of my friend, Bill Ingram, who had formerly coached at Navy before taking the helm at Cal.

The University of California had not won a Big Game matchup since 1923, and there had been only two ties occurring during the interim — the 20-20 emotional thriller in 1924 and the 13-13 frustration in 1928.

Ingram, however, had his squad primed and they won the game, 6-0, in a bitterly-fought contest.

Hank Schaldach was the star for Cal that afternoon as he provided the winning score and broke another exciting run that almost resulted in a touchdown, but the heroic efforts by Jack Hillman of Stanford prevented this from happening.

Following Schaldach's touchdown, Cal was unable to make the point-after conversion. On this play, Stanford's Chuck Ehrhorn blasted through the Cal line and blocked the Bears' attempted dropkick for the extra point, and this gave Cal only a 6-0 lead. (Editor's Note: Although a dropkick being attempted on an extra-point attempt may sound odd in the modern football era, it was a widely-used practice in the early 1900's and was still in use as late as the 1930's. In most cases during this era, a dropkick was used instead of a field goal and counted 3 points.)

The Bears continued their dominance throughout the contest but the Stanford defense kept them from scoring again. On several occasions, the Indians penetrated into the Bears' territory, but the only serious adventure occurred in the fourth quarter when Ernie Caddel reached the Cal 16.

The Bears then held on to win the game, 6-0.

At the end of the 1931 season, during the week of Thanksgiving, Stanford traveled cross-country by train to play Dartmouth at Harvard Stadium, which was located in Cambridge, Mass.

This game, which was played on the Saturday after Thanksgiving, brought back to me many special memories of the journeys that my Carlisle teams had made from eastern Pennsylvania to Boston during the early 1900's. The people of Boston had fallen in love with the crazy antics, determined play and great showmanship that the Carlisle Indians had displayed. And they had packed the grandstand stadiums of that era to watch us play.

Now against Dartmouth, a large and curious crowd filled Harvard Stadium to watch this strange team from California dismantle the Green Indians squad from nearby New Hampshire.

Stanford rolled to a 32-6 victory behind the great play of Phil Moffatt, who was ending his career. The senior back completed eight of 11 passes, including a pair of touchdown aerials to Caddel for 27 and 57 yards, respectively.

Caddel also had a great performance that afternoon as he added two other touchdowns. One was a reverse play around right end that went for 72 yards. And then a few minutes later, he scampered 62 yards on another reverse play.

In all, Dartmouth threw 31 passes but only completed only four for 63 yards. An alert Stanford defense intercepted seven of these errant aerials. On the ground, the Dartmouth offense managed to only rush for 71 yards.

Stanford dominated the action for most of the afternoon by rushing for 364 yards and picked up an additional 111 yards through the air lanes.

Once again, one of my teams had given the town of Boston a heckuva show.

64

My 1931 Stanford squad had finished the season with a record of seven wins, two losses and two ties, which was my worst season there since having arrived in 1924.

At this point, it was my intention to improve upon this record and hopefully dethrone our rival to the south in Los Angeles, who had won the national championship in 1931. The breaking of Howard Jones' and U.S.C.'s four-year strangle-hold on Stanford was unquestionably our top priority.

But these were tumultuous times on the Stanford campus. Besides having to survive the Depression Era of the early 1930's, which hadn't seemed to affect California as much as it had the rest of the country, Stanford, its alumni, faculty and administrators were all locked in a battle to determine the University's future.

Dr. Ray Lyman Wilbur, the President of Stanford University, who was away from the school's campus on a leave of absence while serving as the Secretary of the Interior under President Herbert Hoover, was the source of this maddening confusion. He had originally proposed that the freshman and sophomore classes at Stanford be eventually eliminated and that the school be directed on a new mission of becoming a graduate-level university superpower.

Dr. Wilbur's proposal was also given support due to the growing number of junior colleges that were being opened throughout California. Dr. Wilbur firmly believed that these new two-year schools should be "feeder schools" to the more advanced graduate-level schools.

Many within the Stanford family, including those who had been involved with Leland Cutler in the early 1920's, when I was asked to come to Stanford and build them a great football program, formed a large faction of the opposition to Dr. Wilbur's proposal.

In a heavy airing of protest by the alumni, faculty and the student body, Dr. Wilbur's proposal was eventually withdrawn. But in the process of this institutional tug-of-war, such discussion provided great ammunition to the schools that recruited against us. Quickly, they began to tell prospective freshmen that Stanford would eventually be dropping — either this year or in the next few years — both its freshman and sophomore classes, which would leave the Stanford football program greatly weakened and would eventually bring about its demise.

In newspaper and radio interviews and in talks to Stanford alumni groups, I tried to counter these charges. The University also tried to strengthen their commitment to the Stanford football program by giving me a 5-year extension on my contract.

Such efforts helped temporarily as 101 students reported for fall practice prior to the beginning of the '32 season. But still, no one had a clue how these recent events would effect this Stanford squad or what the season ahead held for us.

In our first five games of the 1932 season, Stanford knocked off the Olympic Club, 6-0; swept past the University of San Francisco, 20-7; blitzed Oregon State, 27-0; corralled Santa Clara, 14-0; and outmaneuvered the West Coast Army team, 26-0.

In all, we outscored our opponents, 93-7.

Next, we faced our old nemesis, U.S.C.

For some strange reason, Stanford was slightly favored in this contest, although the Trojans were undefeated, untied and unscored upon in their first five games.

On the opening drive, the Indians marched to the Trojan 15-yard line before this advance was halted. U.S.C. later added both of their scores on long passes and went on to win, 13-0, which gave the Trojans their fifth straight victory over Stanford and fourth shutout in five attempts.

The next two weeks, U.C.L.A. and Washington added to our misery. The Bruins finally registered their first victory against us, 13-6, and then the Huskies defeated us for the first time since 1925 as they cruised to an 18-13 win.

Afterwards, Stanford took out its frustrations against the California Aggies and crushed them, 59-0, in a one-sided contest. This score, however, could have been much worse. Several of the Stanford starting veterans and I had missed the game with the California Aggies because we had gone to scout the Cal-Idaho game, which was being played at Memorial Stadium in Berkeley. The Bears won this contest, 21-6.

Cal came into the Big Game with a lackluster 6-3-1 record. The Indians didn't have much to be proud of either with our record of six wins and three losses.

During the game, both squads made drives deep into each other's respective territories, but neither team managed to cross the other's goal line.

This uneventful afternoon later ended in a scoreless tie, 0-0.

In the final game of the season, we traveled eastward by train to Pittsburgh to tangle with Jock Sutherland's Pitt Panthers. This is the same Pitt squad, who several weeks later would play in the 1933 Rose Bowl game against U.S.C.

The contest on this chilly, autumn afternoon was a hard-fought battle. The talented Pitt team ruled the line of scrimmage for most of the game, but the valiant Stanford defense was able to stubbornly hold off the Panthers' repeated onslaughts.

But on one brilliant effort, Walter Heller, Pitt's all-America halfback, broke through the Indians' forward wall and scored a touchdown to lead the Panthers to a 7-0 victory.

That evening following the game, a large number of Pitt's football fans, who still held a grudge toward me for my having left Pitt in 1923 to go to Stanford, celebrated their victory as a personal bit of revenge that had been finally enacted. They were also delighted at the fact that their undefeated Pitt Panthers were to be soon playing in the Rose Bowl while my Stanford squad, who was 6-4-1 that season, would be sitting at home on New Year's Day.

Such are the fortunes of football.

65

A few weeks prior to the Stanford-Pitt game, I received a telegram from Charles G. Erny, who was a prominent businessman from the Philadelphia area and a member of the Board of Trustees at Temple University.

I had met Erny a year earlier, in 1931, when I had stopped off in Philadelphia while returning from the Stanford-Dartmouth game in Boston. On this occasion, he gave me a personal tour of the new $450,000 stadium that he had just built and donated to Temple University for its fledgling football program. Needless to say, it was an impressive facility and greatly reinforced the school's and alumni's commitment to field a winning team.

In Erny's telegram, he requested to be able to see me during my team's upcoming visit to Pittsburgh for the Stanford-Pitt game.

After reading the telegram — and being a bit curious — I sent Erny a return wire agreeing to meet with him at the hotel where the Stanford team would be staying on late Saturday afternoon following the Stanford-Pitt game.

I really didn't think much more about the matter until after the Stanford-Pitt game had been completed and there was a knock on my hotel room door. When I opened it, standing there in the doorway was Erny, who was still wearing his heavy winter coat, a wool-brimmed hat and a scarf.

He wasted no time in giving me an enthusiastic greeting and offered encouragement even though my Stanford squad had just been defeated by Pitt, 7-0.

After trading a few hearty laughs over some of the Pitt game's broken plays and near mishaps, I then asked Erny to come in and join me for a bit of refreshment so that we could chat.

It was there in my suite's parlor and by a warm, inviting fire in the high brick fireplace that Erny began to share with me the purpose of his visit.

He told me of Temple's scant football history and how it had fielded informal and infrequent teams in the 1890's and early 1900's, but it wasn't until 1925 — when Heine Miller, the former all-America end at Penn, was hired — that a varsity program was formed. He told me that in the 8-year period since then Temple had amassed a record of 50 wins, 15 losses and 8 ties.

"But now," he explained, "the Temple alumni and administration would like to improve upon their current status as a virtual nobody in college football. In the future, we want to enjoy the successes that Pitt, Army and several other East Coast schools are enjoying."

Erny, who was also the chairman of Temple's athletic committee, proposed that if I was willing to come there to be their head football coach and bring my staff that he would personally insure that I would have the proper backing to build Temple into a first-rate, winning football program.

Suddenly, I couldn't believe what I was hearing. As Erny continued with his proposal, I began to have flashbacks of a very similar conversation that I had with Leland Cutler of the Stanford Board of Trustees, nearly ten years earlier.

With the logs in the fireplace crackling and the smoke from our cigars giving the room a pleasant aroma, Erny then made the conversation even more interesting.

While leaning forward in his seat, he proclaimed, "And to show our sincerity, I'm willing to offer you a 5-year contract that would guarantee to you a total of $100,000 in salary and other benefits."

Now, if I hadn't been thrown for a loop by Erny's first proposal to leave Stanford and coach the Temple football team, this second one with the guaranteed contract definitely got my attention. The economy in this Depression was rather lousy and, personally, I had lost a lot of money when the stock market had crashed in 1929. My salary at Stanford at the time was less than $15,000 a year, so the offer from Temple was indeed appealing.

Erny, by now, was enjoying a few good puffs on his cigar. Realizing that I was definitely interested in his offer, he then unloaded his next salvo.

"Whatever you want, whatever you need to build a winner, I'll back you on it. If you want to travel coast to coast and play the best teams in the country — U.S.C., Georgia Tech, Notre Dame or whoever — then do it. I just want to see Temple playing in New Year's Day bowl games and winning a championship or two."

At that point, I was getting warmed up to the idea, no matter how bold it may have seemed.

Grinning briefly, I then told Erny, "You know, if I do this, a lot of people in California are going to be upset at the both of us."

Erny just chuckled. He had probably made several hundred business deals along the way that were just as risky. Finally, he noted, "And it they get upset at us, don't worry. Whatever the problem is, we'll get through it together."

During the next few moments, a thousand thoughts and questions must have crossed through my mind. The two that loomed largest were the facts that I was now 61 years old and currently, at least, the head football coach at Stanford.

Was it worth it to make one more move to another school? Did I have the ability, the magic and the vision to turn one more lifeless gridiron program into a winner?

While debating these questions, I arose from my seat and slowly walked away from the warmth of the glowing fire and over toward the large double windows that overlooked the Allegheny River below. There, a slight layer of ice was forming around the edges of these picturesque windows.

Across the rising hilltops to the west I was able to see a lumination of orange light that lit up the horizon. And in the valley beneath these hills were dozens of large factories whose tall, brick cylindrical chimneys bellowed large, gray puffs of smoke, serving as a reminder to everyone that steel, which was the primary industry of this area, was being produced and forged.

As I turned my gaze back toward the city, I saw an electric streetcar taking on passengers. Across the street, three mill workers were making their way into a nearby tavern. Not far away was the University of Pittsburgh, where I had once built great football teams and enjoyed many wonderful memories. And just down the street from the hotel was The Pittsburgh Athletic Club, where nearly ten years ago I had made a deal with Leland Cutler to go west and take Stanford into the limelight of college football.

As all of these thoughts seemed to converge together, I then thought of California and its lush scenery and vibrant lifestyle. The people. The energy. And what of Stanford? Their program didn't have much of a history or a tradition until Andy Kerr, Claude Thornhill, Chuck Winterburn and I had gone there and built them into a powerhouse, took them to the Rose Bowl several times and won three conference championships and even a national title in 1926.

Sure, the alumni group in Los Angeles was never gonna be satisfied unless we beat U.S.C. every year. And the academic side at Stanford was always gonna make it more difficult for us to recruit against U.C.L.A., Cal and U.S.C. But somehow, we would always find a way to win and be successful. Sure we would!

Yet down deep inside of me I knew this wasn't to be. The Stanford alumni and administrators had gotten a taste of success from big-time winning and once this happens things were never gonna be the same again there.

And though there seemed to be a temporary truce between the academic and alumni forces on how the school should be run, I also knew that this was going to be a dirty fight that would linger on and perhaps one day get real messy. And at the same time, this fight for power among the various factions of the Stanford family would continue to be used by other schools to hold the Stanford athletic program hostage while we were recruiting.

As this myriad of concerns, solutions and counterviews crossed my mind, I turned my attention to the street below where I saw two young boys who were dressed warmly in wool coats. They were walking with an older gentleman, who was perhaps their father, into the hotel's front lobby entrance. One of the boys had a Pitt pennant in his hand. The other boy had a blue and gold pom-pom shaker.

It was a sight that I had seen a thousand times or more on football Saturdays in the fall. Yet this simple sight captured the entire reason for my involvement in football.

For these two youngsters, today's match between Stanford and Pitt may have been their first time to have ever seen a Pitt game. There, they had the opportunity to cheer loudly for their great Panther team.

It is that tradition that they are now wrapped up in. And I had helped build a large part of that tradition many years earlier during my tenure at Pitt.

Quite vividly, I can still remember when Pitt's football program was in its infancy and didn't have the great teams that they do now. But I can also remember back in 1915, 1916, 1917 and 1918, when the City of Pittsburgh began to take notice of a Pitt football team that was suddenly on the rise up the ladder to the big time of college football. Almost overnight, big crowds flocked to Forbes Field to cheer for a winner. And with a 31-game win streak during this era, Pitt became the best team in the East.

It was those special times of yesteryear that built the foundation for the success that Jock Sutherland's Pitt teams were now enjoying.

I knew that it was indeed possible that another coach could possibly step into my shoes and continue on with the great program that had been built at Stanford. For there was a strong foundation there now and the Stanford players and fans knew what winning and glory was all about.

But could another coach go to Temple and build a program like the ones that I had built at Carlisle, Pitt and Stanford? Could another coach give to the alumni and football fans at Temple the kind of joys and wonderful memories now being shared by these two young boys who I had just seen?

I didn't know if I could rebuild another school's football program into a winner. But in the past I had done it several times and perhaps there was still one more good campaign in me.

After all, the thrill of being a football coach wasn't just being able to win enough games to reach the big time. Instead, the thrill was to be on the ground floor of building a winning team because everyone associated with this kind of team is hungry to be a winner during their brief time together. Also, the enthusiasm, the heartaches and the eventual glory means more to you when you are just getting started.

Yes, these were the reasons that I had hung around this great game for such a long time.

It was at this point that a warm feeling of comfort and reconfirmation began to settle in around me. Slowly, I turned back toward the fireplace and then made my way over to where my guest, Charles Erny, was sitting.

Upon my arrival, I extended my hand in his direction and then spoke: "Mr. Erny, I would be honored to accept your offer."

A brief smile of satisfaction seemed to make its way across Erny's face. Afterwards, he steadily and with tremendous poise rose from his chair and then reached out to grasp my hand with both of his hands in a friendly, sincere handshake.

"No, Coach," he noted in response. "The honor is ours. Temple will now be a much better place because of your efforts."

A bit moved by his kind words, I didn't know what to say, but in reality the silence of the moment spoke more than enough for the both of us to savor and enjoy.

66

In early December of 1932, following our return to Palo Alto from the Dartmouth game, word began to leak out that I might be leaving Stanford.

Our graduate manager of athletics at Stanford, Al Masters, even approached me regarding the validity of these rumors. Initially, I denied them and branded the rumors as "loose talk which had been started by both Cal and U.S.C. alumni and fans." But in actuality I was awaiting the arrival of Temple's contract for my final review before I would discuss this possibility with anyone.

I was also recovering from a bad cold at that time, which I had caught while on our recent trip to Pittsburgh, so my illness provided a good cover during this time of speculation.

Finally, the contract from Temple arrived and I went over its contents and found it to be consistent with the original offer that Charles Enry had made to me when we had met in Pittsburgh a few weeks earlier.

At that point, I went to the local telegram office and dispatched my reply to Enry and the Temple University Council on Athletics. That message read:

> AM MAILING SIGNED CONTRACT AND
> ANNOUNCING MY RESIGNATION HERE
> TOMORROW.
>
> GLENN S. WARNER

The next day, on December 5th, I tendered by resignation over to Al Masters, which even amongst the most recent rumors still seemed to have caught him unexpectedly. Masters then delivered my resignation to Dr. Thomas A. Storey, who was the Director of Athletics at Stanford.

Little did I realize the furor that this move would soon cause. When word of my resignation began to spread, my home was quickly besieged with newspaper writers who either called or were knocking at my front door so that they would confirm the story of my resignation. It was like a frantic madhouse there that day.

With each inquiry by the press, I told them of my plan to take the head-coaching job at Temple. All of them were shocked that I would be making such a bold move, especially so late in my career. And, even more remarkably, considering my tremendous success at Stanford, it was difficult to understand how I could forego all of this to go to a school such as Temple which had only been playing college football for eight seasons.

Perhaps the best example in describing how shocking this move was when one of the most respected sportswriters in San Francisco had called me to discuss the news of my intended departure from Stanford to take the job as head coach at Temple. Inquisitively and earnestly he asked me: "Temple. I never heard of the place. Are you sure that they have a football team there?"

That evening, after confronting a rather long and difficult day, I had to face the largest emotional hurdle of my career. Over eighty members of my Stanford squad came over to our house, which was near the Palo Alto campus. Most of them had tears in their eyes that evening.

Five of the players — Red Targhetta, Jack Hillman, Bill Bates, Bill Sims and George Grey — acted as spokesmen for the rest of the group. These players told me: "Coach, the team would fight their hearts out for you if you would stay at Stanford as our coach."

As I looked out at the assembled group and listened to their pleadings, my insides were tearing at me. It was an emotionally moving sight to see these brave lads, with torches in their hands and enduring the chill of the evening air as they shouted and chanted en masse such heartening cries as "Stay with us, Coach!" or "We need you, too!"

After listening to them for awhile, I stepped forward and with a cracked voice, told them: "Boys, I appreciate what you are doing here tonight and why you are doing it. This means a lot to me. But I can't stay. I have already signed a contract to go to Temple, where, hopefully, I will be able to give them the kind of glory and memories that I have given to both Stanford and to each one of you.

"Stanford is a great school and it will be part of me and a part of you for a long, long time.

"Even though I may be soon leaving, you will still be here. I would like to ask each of you to continue to play for Stanford like you have always played for me. There is still much glory ahead for both you and Stanford football."

I then invited the boys to come inside and have something to eat, which sent my wife, Tibb, into a brief panic, but she was used to having lots of college boys around the house and soon there was enough coffee, tea, milk, cake, cookies and sandwiches to feed everyone.

However later that evening, when everyone had left to return to their dormitories, I sat in the study for a long time, recalling the events of this inspiring, yet very gut-wrenching day. This is one of the sides of college football that I always found most difficult to deal with because, in essence, the game of football is a game for both boys and men to play and enjoy. The camaraderie and the spirit of competition that it fosters and instills are perhaps the best experiences in life that we can enjoy.

These boys of Stanford didn't truly understand all that was going on around them. For them, the game of football was something pure and a dear part of their college life. Yet on a higher level, where alumni and administrators get involved, this purity of sport is diminished somewhat because of the constant clamoring to field undefeated teams and to soundly conquer your big rivals, which in our case was always Cal and U.S.C.

As all of these thoughts and emotions came flooding forth from this very hectic but memorable day, I, too began to briefly weep for Stanford and these boys — all of them from 1922, when I first announced that I would be coming here for the 1924 season but had got to know them during my trips to view spring practice in 1922 and 1923, to those on the Rose Bowl teams of the mid- and late 1920's and the boys on my teams of recent years.

Because of these boys — all of them — I hoped my successor would be able to lead Stanford to much glory.

67

Temple University was originally founded in 1884 as a night
school by the late Dr. Russell H. Conwell, a Baptist minister, who
believed "that everyone, not just the wellborn, should be able to
obtain an education and aspire to a better life." Four years later, in
1888, the school was formally incorporated as a college. In the years
that followed, Temple grew steadily and by 1932 it had achieved a
student body population of nearly 12,500.

The game of football was first introduced to the Temple campus
in the 1890's. During this period, an informal team frequently
patched together a pickup schedule of out-of-town trips to play
against club teams from nearby schools. The most memorable of
these excursions was a trip led by Joe Potts, the team's captain, to play
Franklin & Marshall College at Lancaster, Pa., in 1896. They lost by
the score of 96-0.

In 1900 and 1901, a group of Temple students combined to form
a team which was captained by Joseph Rex. During this era, these
teams practiced primarily on a large field near the 22nd Street Station
of Reading Railroad's Norristown branch line and played their games
at Hunting Park.

But it wasn't until 1925 that Temple formally organized a football
team, with Heine Miller, the former Penn all-America end, being
tapped as their head coach.

Lester Hawns, who had grown up in nearby Ardmore, Pa., and had
been a halfback at Dartmouth, served as Miller's assistant in the
fledgling years of Temple's football program.

Then in 1930, when Hawns was forced to spend more time with
his growing law practice, Miller brought in Bert Bell, the former Penn
halfback, to replace Hawns as the backfield coach. He also brought

in John Da Grossa, a former Colgate star, to coach the linemen.

During an 8-season stretch from 1925 to 1932, Temple's new program forged a record of 50 wins, 15 losses and eight ties.

After I had signed on to take the job at Temple, there was much to be done to begin setting their athletic house in order. Although I had already seen the school's facilities and had visited with Charles Erny, who was Temple's biggest supporter, on two occasions now, I still knew very little about the team or its players.

In late January 1933, I traveled eastward by train with Dick Hanley, the coach at Northwestern University, and Bill Ingram, who was now coaching at Cal.

When we arrived in Chicago, the three of us got off the train. Hanley was returning to his home while Ingram had plans to visit with friends there. My primary purpose for deboarding there was to see Fred Swan, who had been a tackle and the team captain of one of my Stanford squads and was now an assistant line coach for Dr. Clarence Spears at Wisconsin. Swan had traveled from Madison, Wis., to visit with me to discuss the possibility of taking the job as my new line coach at Temple.

Swan was greatly interested in my plans to build a dominant team at Temple in a short period of time. He committed on the spot to join me if offered the job.

Smiling back at him, I said, "Consider the position yours then."

I then traveled on to Philadelphia and arrived after breakfast on the morning of January 30th, where I was met by both Charles Erny and Earl Yoemans, the graduate manager of athletics at Temple. They gave me a tour of the school campus and then took me to visit with Dr. Charles Beury, the president of Temple, at his office in Conwell Hall.

That evening at a private dinner and the Manufacturers' Golf & Country Club, which was located near Oreland, Erny, Yoemans and several others who were prominent supporters of the Temple football program huddled with me.

It was there at this small get-together that a long-term strategy was formulated to build up the Temple football program so that we could compete with Pitt, Notre Dame, Army and other football power-houses in the East and Midwest.

I explained to them that I intended to return to Temple in two months to begin spring practice drills provided that Stanford had been able to find my replacement and if they allowed me to be released from my contract with them prior to August.

The next day, I spoke to the Philadelphia Sportwriters Association banquet at The Benjamin Franklin Hotel. This was my first formal introduction as the new coach at Temple to the City's press.

There, I told them that "It's almost like coming home to be back in this part of the country again. When I coached at Carlisle and Pitt, we had some great games in Philadelphia (with Penn) and always received fine treatment. I hope to spend many happy days here.

"In the East," I added, " football is different from the West. They take their football too fanatically, too fierce out there. There is too much rivalry. It is a case of too much Jones against Warner or Jones against Ingram, etc...

"Here in the East, the sportswriters talk more about the players than the coaches and that is right. It is still a boys game and belongs to them.

"I don't know much about my prospects at Temple. I have met but a few of the players so far and don't know the caliber of the material. A great team can't be developed in a season or two. It may take several seasons and even then the accomplishment rests upon the material (or the level of talent). There are no miracle coaches."

My remarks that evening seemed to hit all of the proper themes that I had hoped to touch upon and were enthusiastically received by the partisan sports crowd. Their applause filled the banquet room and I felt their warmth and sincerity.

Afterwards, following the conclusion of the banquet, an unexpected treat occurred. I was getting ready to leave the head table on the raised platform where all of the evening's speakers had been sitting. Then, unexpectedly, up walked Albert (Chief) Bender, who had been one of my halfbacks at Carlisle and later became a pitching star with the Philadelphia Athletics professional baseball club.

With a big grin on his face, he said, "Hi, Pop!" He then put his arms around me in a great big bear hug.

We stood there for a half hour or longer while talking and reminiscing about those memorable days at Carlisle and what had happened to many of the Indian ballplayers.

Before leaving, Bender wished me "good luck" on building the program at Temple. We then walked out of the large and cavernous Benjamin Franklin Hotel banquet room together. Along the way, the big Indian continued to laugh and started to tell me of the Philadelphia Athletics' upcoming baseball season, yet my mind was wandering to another upcoming season — the 1933 football season at Temple.

Could I once again repeat the magic that I had previously created at Carlisle and Pitt and Stanford? Could this grand experiment at Temple really work? Could I lift this modest football program into the big-time arena of the gridiron world in a short period of time?

These were all difficult questions to answer. The future ahead was unknown and undoubtedly filled with challenge. But I knew that soon I would be rolling up my shirt sleeves and trying to find the answers to all of them.

68

On March 20, 1933, I boarded the train in San Francisco which would take me eastward to Chicago and from there on to Philadelphia and Temple University, where I would begin spring football practice. At the same time, my old friend, Amos Alonzo Stagg, the long-time football coach at the University of Chicago, had already boarded a train in Chicago and was bound westward to Stockton, Calif., where he was to begin his new duties as the head coach of the University of the Pacific.

Somewhere in the late afternoon or early evening of August 21st our trains were expected to pass one another on the transcontinental route. It is an odd twist of fate that two old friends, who both had reached a certain pinnacle of success in college football, would both now be passing each other while traveling by train and en route to take over the coaching reins at what would become the last stops of our coaching careers. What would the odds be of such an occurrence taking place — perhaps 10,000 to 1? 100,000 to 1? Or maybe greater? (Editor's Note: Although Temple and the University of the Pacific would be the final stops on both Warner's and Stagg's coaching journeys as a head coach, both would continue afterwards as "advisory coaches" for several years with Warner serving at San Jose State and Stagg at Susquehanna.)

Chuck Winterburn, who had played for me at Pitt and coached the Stanford freshmen and varsity backfield in recent years, had accompanied me on this trip to Philadelphia. He would be serving as my new backfield coach at Temple. Fred Swan, who had played for me at Stanford and had recently served as a line coach at Wisconsin, was to be my line coach.

Swan had arrived in Philadelphia a few days before both Winterburn and I were scheduled to arrive there. He was supposed to have the initial operational necessities such as offices, practice equipment, student managers and players already organized and waiting for us. My initial strategy was to have five or six weeks of spring practice and I didn't want to waste any time. The first three weeks of spring practice were intended to emphasize the fundamentals of football. Afterwards, we would begin to teach them the basic plays of my single-wing and double-wing system.

A total of 60 candidates reported for spring practice on Monday, March 27th, including 21 veterans of the previous year's team.

At the same time, I had a construction crew come in and erect a series of various blocking-dummy machines, blocking sleds, a coaching tower for me to use in monitoring practices and a dummy-scrimmage machine which I had been tinkering with while at Stanford. In essence, I hoped to turn the Temple football field into an outdoor laboratory.

I know this sounds a bit radical, but Charles Erny had pretty much given me carte blanche to build a football powerhouse at Temple, and with little tradition and only a meager foundation to build upon I realized that it would probably take some ingenuity and forethought to jumpstart the Temple football program and achieve our goals.

To assist me in this transition, I had asked Heine Miller to remain on the Temple staff for the 1933 season and his advice became immeasurable. Bert Bell also assisted us during that initial spring session.

Following a long and often grueling 6-week period of spring practice drills, both Chuck Winterburn and I returned to our homes in Palo Alto, Calif. But since we were neighbors, the two of us got together daily to plan our strategy for the upcoming season.

In our first game of the 1933 season, Temple swept past South Carolina, 26-6.

The following week, Carnegie Tech traveled from Pittsburgh to defeat us, 25-0, and quickly humbled whatever grand illusions we might have had about ourselves.

The players must have gotten the message from the Carnegie Tech trouncing because the next two weeks they romped over the Haskell

Indian Institute, 31-0, and knocked off West Virginia, 13-7, before finally being stopped by Bucknell, 20-7.

By now, however, my backfield of Eddie Zukas, George Paul, Danny Testa and Johnny Stonik was clicking.

We next disposed of Drake, who was from Des Moines, Ia., by a 20-14 score and shutout Washington & Jefferson, 13-0.

But in our season finale against cross-town rival Villanova, we were blitzed, 24-0.

Overall, we wound up with a record of five wins and three losses for the season, which was a respectable finish for most schools. Yet it paled in comparison to my first-year records at Pitt (8-0-0) and Stanford (7-1-1).

The next season, the seeds of our hard work began to yield some fruitful results.

A strong freshman class had been brought in at Temple in the fall of 1933 and these youngsters would now be sophomores. In addition, the upperclassmen were now more experienced in using the single-wing and double-wing system and their confidence and superb execution was beginning to show up on the gridiron each Saturday.

In the off-season, following spring practice drills, I had greatly upgraded our schedule so that we would be playing much stronger competition. The new schools that I added were V.M.I., Texas A&M, Indiana, Marquette and Holy Cross. The schools that I had retained from the 1933 schedule were West Virginia, Carnegie Tech, Villanova and Bucknell. Together this group would form one of the most difficult schedules in the country for any major football power to play against.

But the 1934 schedule also had some advantages. I had arranged this difficult list of opponents while also structuring it so that Temple would only have to play one road game — and this would be against Marquette in Milwaukee, Wis. The remainder of our schedule was to be played at our home field, Memorial Stadium, in Philadelphia.

Temple would post a record of seven wins and two ties in 1934, with the ties coming against Indiana and Bucknell. Danny Testa, Don Watts, Horace Mowray, Dave Smuckler and Wilfred Longsderff were among the leaders on this undefeated squad.

Our season opened with a 34-0 romp over Virginia Tech, with Testa turning in three touchdowns to lead the Owls' offensive effort.

A week later, while Fred Swan and I had traveled to Columbus, Ohio, to get a close-up of Indiana coach Bo McMillin's much-discussed five-man backfield against Ohio State and Chuck Winterburn journeyed to Morgantown, W. Va., to view the West Virginia-Pitt battle, my Temple squad was left in the hands of Pete Stevens, the team's captain, to take on Texas A&M on a rainy Friday evening.

On the game's opening kickoff and the first play from scrimmage, Temple managed to take all of the fire out of the visiting Texans. Stonik fielded the Aggies' kick at the 7-yard line and then proceeded to scoot for 52 yards upfield. Then on the first play from scrimmage, Testa swept around left end for 41 yards and a touchdown.

Suddenly, the hopes of the Aggie team were dashed.

Testa would go on to score on two more occasions amongst the growing sea of mud that evening and Don Watts scampered 80 yards on a punt return as Temple flattened Texas A&M, 40-6.

After a humbling 6-6 struggle with Indiana, my young Owls bounced back and knocked off West Virginia, 28-13, and Marquette, 28-6. Testa added two more tallies in Milwaukee that afternoon.

Now, with a full steam of momentum, we then swept past Holy Cross, 14-0; crushed Carnegie Tech, 34-6; and shutout cross-town rival Villanova, 22-0.

On Thanksgiving Day, the Owls were unable to get past a testy Bucknell squad and the contest ended up in a 0-0 tie.

Through 9 games, Temple had racked up a total of 2,605 yards of total offense. 2,131 yards had been gained on the ground and 474 yards through the air. This gave us an average of nearly 300 yards per game. Our opponents, however, were only able to mount 1,290 on offense — 971 in rushing yardage and 319 yards in aerials.

Only twice in the season did we go below the 200-yard mark on offense — against Indiana and Bucknell — and both of these games ended in ties.

At the end of the season, with the Philadelphia and East Coast newspapers now hailing our successes, Temple was invited to play against Tulane in the inaugural Sugar Bowl Classic which would be played on New Year's Day in New Orleans, La.

For Charles Erny and the others who had hatched this radical experiment at Temple, it was a thrilling and joyous time. As youngsters during the turn of the century and in the early 1900's, Erny and these gentlemen had been raised during the era of George Woodruff's mighty Penn teams that had ruled the gridirons of the East.

Now, they were intimately involved with the building of a football powerhouse.

69

Our selection to play in the first Sugar Bowl game was both a surprise and a stamp of approval for the progress that Temple was making in its much-hastened "great football experiment."

Representatives of the New Orleans Mid-Winter Sports Association had initially contacted me about playing in such a game during the middle of the 1934 season. The Southerners promised to put on a true extravaganza filled with lots of good eating, wonderful sightseeing and a large vocal football crowd on gameday. It was their goal to have a bowl game that eventually would rank up there with the Rose Bowl.

At this point in time, the Cotton Bowl game had not arrived on the scene just yet. Their first matchup, which would pit T.C.U. against Marquette, wasn't played until January 1, 1937. The initial Orange Bowl game, however, was just getting launched. It paired Bucknell and the University of Miami (Fla.) and was to be played on New Year's Day 1935.

The final team selections for the inaugural Sugar Bowl game were announced in early December and the Temple football fans in Philadelphia were wildly enthusiastic over our being picked. Even the Philadelphia press, who had been used to the staid tradition of Penn football and wasn't quite sure what to make of the growing football phenomenon at Temple, began to join in the maddening hysteria.

The Owls, who were ranked third nationally in the Williamson Poll, were undefeated and though tied twice were considered the "Northern Champion" for the Sugar Bowl contest. Tulane, who hailed from New Orleans and was ranked 13th nationally, with a 9-1-0 record, was chosen to be the "Southern Champion" and home team.

The Mid-Winter Sports Association representatives gave us a guarantee of $15,000 to play in the Sugar Bowl. And with little hesitation, we quickly accepted their offer.

On a cool, cloudy New Year's Day afternoon, a crowd of more than 22,000 packed the brick stands of Tulane Stadium for the contest between Temple and Tulane.

The Temple team had brought along several hundred Owl fans on the train trip to New Orleans. And our Temple band, which was also formed in 1925 and originally outfitted with $800 in uniforms and instruments ordered from the Sears catalog, made the trip, too. They traveled for nearly two days by bus to get there. And their presence was greatly appreciated because it did a lot to help us feel at home amongst this largely Southern, hostile crowd.

In the game's opening quarter, the Temple line managed to take control of the line of scrimmage and this allowed our youthful squad to play with a bit more reckless abandon.

Late in the first quarter, Tulane halfback Barney Mintz fumbled at the Green Wave 10-yard line and Owl lineman Stan Gurzinski wasted no time in recovering the ball. This, of course, put us in easy scoring position.

On the first play, Dave Smuckler, our big fullback, gained 3 yards while smashing off-tackle. Then on the next play, the Owls used a little razzle-dazzle that reminded me of the shenanigans that my Carlisle teams once used.

As soon as the teams lined up again to await the next play, the Temple center immediately snapped the ball. The pigskin was then handed off to Smuckler who began to sweep around right end. However, as the Green Wave players began to zero in on Smuckler, he fired a pass to Owl halfback Danny Testa who had floated into the end zone undetected by Tulane's great defensive halfback, Monk Simmons. Smuckler's pass to Testa was quickly snagged for the touchdown. After Smuckler added the extra-point kick, Temple now led, 7-0.

In the second period, Owl quarterback Glenn Frey hit a booming punt that went out-of-bounds deep in Green Wave territory. While trying to advance Tulane out of this difficult spot, Green Wave fullback Stanley Lodrigues coughed up the ball on a fumble which was recovered by one of our linemen, Bill Docherty, at the Tulane 18-yard line.

Two consecutive reverse plays moved the ball to the Tulane 4. Afterwards, the Green Wave stopped two of our advances, netting us only 2 yards. But on the next play, Smuckler blasted over center to reach the Green Wave end zone. Following the conversion kick, Temple's lead was increased to 14-0.

At this point in the contest, our prospects for victory were looking pretty good.

However, in the third quarter, that outlook began to change.

Tulane quarterback Johnny McDaniel fielded Temple's second-half opening kickoff near the sidelines at the Green Wave 10. After running a few yards, thus attracting the attention of the Owls' kick coverage, McDaniel quickly lateralled to an awaiting Simmons who was 5 yards behind him and running in the opposite direction.

Simmons then headed up the opposite sideline running like a scared rabbit. One or two of our kick coverage players managed to figure out what was going on and made an attempt to corral Simmons at the Tulane 35. But as they moved in to stop the fleet-footed Green Wave back, a couple of Simmons' teammates seemingly came out of nowhere and wiped out the Owl pursuers.

With nothing but open field in front of him, Simmons raced toward the Temple goal line. The score was Simmons' 11th touchdown of the season. Afterwords, the point-after kick allowed Tulane to narrow Temple's lead to 14-7.

Tulane, however, was just getting cranked up.

Bucky Bryan, a reserve Green Wave halfback, got Tulane moving again late in the third quarter when he turned in a spectacular 28-yard run that moved the ball deep into Owl territory.

A few plays later, with Tulane at the Owls' 4-yard line, Byran passed to Dick Hardy in the end zone, who had to leap high into the air and between two Temple defenders to grab the catch for the score. Mintz than booted the conversion kick which tied the score at 14-14.

A second Hardy reception — this one for 12 yards — early in the fourth quarter got the Green Wave moving again. Hardy's catch edged into Owl territory at the 48-yard line.

Joe Lofton then picked up 6 yards on the ground to advance the Tulane offense to the Owl 42. On the next two plays, Mintz tried passes on both attempts. The first one ended up falling incomplete. However, on the second attempt, Horace Mowrey, a reserve halfback, stepped in front of Hardy, the Tulane receiver, to steal the pass. But in an eagerness to field the ball, the ball brushed off Mowrey's fingertips and bounced up into midair.

An alert Hardy rushed over to lasso the floating ball and quickly headed on toward the Temple end zone which was just 15 yards away.

Wilfred Longsderff attempted to stop Hardy from reaching the goal line and dove desperately at Hardy's heels, but he wasn't able to slow him up.

On the conversion attempt, Longsderff blocked Mintz's kick which kept Temple's hopes alive.

But Tulane, who was now leading, 20-14, wouldn't let go of their growing momentum and held on for the victory.

With a large crowed on hand, the exciting game also turned out to be a financial success. Each team was given a check for $20,759.20 which was 38 percent more than what we had been promised.

In the years that followed, the Sugar Bowl would be the home to many more exciting New Year's Day contests.

70

Our loss to Tulane in the inaugural Sugar Bowl Classic was a big disappointment, but it was not a setback to our program. Instead, it served to gauge where we were in the building process at Temple.

Within two years, the Owls had been lifted from a level of mediocrity to one of being a rising contender on the national scene. Now, we were being quoted often in the daily newspaper columns and stories when big-time college football was the subject matter. And on autumn Saturdays, the big-city newspapers sent their writers and photographers to cover our games. Then in Sunday's morning edition there would be bold headlines, photographs and several columns of news stories dedicated to Temple's recent gridiron exploits.

And if you were a Temple fan, these were heady times.

After we had captured a nice taste of success in 1934, several of the key Temple supporters and I got together and decided that it might prove to be a bit more interesting to turn up the pace of our grand gridiron experiment and beef up the Temple schedule even more for 1935.

Normally, I would have hesitated at trying to move so quickly because a young team that is in the midst of a building phase needs time to mature and the strength of one's schedule can either help or hinder your efforts. But this wasn't your traditional effort, so I threw out all of the rules of the past and added Vanderbilt, who had been having a lot of success under Dan McGugin, and Michigan State to our schedule for 1935. (Editor's Note: McGugin retired from Vanderbilt after the 1934 season. During his 30-year reign there, the Commodores had achieved a record of 197-55-19.)

We opened the 1935 season against St. Joseph's who was now

being coached by Heine Miller, my predecessor at Temple. The Owls crushed them, 51-0, in front of a hometown crowd in Memorial Stadium.

Continuing our winning ways, we defeated Centre, 25-13, and then traveled to Tyler, Tex., where we rolled over the Texas A&M Aggies, 14-0.

Afterwards, the Owls managed to overcome the feisty Commodores, 6-3, in a hard-fought contest.

The next two weeks, my Temple squad rode the rails of Penn Central as we journeyed west to Pittsburgh to beat Carnegie Tech, 13-0, and then went south and west into the Appalachian coal field area where we romped West Virginia, 19-6.

At this point, Temple was at a high-water point in my tenure there. We were undefeated, with six wins under out belt, and now facing the most difficult stretch in the 1935 schedule.

But with our spectacular backfield of Dave Smuckler, Vince Renzo, Glenn Frey and Wilfred Longsderff, who had racked up a nice string of victories, we were ready for the big task ahead.

In front of a capacity crowd at Memorial Stadium, Michigan State narrowly won, 12-7, in a nail-biter of a contest.

The Owls recovered the next week to handily beat Marquette, 26-6. However in the final two games of the season, cross-town rival Villanova, who was being coached by former Four Horseman Harry Stuhldreher, defeated us 21-14 and Bucknell eked out a 7-6 victory.

When the season was over, the Owls had racked up a record of 7 wins and three losses against a tremendously difficult schedule.

Temple had now put together three successive winning seasons and the past two had been especially successful. With these encouraging signs to point to, I felt that our outdoor football laboratory on the practice fields at Temple was beginning to yield some significant results. As to be expected, our alumni and student body were immensely jubilant over our new-found prosperity.

Still, I knew that although there had been some early success with our efforts, the next year or two ahead would give us a good glimpse of what the future held.

71

During the 1935 season, I had been offered two coaching offers that presented an interesting dilemma.

One was from my alma mater, Cornell, who was be seeking a replacement for my good friend, Gil Dobie. Doobie had been forced out after having been the coach of the Redmen for 16 seasons.

The second opportunity was at the University of California, who had been one of Stanford's big rivals. Stub Allison had replaced Bill Ingram after the 1934 season. And like the others who had followed Andy Smith, he was having a difficult time in trying to find the magical winning formula that Smith had once possessed while coaching there from 1916 to 1925 and compiling a record of 74 wins, 16 losses and 7 ties.

As I assessed these two offers, I became torn in three completely different directions.

Part of me would have loved to have taken the Cornell job and returned to those hallowed halls that were covered in ivy and to be reunited with the school where I had first started my football career as a player and later coached and, of course, had received my law degree from Cornell. It was also near my boyhood home and the farm in Springville, N.Y., that I still owned. But Gil Dobie was a long-time friend of mine and whom I had spent many special times with. To replace him under these circumstances would not have been the right thing to do. To me, I'd rather retain an old friendship than to return to Cornell in this manner.

The Cal job offer was an intriguing one because the Golden Bears had everything going for them — a great winning tradition, a large stadium that usually sold out at each home game, a big alumni following and, most importantly, being in a great location. The State of California was a growing mecca for football talent and the people there loved the fast-paced, swift style of football that the gridiron powerhouses in California were now playing.

And besides, I had already made a good name for myself out there with my great teams at Stanford. All Cal really needed was a strong personality and a firm guiding hand to help them rediscover their winning ways of the past.

Agreeably, these were great opportunities to be facing, but the overwhelming factor that held me back was my existing commitment to Temple. I felt that my obligation to Temple had not been fully met and it was important to help them reach a certain level of success as well as be able to win there on a consistent basis. If these objectives had already been achieved and I was in good health, then I later might have considered other schools' offers.

But the timing had to be right to consider making a move and at this point, in the late fall of 1935, this was not the right time.

Following the 1935 Sugar Bowl Classic, Charles Enry had wanted to extend my contract with Temple for another 2 or 3 seasons, but I managed to talk him out of it when I explained that although my health was fine at the present it may not stay this way as I got into my mid-sixties. I was already using a cane to assist me a lot in my walking and, perhaps, I wasn't sure if I had really wanted to coach beyond the 1937 season when my original contract was due to expire.

In 1936, the Owls posted a 6-3-2 record while playing against a significantly more difficult schedule that included Ole Miss (the University of Mississippi), Boston College, Carnegie Tech, Holy Cross, Michigan State, Villanova, Iowa and St. Mary's. Undoubtedly, this was one of the most difficult schedules in the country.

The great freshman class that had been recruited to Temple in 1934 — and who was undefeated in their freshman season — was now at the top of their game. But the swift ascent up the ladder of gridiron success was beginning to show signs of stagnation.

At the end of the 1936 season, I finally agreed to a two-year extension to my original contract, which would have carried me through the 1939 season.

Knowing that my health was slowly getting the best of me and hindering my considerable travel routine, I told both Charles Enry and Dr. Charles Beury, the University's president, that I felt like I could have the football program poised to continue its winning ways and everything in its proper place for my successor by 1939 if I wanted to retire at that point.

I also agreed to the 2-year extension because I hoped to put together a championship team by 1939.

In 1937, I added the University of Florida to our schedule and we barely defeated them, 7-6, in our own ballpark, Memorial Stadium.

Along the way that season, Temple racked up four ties in hard-fought battles against Ole Miss, Boston College, Holy Cross and Bucknell while we earned an overall record of three wins, two losses and four bruising ties.

Then in 1938, I added two more powerhouses to our schedule, Pitt and Texas Christian University. We struggled against both schools.

This would be Jock Sutherland's last season at Pitt before departing to coach the Philadelphia Eagles of the National Football League. Pitt ended up plastering us, 28-6, as Dick Cassio, the stellar Panther halfback, put on an impressive performance that afternoon while racing for two touchdowns.

Next, we took on T.C.U., who was led by their great halfback, Davey O'Brien, the 150-pound, five-foot, seven-inch mighty mite. The Horned Frogs were able to repeat Pitt's earlier success story and won, 28-6, as O'Brien won accolades for his wonderful running and passing performance in this contest. T.C.U. would go on to post an undefeated season in 1938 and defeat Carnegie Tech, 15-7, in the 1939 Sugar Bowl Classic. (Editor's Note: At the conclusion of the 1938 season, O'Brien's gridiron prowess earned him considerable praise and he was selected as a consensus all-America and swept all three of the country's prominent most valuable players — The Heisman Memorial Trophy, The Maxwell Trophy and The Walter Camp Trophy.)

Against a remaining rugged schedule of Bucknell, Boston College, Georgetown, Holy Cross, Villanova, Michigan State and Florida, my Temple squad faltered badly. We ended up with three wins that season while losing six others and tying one, a 26-26 tug-of-war with Boston College.

After we had defeated Florida, 20-12, in Gainesville, Fla., I knew that it was time for a change. The Temple football program had suffered several setbacks to some great teams during the past two seasons, but I sincerely believed that the Owls could have a perennial powerhouse if the lofty ambitions of my great gridiron experiment could be scaled back a bit and the football program be given an opportunity to mature and catch up with its earlier successes.

Knowing that I could not lead this kind of pace of continuing cross-country travel while also trying to build-up the Temple football program, I felt it would be best to step back and let a younger coach take the helm, which my assistant, Fred Swan, did for one season. In 1940, Ray Morrison was then chosen to lead the Owls' football program, which he did for a 9-year stretch.

As I closed the book on my tenure at Temple and returned by train to my home in Palo Alto, Calif., I must note that my career there was a memorable one.

Against the backdrop of the Depression Era and a new revival under President Franklin D. Roosevelt, I was able to openly experiment and develop an almost unknown football program into a team that in six short seasons was playing top-notch football against the best teams in the country. My only regret was that I wasn't able to help them win a national championship or earn a trip to play in the Rose Bowl.

But in the end, it was a great run. And for Charles Erny, Earl Yoemans, Dr. Beury, myself and the Temple fans, we all had a lot of fun watching this unlikely football squad rise to become a national contender.

The Final Years
By MIKE BYNUM

In early January 1939, rumors began to circulate among several prominent circles of West Coast sportswriters and athletic officials that Warner might not be returning to Temple for the 1939 season. These rumors eventually made their way eastward and surfaced in the Philadelphia newspapers a week later.

These rumors were given added weight in mid-January when several powerful Stanford University alumni began to publicly suggest that Warner be named as an "advisory coach" to assist Stanford head tutor Claude Thornhill, whose Indian football squad had turned in three straight losing seasons following their earlier three straight Pacific Coast Conference championships and record-setting Rose Bowl berths in 1934, 1935 and 1936. With Thornhill's teams now struggling, Warner's brilliant coaching wisdom and uncanny ability to breathe life into downtrodden football programs suddenly seemed to be the perfect prescription for what Stanford needed.

This scenario was eventually revealed in a United Press newswire story from the West Coast in mid-January.

Once this flurry of rumors began to become public in the East, several Temple heavyweight alums who had previously been critics of Warner's lackluster 1937 and 1938 seasons saw this as an opportunity that they had been waiting for. They responded by informing the Philadelphia press of some of Temple's "behind-closed-doors-only privileged athletic secrets."

It was a widely known fact in the Quaker City that certain factions of the Temple alumni, faculty and administration, who had gotten caught up in the Owls' newly-found gridiron success and growing status in the college athletic world, had become frustrated with

Temple's recent leveling off in terms of victories following their earlier meteoric rise during Warner's first four years there.

Finally, on January 28th, the rumors began to take on a new dimension when *The Philadelphia Evening Bulletin* broke the story that Warner's contract with Temple had a disability clause and that school officials had forced Warner to take a physician's exam prior to the beginning of the 1938 season.

The Evening Bulletin story noted: "Warner was examined by Dr. John Royal Moore, a prominent surgeon, who submitted a report that Pop was in no condition to actively assume charge of a football squad."

The Evening Bulletin story then added: "Warner has a hip ailment, finding it necessary to lean heavily on a cane. When he gets up from a chair it requires a great deal of effort. The physicians said they were certain Warner suffered excruciating pains (from the hip ailment), yet Pop insisted he could carry on (during the 1938 season) and refused to join the idle."

As the controversy began to mount, Temple administrators and key alumni gathered to seek a solution.

Knowing that Warner, himself, had been quite concerned for his mobility problems and inability to continue the tremendous cross-country travel that the Temple job had required, yet still desired to finish out his tenure there with a winner so that his successor would have the athletic talent and much-needed momentum to carry-on with his "great football experiment," Dr. Charles E. Beury, Temple's president, and Earl R. Yoemans, Temple's graduate manager of athletics, drafted a proposal which might accommodate everyone.

The proposal suggested that if Warner would go ahead and retire with one year still remaining on his contract extension of 1936, then Temple would honor the payment of his salary and other perks that he otherwise would have received for the 1939 season. This arrangement would allow Warner to forego having to return to Temple for both spring practice and the fall season as well as the hectic demands that his job had been requiring.

Beury and Yoemans also proposed that Warner's number-one assistant, Fred Swan, the Owls' line coach, be elevated to become head coach and Charlie Winterburn be retained as the Owls' backfield coach. Both had been associated with Warner for over 15 years and still had one year remaining on their contracts.

When the draft proposal was ready to be discussed, Yoemans then called Warner who was at his residence in Palo Alto, Calif., which was located near the Stanford campus. The two reviewed the details of the proposal in great depth that afternoon.

As it turned out, Warner was receptive to most of what Yoemans proposed and after 30 minutes of conversation they finally worked out the remaining details.

The next morning when Yoemans arrived at his office, he found a telegram sitting on top of his desk. If was from Warner.

Upon opening the telegram, Yoemans read its contents.

"You will recall that at the close of the (1938) football season, I expressed my desire to resign," the wire noted. "It was arranged that I delay my final decision until the first of March.

"There is no need for further delay because I still feel the same way about it and I hereby tender my resignation.

"During the six years I have been at Temple, I have not heard one word of criticism of my work from anyone connected with the university. I mention this because I deeply appreciate it and that it is an unusual experience for a football coach.

"I want to thank you and everyone at Temple for the cooperation I have had and I wish for my successor and the football team every possible future success."

After conferring with Dr. Beury, Yoemans then dispatched a return telegram to Warner.

"The football committee of the Council on Athletics, through me, deeply regrets your decision to withdraw as coach of the Temple University football team," the wire stated.

"I can sincerely say that the athletic authorities were well satisfied with your efforts and appreciate the contribution you have made to Temple football. We are reluctant to accept your resignation but are abiding by your wishes. We sincerely hope you will continue to coach football for years to come."

Around the college football world, Warner's resignation at Temple raised many eyebrows. But those who knew him also believed that

Warner would not simply retire and leave football entirely.

And when the dust settled a few weeks later, Warner chose not to follow the course that many sportswriters had predicted by becoming an advisory coach to assist his long-time friend and former assistant, Claude Thornhill. Although the temptation seemed perhaps too great for both Warner and Stanford to re-unite once again, Warner shied away from such overtures because he did not want to undercut Thornhill's presence there.

Stanford, however, did eventually name Lawrence (Spud) Lewis, the former coach at the University of San Francisco, to replace backfield coach Bobby Grayson, a former Stanford all-America fullback, who was departing to take up a career as an attorney.

Then, in early March, Warner was offered a coaching job that fit nicely with his new semi-retirement plans — it was near his home in Palo Alto and it offered him both a challenge and an opportunity to prove his talents once again.

Dudley DeGroot, who had been a captain on the 1922 Stanford team that Andy Kerr and Claude Thornhill had coached for Warner and was now the head football coach at San Jose State College, invited Warner to accept the position of advisory coach on his staff. Wasting little time deliberating the offer, Warner quickly agreed to take charge of the San Jose State offense practice drills that spring. However in accepting the San Jose offer, Warner stated that he did not want a salary for taking the advisory coach position. Instead, he asked only for a reimbursement of his commuting expenses and meals.

That fall, San Jose State, which had a student body of only 3,000 and a small wooden bleacher stadium seating only 12,000, went undefeated with a 13-0-0 record. One of their more memorable wins that season was a 13-3 victory over Amos Alonzo Stagg's savvy College of the Pacific squad on their home field in Stockton, Calif.

Following the 1939 season, DeGroot resigned his position as head coach of the Spartans to take the top coaching spot at Rochester University in Rochester, N.Y. His replacement was Ben Winkleman, who had previously been an assistant at Stanford.

It took a bit of coaxing by San Jose State president T.W. McQuarrie and newly-appointed athletic director Glenn Hartranft, but Warner agreed to remain on and assist Winkleman for the 1940 season. That fall, the Spartans romped to a 10-1-0 record.

By now, Warner, who was nearing 70, was ready to step away from the sidelines. He retired at the conclusion of the 1940 season.

In retirement, Warner spent a lot of time at his home in Palo Alto and on occasion journeyed to Springville, N.Y., to visit his family farm.

He spent a considerable amount of time corresponding with former players, coaches and sportswriters whom he had known from his coaching career and finished a number of watercolor paintings. He also enjoyed watching college and professional football games being played on weekends in the San Francisco area.

Before retiring, Warner had helped stage a college all-star football game in Chicago's Soldier Field in 1933 with nearly 100,000 in attendance. The Pacific Coast team was coached by U.S.C. coach Howard Jones and the Midwest squad was coached by Northwestern's Dick Hanley. This game would serve as a forerunner to the splashy annual, late summer College All-Star Game that Arch Ward, the sports editor of *The Chicago Tribune,* would launch in 1936.

In 1935, he joined Fielding Yost, the former coach at the University of Michigan; Dan McGugin, the former coach at Vanderbilt University; Amos Alonzo Stagg, Pudge Heffelinger and several others in setting up the National Amateur Football Association. This league of amateur teams across the country was established to stage a series of football games in key cities in each state, with the winners advancing to state and national championships. One division of teams was for kids younger than 17 years old. The other division was for those over the age of 17. Receipts of the games were to be used to fund an educational fund to assist needy students who would be attending college. Although it was set up under the Amateur Athletic Union, the N.A.F.A. never really got off the ground.

In 1939, Warner was offered the league presidency of the American Professional Football League but he turned it down.

In 1941, he attended a reunion of Carlisle students at the New York State Fair which was being held in Syracuse. The gathering brought Warner together with many of his former Indian players — some of whom he hadn't seen for 35 years — and it turned out to be a nostalgic time for everyone.

In 1945, he attended a 50-year reunion weekend of his first team at Iowa State. Iowa State celebrated Warner's return by walloping Nebraska, 27-7.

Two years later, in 1947, Warner was honored by the Touchdown Club of New York City with their Outstanding Contributions to Football Award.

In 1949, the Palo Club of Palo Alto, Calif., announced that it would honor Warner by launching a new award that would be named for him and given each year thereafter to the West Coast's most valuable senior college football player. The award was christened "The Pop Warner Trophy" and has been given each year to some of the biggest names in college football, including Eddie LeBaron, Ollie Matson, Mike Garrett, Gary Beban, O.J. Simpson, Jim Plunkett, Lynn Swann, Marcus Allen and John Elway. For many years until his death in 1976, Ernie Nevers — who was perhaps Warner's greatest player — was on hand to personally hand out this prestigious award.

The early 1950's would prove to be an eventful period for Warner.

In 1951, he was honored by being inducted into both the Helm's Athletic Foundation Hall of Fame and in the first class of the National Football Foundation's College Football Hall of Fame.

Shortly thereafter, he was voted the "Coach of The Era" by the American Football Coaches Association and honored at a big banquet in his honor at The Netherland Plaza Hotel in Cincinnati, Ohio, on January 10, 1952.

Old age, however, was catching up with the legendary coach.

In July 1954, Warner was operated on to remove a throat tumor. During early August, the tough-minded old coach seemed to be rallying during his post-surgery recovery. But in mid-August, his progress began to falter and he eventually fell into a coma. He finally passed away on Monday, September 7th. He was 83.

POP WARNER'S LEGACY

By MIKE BYNUM

The gray clouds in the late morning sky continued to grow darker as the day began to move toward mid-afternoon.

It was April 19, 1934, a day when spring should have been welcoming the budding, vivid hues of flowers in bloom and the sun's radiant sunshine. Instead, a blustery late winter storm was setting in on the City of Philadelphia and its surrounding suburbs. As the afternoon workday concluded, the sleet and freezing rain sent the downtown business commuters into a frenzy as they made a mad dash to catch the electric trains which would carry them back to their neighborhoods and the nearby towns and villages.

The culprit for such maddening activity with the Philadelphia community trains was treacherous ice which had begun to form on the rails and the bridges. This peril was forcing the trains to travel at a much slower speed than usual, which resulted in many of them being pushed behind schedule as they continued to journey to their destinations through the late afternoon and early evening hours. At the Broad Street and 30th Street Stations, long lines of commuters waited anxiously through these delays for their intended trains. And as the afternoon's train schedules continued to back up, the crowd's tempers also heightened.

Those who had attempted to travel home by automobile on this obstreperous afternoon were confronted by a similar problem. Most of the roads had become icy and were deemed impassable to drive on.

Later that evening, amongst all of this confusion and congestion, a coaching clinic for a youth football league and its coaches and players had been scheduled to begin at 7:30 p.m. A dozen prominent coaches from the Philadelphia area had committed to lecture at the youth league's coaching clinic, which would be held at a Philadelphia junior high school auditorium. For the fledgling five-year-old league, which was known as the Junior Football Conference and had begun its operations in 1929, this was supposed to be a big evening.

Unfortunately, Fate was not cooperating. The winter storm continued to grow worse with the evening hour.

As the start of the clinic drew near, many of the coaches who were to be guest lecturers on the program began to call in and cancel their plans, explaining that the weather had made it virtually impossible for them to travel to the coaching clinic.

By 8:15 p.m., eleven of the coaches had telephoned to give their regrets.

Still, one of the coaches had not been heard from.

Then at 8:30, as an audience of nearly 350 at the coaching clinic was beginning to grow restless, the doors at the back of the school auditorium swung open and an elderly gentleman with spectacles and who leaned heavily on a cane slowly made his way up the aisle to the front stage.

All eyes in the audience followed the visitor as he moved through the auditorium. Several of the boys and the grown-ups recognized the identity of their visitor and in quiet whispers began to share this with others who were sitting nearby.

Yes, it was Glenn S. (Pop) Warner, the great football coach who had built legendary programs at Carlisle, Pittsburgh and Stanford, and who was now attempting to take Temple University to the bright lights of glory at the top of the college football world.

Pop Warner had originally planned to come to this assembly to say a few words of encouragement to the coaches and young ballplayers. But when notified that he was the only guest lecturer to make it through the arduous winter storm to the clinic, Warner offered to fill-in for those who were unable to attend so that the boys and grown-ups in the assembled group would not be disappointed.

With no notes or an agenda, Warner then took the stage to address the gathering. He drew on his rich past and long-time association with the many greats of college football and poured forth his wisdom and insights to the game. He also shared several amusing anecdotes and stories from his many adventures as both a player and a coach.

Afterwards, he offered to let the audience ask any questions which they might have. Eagerly, many of the youngsters and a few of the grown-ups raised their hands.

There was laughter and giggling, both silly questions and smart ones. There were questions about Jim Thorpe and Ernie Nevers, the Rose Bowl and one or two concerning Warner's plans for the Temple football program.

With the audience listening intently, Warner answered all of their questions. And in the smiles on the youngsters' faces, it was quite evident that a special warmth and mutual affection had settled in on the auditorium gathering this evening.

Finally when it was almost 10 p.m., the grand old coach brought the program to a close. There was then a thundering applause by the youngsters and grown-ups which was warm, enthusiastic and heartfelt.

But before leaving, Warner stayed for another half hour to sign autographs for his new friends. And with each signature, he offered a note of encouragement.

Warner Adopted

In the months following the coaching clinic, Warner continued to assist and encourage the coaches in the Junior Football Conference. Finally, prior to the beginning of the 1934 fall season, the Junior Football Conference coaches and officials voted to rename their league in honor of their new patron. From that point forward, the youth organization would be known as "The Pop Warner Football Conference."

Almost immediately, Warner's affiliation with the youth football league attracted both attention and new teams like a magnet. After starting with 16 teams which had been primarily based in the Northeast Philadelphia suburbs, the Pop Warner Football Conference grew to 157 teams by 1938.

In the early years of the Pop Warner Football Conference, its teams consisted of kids who were 15 years and older. Some teams were even stocked with players who were over 30 years old.

In 1937, the league's age limit for players was dropped to 13 years of age and a greater emphasis was put on fielding "midget" football teams.

During this period, the structure of the league was such that teams in the City of Philadelphia represented their respective neighborhoods, while suburban teams represented their local towns and villages. Competition among the teams was organized by weight limits of the players.

Humble Beginnings

The Junior Football Conference began in Northeast Philadelphia in 1929 as an attempt to give the town's idle youth something to participate in following school. The founder of the league was Joe Tomlin, a prosperous young stockbroker from Philadelphia.

Northeast Philadelphia was a factory town and there were a lot of children in the local neighborhoods.

Once, while on a visit to Northeast Philadelphia, Tomlin noticed a new building which had recently been built and was now open for business. Its owner was the Horace T. Potts Company. The building was graced with ornate brickwork and several large front windows, which extended from the floor to the ceiling.

Tomlin also noticed that a few of the kids from the neighborhood were throwing rocks at the new building's windows, while standing in a nearby vacant lot. After asking around, Tomlin soon learned that in a period of one month this group of kids had broken more than 100 of Potts' windows.

Realizing that this problem needed a quick solution, Tomlin met with Mr. Potts, the company's owner, and suggested a possible solution which might alleviate his problems with broken windows.

Tomlin suggested that Potts get all of the area's mill owners together and each owner put up an equal amount of money to start an athletic program for the neighborhood kids. At the time, there were no existing recreation programs or other organized youth athletic programs in the factory town, except for those in scattered Catholic parishes.

Within a few weeks, the mill owners eventually agreed to back Tomlin's plan, but there was one condition: he was to take charge of the athletic program and get it off the ground.

That fall, Tomlin worked at his job at the brokerage house in downtown Philadelphia and on the weekends commuted to Northeast

Philadelphia, where he launched the Junior Football Conference. There were four teams in that initial season. But it was the beginning of much more to come.

Beating the Odds

During the early years of the Depression, Joe Tomlin solicited financial support from many of the leaders of the Philadelphia community to underwrite the activities of the Pop Warner Football Conference. One of the league's more active benefactors was A. J. Drexel Paul, who was an heir to the Drexel family wealth.

The Depression of the 1930's had caused much poverty in the Philadelphia area as well as in most parts of the country. Many kids were unable to attend school and thus had a lot of idle time to get into trouble. Tomlin and an expanding Pop Warner Football Conference tried to occupy these youngsters' time by supplying them with books and guest speakers. And for those who wanted, tutors were provided to assist the youngsters in their studies.

Mr. Paul was impressed with the Pop Warner Football Conference's ability to keep the Philadelphia kids out of trouble and the emphasis on education which it instilled. He backed his support of the Pop Warner Football Conference with a large financial donation and quickly enlisted the support of his friends in the Philadelphia Social Register to join him.

Mr. Paul's influence, along with that of his friends, eventually led to the formation of the Sandlot Sports Association, which was a fund-raising umbrella for the Pop Warner Football Conference and the Connie Mack Baseball Conference, a Philadelphia area youth baseball league which Joe Tomlin had also founded and promoted.

Philadelphia shipbuilding magnate H. Birchard Taylor served as president of the Sandlot Sports Association during its early years and led the group's fund-raising activities. In addition, four volunteers joined Tomlin to add structure to the Pop Warner Football Conference. Andrew J. Turish oversaw the football league's officiating and scheduling, while Joseph L. Vetter ran the fast-growing midget football program. William A. Gillen and John D. Scott handled the football league's many administrative duties. Their efforts allowed Tomlin to concentrate on developing the framework for the Pop

Warner Football Conference to eventually expand on a national level.

As World War II continued to become a larger part of the daily lives of most Americans, it also had a significant impact on the Pop Warner Football Conference. Because of the war, the league's older players were being drafted into the military. This caused many of the youth football teams to either fold or merge. The decrease in the number of teams also caused a financial drain on the Sandlot Sports Association.

It was at this point that H. Birchard Taylor recommended that the Sandlot Sports Association, including the Pop Warner and Connie Mack youth leagues, be closed for the duration of the war. Taylor, who was a big believer of Tomlin's youth sports program, then offered Tomlin a job to work for him as a foreman at his shipbuilding yard. There, Tomlin was given an office and a secretary. His responsibilities were to oversee a crew in the shipbuilding yard each day and continue to keep alive the spirit and the framework of the Pop Warner and Connie Mack youth sports leagues.

For two years, both the Pop Warner and Connie Mack leagues would remain inactive. Then in late 1944, when it appeared that the Allies were beginning to get the upper hand against the Germans and the Japanese, Taylor suggested to Tomlin that the two youth sports leagues might soon be coming to life once again. Knowing that the postwar era would bring a significant boom to the youth sports leagues, Taylor then dispatched Tomlin to begin scouting for possible new sights for recreation fields, which Philadelphia and its suburbs would undoubtedly need to build.

As it turned out, Taylor's vision was keenly accurate. Returning military servicemen, who had grown up in downtown Philadelphia, came back to their sweethearts, got married and moved to the suburbs to begin a new life.

A revived Pop Warner Football Conference adopted a new set of rules which put a strong emphasis on the midget football program and restricted the older players from joining. There were also restrictions on minimum and maximum weights for the players, as well as new limits on 8- and 10-minute quarters. The Pop Warner Football Conference also debuted its new regulation size football field for the younger teams. Its dimensions were 40 yards wide and 80 yards in length.

Of the 88 teams which were fielded in 1946, 36 of these teams had players who were 15 years old or younger.

The Boom Begins

At the conclusion of the 1938 college football season, Pop Warner retired as the head football coach at Temple, while at the age of 68, and returned to Palo Alto, Calif., where he had previously lived during his years of coaching at Stanford University. Warner then served as an advisory coach to Dudley DeGroot at San Jose State for two seasons before finally retiring from football for good. DeGroot had previously played for Stanford in the early 1920's prior to Warner's arrival there.

However after leaving Philadelphia to return to the West Coast, both Warner and Joe Tomlin stayed in frequent contact by telephone and correspondence in letters. Warner continued to be a strong supporter of Tomlin's vision of a national youth football league and offered many suggestions and contacts for Tomlin to follow during his growing efforts to take the Pop Warner Football Conference to broader horizons.

Following World War II, one of Tomlin's and the Pop Warner Football Conference's biggest boosters was Frank Palumbo, who owned three restaurants in the Philadelphia area. Palumbo often hosted Pop Warner Football Conference meetings at his restaurants and always picked up the tab whenever league coaches and officials dined there.

In 1947, in an effort to bring national publicity to his restaurant chain, Palumbo suggested the idea that the Pop Warner Football Conference stage the nation's first inner-city "Kiddie Bowl," which would pit an outside opponent against a local Pop Warner team. Palumbo also offered to sponsor the local Pop Warner team and assist in promoting the event. Then in a master public relations move to get the big-city newspapers and radio stations interested in the game, Palumbo arranged to have the visiting team sponsored by his good friend, Frank Sinatra.

Finally on December 28, 1947, the initial Santa Claus Bowl was played. The contest matched Frank Palumbo's Clickets against Frank Sinatra's Cyclones, which was an all-star squad who hailed from the New York City area. It was played at South Philadelphia High School. The Santa Claus Bowl was co-promoted by *The Philadelphia Daily News* and had an advance sale of 5,000 tickets. In a hard-fought game, the Clickets won, 6-0.

The Santa Claus Bowl proved to be a major public relations bonanza for Palumbo's Click Supper Club, the restaurant chain for whom the Clickets team was named. Wire service stories of the game were picked up by newspaper and radio stations all across the country.

The Santa Claus Bowl series would enjoy many successes. A second competition was held the next season with the Clickets taking on a team from Durham, N.C. Later, matches against teams from Omaha, Neb., and Lynchburg, Va., were added and the teams played for a mythical "National 100-Pound Midget Football Championship."

The Santa Claus Bowl moved to Omaha in 1949 and then on to Lakeland, Fla., in 1951. There, it was broadcast nationally on the Mutual Radio Network for two years.

Joe Tomlin also helped to set up and promote other midget football Kiddie Bowl games. By 1954, he had already launched the Piggy Bank Bowl, the Toys for Tots Bowl and the Kids Army-Navy Game.

Then in 1956, the Pop Warner Football Conference took its most daring step since the boys football league in Northeast Philadelphia had been formed 27 years earlier when league officials voted to exclusively become a "midget" youth football association.

The Big Break

With the success of the Santa Claus Bowl and a strong network of Pop Warner teams in the greater Philadelphia area to build upon, Joe Tomlin continued to broaden the base of the Pop Warner Football Conference.

In the early 1950's, he was put on the payroll of Albert Zachary, who was another Pop Warner benefactor. Tomlin was paid $300 per week and only showed up at the office on Friday afternoons to pick up his paycheck. His sole task with Zachary's firm was to promote Pop Warner youth football.

Tomlin spent a considerable amount of time on the telephone with

Pop Warner during this period. Their strategy was to build a national youth football league very similar to that of Little League Baseball, which had also gotten its start in Pennsylvania. With a kitchen cabinet of Frank Palumbo, University of Pennsylvania athletic director George Munger and Tomlin, the national growth of the Pop Warner Football Conference began to slowly take shape.

This growth started with a Pop Warner youth football league being established in Northern California in the early 1950's. A second Pop Warner youth football league was later added in Southern California, near Los Angeles, in 1958.

It was the installation of the new Pop Warner franchise in Southern California that opened the long-awaited dose of public exposure which both Tomlin and the Pop Warner Football Conference needed to get their program to a new level of growth.

A few months after the Southern California youth football program had begun, Tomlin received a call from Walt Disney Studios, which is based in the Los Angeles suburb of Anaheim. The Disney officials asked Tomlin if the Pop Warner Football Conference would be willing to participate in the filming of a television program.

Years later, Tomlin would recall the experience. He explained; "So there we were. We had $500 in the bank and then came this call from Disney. We knew there wouldn't be another chance, so we said, 'We'd do it.' "

Suddenly, a decade of dreaming and much hard work had paid off.

The show, "Moochie of Pop Warner Football," was aired in 1960 on the Disney Television show on the ABC Network. (Note: This show is still occasionally aired on The Disney Channel on Cable T.V.)

Walt Disney, himself, took an interest in the Pop Warner-Disney project and was greatly impressed with Pop Warner Football's commitment toward academics. He later agreed to lend the Disney name to a new series of Kiddie Bowls which would be known as the "Pop Warner-Disneyland Bowl." In 1969, following the opening of Disney's second theme park in Orlando, Fla. Walt Disney World, the Pop Warner-Disney Kiddie Bowl series was expanded to include the "Walt Disney World Bowl."

These Disney-sponsored post-season games would continue until 1978.

Going National

The late 1950's brought much change to the Pop Warner Football Conference. It had been established some thirty years earlier in 1929, but the struggle to build a national organization had proved to be a difficult one.

The addition of the new leagues in Northern and Southern California had given hope to Joe Tomlin's dream of a national Pop Warner organization, but the other necessary ingredients to realize such a dream had yet to fall into place. Primarily, it needed a corporate sponsor.

Pop Warner, the great football coach who had originally inspired the fledgling youth league in the early 1930's and for whom the youth league was named, had died in 1954. He had been working on arranging a corporate sponsor for the Pop Warner Football Conference which would be a similar arrangement to Little League Baseball's sponsorship by the U.S. Rubber Company. But unfortunately, those plans weren't completed.

Now without a guiding influence to inspire him, Tomlin and his small army of league officials had to continue the work of building a national organization by themselves. In the years to come, they would be faced with many difficult obstacles.

The most pivotal of these occurred in 1958, when Pop Warner Football Conference officials were forced to notify the local leagues that it would not be able to continue overseeing their local leagues in the upcoming season. It was then that one of the local league presidents, Robert Miller, stepped forward in an attempt to salvage the Pop Warner Football Conference and hold the many local leagues together as an association.

The next year, in September 1959, Miller's efforts reached fruition when the Pop Warner Football Conference was reorganized and legally incorporated as "Pop Warner Little Scholars, Inc." Miller then set up a national organization, "The National Pop Warner Football Conference," which would oversee its many local leagues. Several years later, the League's name would be changed once more. This time it would adopt the title of "Pop Warner Junior League Football."

In an effort to fund the initial operations of The National Pop

Warner Football Conference, Miller and Tomlin asked the group's sixty trustees to each contribute $100. An office was then set up in the Northeast Philadelphia Chamber of Commerce Building, where, ironically, the Junior Football Conference had opened its original office thirty years earlier.

Knowing that their meager nest egg would not last long, Joe Tomlin and other Pop Warner officials next tried to secure permanent funding and support for its operations from an old friend of the Pop Warner youth football movement, Bert Bell, who had been an assistant to Pop Warner at Temple in 1933, then became the owner of the Philadelphia Eagles and, at the time was the Commissioner of the National Football League.

According to Tomlin, "a link-up with the N.F.L. looked promising at the time." Unfortunately, the link-up was never realized.

On October 11, 1959, Bell died while watching the closing minutes of a professional football game between the Philadelphia Eagles and the Pittsburgh Steelers. Sitting with him at the game that afternoon was his long-time friend, Tomlin. Several hours before the game, the two had discussed the details of wrapping up an N.F.L. sponsorship of the National Pop Warner Football Conference.

With the Pop Warner youth football program's future now uncertain and lacking a firm financial footing, Sam Daroff, a Pop Warner trustee from the Philadelphia area who had recently been named the chairman of The National Pop Warner Football Conference, stepped forward and organized a charity dinner to benefit the Pop Warner youth football program.

Daroff, who was an executive with Botany 500, the men's apparel firm, then called on all of his friends in the Philadelphia business community to buy tickets for the charity dinner. This event took place in the winter of 1961 and honored Joe Scott, one of the co-owners of the N.H.L.'s Philadelphia Flyers professional hockey franchise. The combination of professional and collegiate sports celebrities and prominent local business leaders insured that the affair would be a large success.

These banquets would become a permanent annual fixture beginning in 1964, and have since grown to become a vital part of the Pop

Warner Junior League Football program.

Initially, the annual banquets were called "The All-American Eleven Banquets" and honored eleven honorees each year, who were presented gold footballs by a Pop Warner "Little Scholar."

The banquet format was later revised in 1979 to honor a select number of Little Scholars from the many Pop Warner local youth leagues across the country.

Expansion Finally Arrives

In the early 1960's, the Pop Warner youth football program began a period of rapid expansion. The support of Walt Disney and the Walt Disney Studios gave the youth football league a strong dose of much-needed exposure. Eventually, Pop Warner leagues were formed in Florida, Georgia, Texas, North Carolina, Illinois, throughout California and in the Pacific Coast states.

In 1962, Joe Tomlin retired from his limousine business which he had set up in 1954 and began to run the Pop Warner youth football league's business activities full-time. Shortly thereafter, he moved their offices to downtown Philadelphia and quickly began to ride herd over a program that had finally started to grow into its potential.

In 1979, Pop Warner Junior League Football celebrated the 50th anniversary of its original formation in 1929 as the Junior Football Conference in Northeast Philadelphia. More than 1,000 people attended the league's golden anniversary dinner in downtown Philadelphia, which was put together by CBS-TV sports commentator Irv Cross.

At that point, the Pop Warner youth football program had a total of 130,000 players on 3,700 teams. This number included over 200 Pop Warner teams which were playing in Mexico.

During the 1970's, the Pop Warner movement expanded to bring girls into their newly-created Pop Warner Cheerleading Program. This new addition has since achieved tremendous growth.

In 1983, a major milestone was reached when the Russell Corporation, one of the largest manufacturers of athletic uniform and sports apparel in the U.S., entered into an agreement to be the corporate sponsor for the first-ever Pop Warner Junior Football League National Championships, which were to be held in Alexander City, Ala.

The Russell Corporation's sponsorship of these championships would continue for three years.

Also in 1983, flag football was added to the Pop Warner youth program as an alternative to the tackle football program.

In 1987, Nickelodeon, the children's cable T.V. channel, began to broadcast highlights of the Pop Warner national midget football championships on a one-hour, prime-time television show. This coverage would continue on through 1990 and provided the Pop Warner youth program with lots of exposure across the country.

In 1988, Pop Warner expanded across the Pacific and fielded its first local league in Japan. The Pop Warner National Cheerleading Championships also began that year and were held in conjunction with the youth program's national football championships.

Finally, after nearly sixty years of struggling, it seemed that the Pop Warner youth football program had arrived.

But on May 16, 1988, it, instead, faced one of its darkest hours when Joe Tomlin, the saintly founder of the Pop Warner organization passed away.

Tomlin, who was 85 at the time of his death, had nurtured the Pop Warner youth league since it was founded as the Youth Football Conference in Northeast Philadelphia in 1929. Together, they had weathered and overcome many difficulties, yet at the time of his death he had built a strong organization of over 175,000 boys and girls who were participating in the Pop Warner football and cheerleading programs.

The Journey Continues

In 1991, Pop Warner Little Scholars, Inc. hired Jon C. Butler, an executive with the Rae Crowther Company, a long-time successful manufacturer of football blocking sleds, which was located in the Philadelphia area, to become the organization's new executive director and fill the void that had been caused since Joe Tomlin's death.

With youth, a strong business acumen and a bundle of energy, Butler has begun to pick up where Joe Tomlin had left off in building an international youth football and cheerleading program.

Today, over 190,000 boys and girls are enjoying the fruits of the hard work that has gone into building the Pop Warner youth program.

Still, as one looks back to that modest neighborhood football coaching clinic that was held on an evening in April 1934, when sleet and freezing rains could have just as easily destroyed Joe Tomlin's dream of building a youth football program in the Philadelphia area, that dream was, instead, saved by a grandfatherly gentleman by the name of Glenn S. (Pop) Warner, who happened to be a legendary football coach and had believed in the promise of Tomlin's ambitious dream enough that evening to make it through the bad weather to support it.

Such an event inspired Tomlin to spend the rest of his life trying to make that dream come true. And at the time of his death in 1988, Joe Tomlin's dream had reached its full promise.

So this fall, when the football is being kicked off to begin another season of laughter, of glory and memories, it is inspiring to know that the legacy and the spirit of Pop Warner continues to live on in the neighborhood sandlot recreation fields and in the hearts of the youth of America and elsewhere around the world.

It is a special story that we can all be proud of.

Appendix

Pop Warner's
Career Highlights

ALL-TIME WINNINGEST COACH IN
MAJOR COLLEGE FOOTBALL
341 Wins, 118 Losses and 33 Ties

NEW YORK TOUCHDOWN CLUB'S
OUTSTANDING CONTRIBUTIONS TO FOOTBALL AWARD
Recipient - 1947

AMERICAN FOOTBALL COACHES ASSOCIATION
"COACH OF ALL AGES" AWARD
Recipient - 1951

NATIONAL FOOTBALL FOUNDATION'S
COLLEGE FOOTBALL HALL OF FAME
Inducted - 1951

HELM'S ATHLETIC FOUNDATION HALL OF FAME
Inducted - 1951

COLLEGE FOOTBALL NATIONAL CHAMPIONS
Pittsburgh - 1915
Pittsburgh - 1916
Pittsburgh - 1918
Stanford - 1926

PACIFIC COAST CONFERENCE FOOTBALL CHAMPIONS
Stanford - 1924
Stanford - 1926
Stanford - 1927

ALL-AMERICA PLAYERS - 30

Glenn S. (Pop) Warner
Season-By-Season Record

Year	School	Won	Lost	Tied	Pts.	Opp.
1895	Iowa State (1)	3	3	0	102	53
	Georgia	3	4	0	98	44
1896	Iowa State (1)	8	2	0	305	46
	Georgia	4	0	0	88	22
1897	Iowa State (1)	3	1	0	34	22
	Cornell	5	3	1	133	42
1898	Iowa State (2)	3	2	0	49	50
	Cornell	10	2	0	296	29
1899	Iowa State (2)	5	4	1	118	78
	Carlisle Indian School	9	2	0	364	50
1900	Carlisle Indian School	6	4	1	211	92
1901	Carlisle Indian School	5	7	1	133	168
1902	Carlisle Indian School	8	3	0	251	51
1903	Carlisle Indian School	11	2	1	274	52
1904	Cornell	7	3	0	226	92
1905	Cornell	6	4	0	173	59
1906	Cornell	8	1	2	237	37
1907	Carlisle Indian School	10	1	0	267	62
1908	Carlisle Indian School	11	2	1	234	55
1909	Carlisle Indian School	8	3	1	243	94
1910	Carlisle Indian School	8	6	0	235	68
1911	Carlisle Indian School	11	1	0	298	49
1912	Carlisle Indian School	12	1	1	504	114
1913	Carlisle Indian School	10	1	1	296	63
1914	Carlisle Indian School	5	9	1	125	174
1915	Pittsburgh	8	0	0	247	26
1916	Pittsburgh	8	0	0	255	25
1917	Pittsburgh	10	0	0	260	31
1918	Pittsburgh	4	1	0	140	16
1919	Pittsburgh	6	2	1	119	66

1920	Pittsburgh	6	0	2	146	44
1921	Pittsburgh	5	3	1	133	50
1922	Pittsburgh	8	2	0	190	43
1923	Pittsburgh	5	4	0	83	45
1924	Stanford	7	1	1	179	69
1925	Stanford	7	2	0	230	71
1926	Stanford	10	0	1	268	86
1927	Stanford	8	2	1	151	75
1928	Stanford	8	3	1	274	69
1929	Stanford	9	2	0	288	53
1930	Stanford	9	1	1	252	69
1931	Stanford	7	2	2	160	44
1932	Stanford	6	4	1	171	58
1933	Temple	5	3	0	110	96
1934	Temple	7	1	2	220	57
1935	Temple	7	3	0	181	68
1936	Temple	6	3	2	117	66
1937	Temple	3	2	4	38	59
1938	Temple	3	6	1	97	170
		341	118	33	9,584	3,121

(1) - Bert German, an assistant coach, filled in for Pop Warner in coaching the Iowa State team during a portion of the 1895, 1896 and 1897 seasons.
(2) - Joe Meyers, an assistant coach, filled in for Pop Warner in coaching the Iowa State team during a portion of the 1898 and 1899 seasons.

All-America Players

Year	Player	School	Position
1899	Isaac Seneca	Carlisle	Back
1903	Jimmy Johnson	Carlisle	Back
1906	Bill Newman	Cornell	Center
	Elmer Thompson	Cornell	Guard
1907	Albert Exendine	Carlisle	End
	Peter Hauser	Carlisle	Back
1911	Jim Thorpe	Carlisle	Back
1912	Jim Thorpe	Carlisle	Back
1915	Bob Peck	Pittsburgh	Center
1916	Bob Peck	Pittsburgh	Center
	Andy Hastings	Pittsburgh	Back
	James Herron	Pittsburgh	End
	Claude Thornhill	Pittsburgh	Guard
1917	H.C. Carlson	Pittsburgh	End
	Jock Sutherland	Pittsburgh	Guard
	Dale Seis	Pittsburgh	Guard
	George McLaren	Pittsburgh	Back
1918	Tom Davies	Pittsburgh	Back
	Leonard Hilty	Pittsburgh	Tackle
	George McLaren	Pittsburgh	Back
1920	Herb Stein	Pittsburgh	Center
	Tom Davies	Pittsburgh	Back
1921	Herb Stein	Pittsburgh	Center
1924	Jim Lawson	Stanford	End
1925	Ernie Nevers	Stanford	Back
1926	Ted Shipkey	Stanford	End
1928	Seraphim Post	Stanford	Guard
	Don Robesky	Stanford	Guard
1930	Phil Moffatt	Stanford	Back
1932	Bill Corbus	Stanford	Guard

Glenn S. (Pop) Warner Career Coaching Record

IOWA STATE COLLEGE ERA

1895
(3-3-0)
Captain: Ed Mellinger

Date	Opponent	Where	I.S.C.	Opp.	
Sept. 15	Butte Athletic Club	Butte, Mont.	10	13	L
Sept. 28	Northwestern	Evanston, Ill.	36	0	W
Sept. 30	Wisconsin	Madison, Wis.	6	12	L
Oct. 12	Sioux City Athletics	Sioux City, Ia.	26	4	W
Oct. 19	Minnesota	Minneapolis, Minn.	0	24	L
Oct. 28	Iowa	Iowa City, Ia.	24	0	W
			102	53	

1896
(8-2-0)
Captain: Jim Wilson

Date	Opponent	Where	I.S.C.	Opp.	
Sept. 4	Iowa Falls	Eldora, Ia.	46	0	W
Sept. 5	Cornell (Iowa)	Eldora, Ia.	50	0	W
Oct. 2	Missouri	Columbia, Mo.	12	0	W
Oct. 17	Des Moines Y.M.C.A.	Des Moines, Ia.	24	16	W
Oct. 24	Minnesota	Minneapolis, Minn.	6	18	L
Oct. 30	Simpson	Ames, Ia.	44	0	W
Nov. 7	Grinnell	Des Moines, Ia.	42	0	W
Nov. 19	Nebraska	Lincoln, Neb.	4	12	L
Nov. 21	Des Moines Y.M.C.A.	Des Moines, Ia.	15	0	W
Nov. 28	Eldora	Eldora, Ia.	62	0	W
			305	46	

1897
(3-1-0)
Captain: None

Date	Opponent	Where	I.S.C.	Opp.	
Oct. 8	Nebraska	Ames, Ia.	10	0	W
Oct. 23	Minnesota	Minneapolis, Minn.	12	10	W
Oct. 30	Grinnell	Grinnell, Ia.	6	12	L
Nov. 5	Iowa	Iowa City, Ia.	6	0	W
			34	22	

1898
(3-2-0)
Captain: Simon Tarr

Date	Opponent	Where	I.S.C.	Opp.	
Oct. 1	Rush Medical College	Ames, Ia.	10	0	W
Oct. 8	Nebraska	Lincoln, Neb.	10	23	L
Oct. 15	Kansas	Lawrence, Kan.	6	11	L
Oct. 22	Minnesota	Minneapolis, Minn.	6	0	W
Oct. 29	Drake	Ames, Ia.	17	16	W
			49	50	

1899
(5-4-1)
Captain: C. J. Griffith

Date	Opponent	Where	I.S.C.	Opp.	
Sept. 16	Panora	Panora, Ia.	23	0	W
Sept. 30	Cornell (Iowa)	Mt. Vernon, Ia.	32	0	W
Oct. 6	Nebraska	Ames, Ia.	34	0	W
Oct. 11	Simpson	Indianola, Ia.	18	0	W
Oct. 14	South Dakota	Souix City, Ia.	11	6	W
Oct. 21	Minnesota	Minneapolis, Minn.	0	6	L
Oct. 28	Iowa	Iowa City, Ia.	0	5	L
Nov. 4	Grinnell	Des Moines, Ia.	0	55	L
Nov. 11	Northern Iowa	Cedar Falls, Ia.	0	0	T
Nov. 18	Grinnell	Ames, Ia.	0	6	L
			118	78	

UNIVERSITY OF GEORGIA ERA

1895
(3-4-0)
Captain: H. W. Stubbs

Date	Opponent	Where	Ga.	Opp.	
Oct. 19	Wofford	Athens, Ga.	34	0	W
Oct. 26	North Carolina	Atlanta, Ga.	0	6	L
Oct. 31	North Carolina	Atlanta, Ga.	6	10	L
Nov. 2	Alabama	Columbus, Ga.	30	6	W
Nov. 18	Sewanee	Atlanta, Ga.	22	0	W
Nov. 23	Vanderbilt	Nashville, Tenn.	0	6	L
Nov. 28	Auburn	Atlanta, Ga.	6	16	L
			98	44	

1896
(4-0-0)
Captain: R. B. McNalley

Date	Opponent	Where	Ga.	Opp.	
Oct. 24	Wofford	Spartanburg, S.C.	26	0	W
Oct. 31	North Carolina	Atlanta, Ga.	24	16	W
Nov. 9	Sewanee	Athens, Ga.	26	0	W
Nov. 26	Auburn	Atlanta, Ga.	12	6	W
			88	22	

CORNELL UNIVERSITY ERA

1897
(5-3-1)
Captain: William McKeever

Date	Opponent	Where	C.U.	Opp.	
Sept. 25	Colgate	Ithaca, N.Y.	6	0	W
Oct. 2	Syracuse	Ithaca, N.Y.	16	0	W
Oct. 9	Tufts	Ithaca, N.Y.	15	0	W
Oct. 16	Lafayette	Easton, Pa.	4	4	T
Oct. 23	Princeton	Ithaca, N.Y.	0	10	L
Oct. 30	Harvard	Cambridge, Mass.	5	24	L
Nov. 6	Penn State	Ithaca, N.Y.	45	0	W
Nov. 13	Williams	Buffalo, N.Y.	42	0	W
Nov. 25	Pennsylvania	Philadelphia, Pa.	0	4	L
			133	42	

1898
(10-2-0)
Captain: Allen E. Whiting

Date	Opponent	Where	C.U.	Opp.	
Sept. 21	Syracuse	Ithaca, N.Y.	28	0	W
Sept. 24	Colgate	Ithaca, N.Y.	29	5	W
Sept. 28	Hamilton	Ithaca, N.Y.	41	0	W
Oct. 1	Trinity	Ithaca, N.Y.	47	0	W
Oct. 5	Syracuse	Syracuse, N.Y.	30	0	W
Oct. 8	Carlisle	Ithaca, N.Y.	23	6	W
Oct. 15	Buffalo	Ithaca, N.Y.	27	0	W
Oct. 22	Princeton	Princeton, N.J.	0	6	L
Oct. 29	Oberlin	Ithaca, N.Y.	6	0	W
Nov. 5	Williams	Buffalo, N.Y.	12	0	W
Nov. 12	Lafayette	Ithaca, N.Y.	47	0	W
Nov. 24	Pennsylvania	Philadelphia, Pa.	6	12	L
			296	29	

CARLISLE INDIAN SCHOOL ERA

1899
(9-2-0)
Captain: Martin Wheelock

Date	Opponent	Where	C.I.S.	Opp.	
Sept. 23	Gettysburg	Carlisle, Pa.	21	0	W
Sept. 30	Susquehanna	Carlisle, Pa.	56	0	W
Oct. 14	Pennsylvania	Philadelphia, Pa.	16	5	W
Oct. 21	Dickinson	Carlisle, Pa.	16	5	W
Oct. 28	Harvard	Cambridge, Mass.	12	22	L
Nov. 4	Hamilton	Utica, N.Y.	32	0	W
Nov. 11	Princeton	New York, N.Y.	0	12	L
Nov. 18	Maryland (1)				
Nov. 25	Oberlin	Carlisle, Pa.	81	0	W
Nov. 30	Columbia (2)	New York, N.Y.	45	0	W
Dec. 22	California	San Francisco, Calif.	2	0	W
Jan. 1, 1900	Phoenix Indian School	Phoenix, Ariz.	83	6	W
			364	50	

(1) - Game cancelled.
(2) - Game played at the Polo Grounds, New York, N.Y.

1900
(6-4-1)
Captain: Edward Rogers

Date	Opponent	Where	C.I.S.	Opp.	
Sept. 22	Lebanon Valley	Carlisle, Pa.	34	0	W
Sept. 26	Dickinson	Carlisle, Pa.	21	0	W
Sept. 29	Susquehanna	Carlisle, Pa.	46	0	W
Oct. 6	Gettysburg	Carlisle, Pa.	45	0	W
Oct. 13	Virginia	Washington, D.C.	16	2	W
Oct. 15	Maryland	Baltimore, Md.	27	0	W
Oct. 27	Harvard	Cambridge, Mass.	5	17	L
Nov. 10	Yale	New Haven, Conn.	0	35	L
Nov. 17	Pennsylvania	Philadelphia, Pa.	6	16	L
Nov. 24	Washington & Jefferson	Pittsburgh, Pa.	5	5	T
Nov. 29	Columbia	New York, N.Y.	6	17	L
			211	92	

1901
(5-7-1)
Captain: Isaac Seneca

Date	Opponent	Where	C.I.S.	Opp.	
Sept. 21	Lebanon Valley	Carlisle, Pa.	28	0	W
Sept. 28	Gallaudet	Carlisle, Pa.	19	6	W
Oct. 2	Gettysburg	Harrisburg, Pa.	5	6	L
Oct. 5	Dickinson	Carlisle, Pa.	15	11	W
Oct. 12	Bucknell	Williamsport, Pa.	6	5	W
Oct. 16	Haverford	Carlisle, Pa.	29	0	W
Oct. 19	Cornell	Buffalo, N.Y.	0	17	L
Oct. 26	Harvard	Cambridge, Mass.	0	29	L
Nov. 2	Michigan	Detroit, Mich.	0	22	L
Nov. 9	Navy	Annapolis, Md.	5	16	L
Nov. 16	Pennsylvania	Philadelphia, Pa.	14	16	L
Nov. 23	Washington & Jefferson	Pittsburgh, Pa.	0	0	T
Nov. 28	Columbia	New York, N.Y.	12	40	L
			133	168	

1902
(8-3-0)
Captain: Charles Williams

Date	Opponent	Where	C.I.S.	Opp.	
Sept. 20	Lebanon Valley	Carlisle, Pa.	48	0	W
Sept. 27	Gettysburg	Carlisle, Pa.	25	0	W
Oct. 4	Dickinson (1)				
Oct. 11	Bucknell	Williamsport, Pa.	0	16	L
Oct. 15	Bloomsburg Normal	Carlisle, Pa	50	0	W
Oct. 18	Cornell	Ithaca, N.Y.	10	6	W
Oct. 25	Medico Chi	Carlisle, Pa.	63	0	W
Nov. 1	Harvard	Cambridge, Mass.	0	23	L
Nov. 8	Susquehanna	Carlisle, Pa.	24	0	W
Nov. 15	Pennsylvania	Philadelphia, Pa.	5	0	W
Nov. 22	Virginia	Norfolk, Va.	5	6	L
Nov. 27	Georgetown	Washington, D.C.	21	0	W
			251	51	

(1) - Game cancelled.

1903
(11-2-1)
Captain: James Johnson

Date	Opponent	Where	C.I.S.	Opp.	
Sept. 19	Lebanon Valley	Carlisle, Pa.	28	0	W
Sept. 26	Gettysburg	Carlisle, Pa.	46	0	W
Sept. 30	Mt. St. Mary's (1)				
Oct. 3	Bucknell	Williamsport, Pa.	12	0	W
Oct. 7	Bloomsburg Normal (1)				
Oct. 10	Franklin & Marshall	Lancaster, Pa.	30	0	W
Oct. 17	Princeton	Princeton, N.J.	0	11	L
Oct. 24	Swarthmore	Carlisle, Pa.	12	5	W
Oct. 31	Harvard	Cambridge, Mass.	11	12	L
Nov. 7	Georgetown	Washington, D.C.	28	6	W
Nov. 14	Pennsylvania	Philadelphia, Pa.	16	6	W
Nov. 21	Virginia	Norfolk, Va.	6	6	T
Nov. 26	Northwestern	Chicago, Ill.	28	0	W
Dec. 19	Utah	Salt Lake City, Ut.	22	0	W
Dec. 25	Reliance A.A.	San Francisco, Calif.	23	0	W
Jan. 1, 1904	Sherman Institute	Riverside, Calif.	12	6	W
			274	52	

(1) - Game cancelled.

CORNELL UNIVERSITY ERA

1904
(7-3-0)
Captain: James Lynch

Date	Opponent	Where	C.U.	Opp.	
Sept. 28	Colgate	Ithaca, N.Y.	17	0	W
Oct. 1	Rochester	Ithaca, N.Y.	29	6	W
Oct. 5	Hobart	Ithaca, N.Y.	24	0	W
Oct. 8	Hamilton	Ithaca, N.Y.	34	0	W
Oct. 15	Bucknell	Ithaca, N.Y.	24	12	W
Oct. 22	Franklin & Marshall	Ithaca, N.Y	36	5	W
Oct. 29	Princeton	Ithaca, N.Y.	6	18	L
Nov. 5	Lehigh	Ithaca, N.Y.	50	5	W
Nov. 12	Columbia	New York, N.Y.	6	12	L
Nov. 24	Pennsylvania	Philadelphia, Pa.	0	34	L
			226	92	

1905
(6-4-0)
Captain: James Castello

Date	Opponent	Where	C.U.	Opp.	
Sept. 27	Hamilton	Ithaca, N.Y.	5	0	W
Sept. 30	Colgate	Ithaca, N.Y.	12	11	W
Oct. 4	Hobart	Ithaca, N.Y.	28	0	W
Oct. 7	Bucknell	Ithaca, N.Y.	24	0	W
Oct. 21	Pittsburgh	Ithaca, N.Y.	30	0	W
Oct. 28	Haverford	Ithaca, N.Y.	57	0	W
Nov. 4	Swarthmore	Ithaca, N.Y.	0	14	L
Nov. 11	Princeton	Princeton, N.J.	6	16	L
Nov. 18	Columbia	Ithaca, N.Y.	6	12	L
Nov. 30	Pennsylvania	Philadelphia, Pa.	5	6	L
			173	59	

1906
(8-1-2)
Captain: George Cook

Date	Opponent	Where	C.U.	Opp.	
Sept. 29	Colgate	Ithaca, N.Y.	0	0	T
Oct. 3	Hamilton	Ithaca, N.Y.	21	0	W
Oct. 6	Oberlin	Ithaca, N.Y.	25	5	W
Oct. 10	Niagra	Ithaca, N.Y.	23	6	W
Oct. 13	Bucknell	Ithaca, N.Y.	24	6	W
Oct. 20	Bowdoin	Ithaca, N.Y.	72	0	W
Oct. 27	Princeton (1)	New York, N.Y.	5	14	L
Nov. 3	Pittsburgh	Ithaca, N.Y.	23	0	W
Nov. 10	Holy Cross	Ithaca, N.Y.	16	6	W
Nov. 17	Swarthmore	Ithaca, N.Y.	28	0	W
Nov. 29	Pennsylvania	Philadelphia, Pa.	0	0	T
			237	37	

(1) - Game played at the Polo Grounds, New York, N.Y.

CARLISLE INDIAN SCHOOL ERA

1907
(10-1-0)
Captain: Antonio Lubo

Date	Opponent	Where	C.I.S.	Opp.	
Sept. 21	Lebanon Valley	Carlisle, Pa.	40	0	W
Sept. 28	Villanova	Carlisle, Pa.	10	0	W
Oct. 2	Susquehanna	Carlisle, Pa.	91	0	W
Oct. 5	Penn State	Williamsport, Pa.	18	5	W
Oct. 12	Syracuse	Buffalo, N.Y.	14	6	W
Oct. 19	Bucknell	Carlisle, Pa.	15	0	W
Oct. 26	Pennsylvania	Philadelphia, Pa.	26	6	W
Nov. 2	Princeton	New York, N.Y.	0	16	L
Nov. 9	Harvard	Cambridge, Mass.	23	15	W
Nov. 16	Minnesota	Minneapolis, Minn.	12	10	W
Nov. 23	Chicago	Chicago, Ill.	18	4	W
			267	62	

1908
(11-2-1)
Captain: Emil Wauseka

Date	Opponent	Where	C.I.S.	Opp.	
Sept. 19	Conway Hall	Carlisle, Pa.	53	0	W
Sept. 23	Lebanon Valley	Carlisle, Pa.	39	0	W
Sept. 26	Villanova	Carlisle, Pa.	10	0	W
Oct. 3	Penn State	Wilkes-Barre, Pa.	12	5	W
Oct. 10	Syracuse	Buffalo, N.Y.	12	0	W
Oct. 17	Susquehanna (1)				
Oct. 24	Pennsylvania	Philadelphia, Pa.	6	6	T
Oct. 31	Navy	Annapolis, Md.	16	6	W
Nov. 7	Harvard	Cambridge, Mass.	0	17	L
Nov. 14	Pittsburgh	Pittsburgh, Pa.	6	0	W
Nov. 21	Minnesota	Minneapolis, Minn.	6	11	L
Nov. 26	St. Louis	St. Louis, Mo.	17	0	W
Nov. 30	Haskell	Lawrence, Kan.	12	0	W
Dec. 2	Nebraska	Lincoln, Neb.	37	6	W
Dec. 5	Denver	Denver, Colo.	8	4	W
			234	55	

(1) - Game cancelled.

1909
(8-3-1)
Captain: Joseph Libby

Date	Opponent	Where	C.I.S.	Opp.	
Sept. 18	Steelton Athletic Club	Carlisle, Pa.	35	0	W
Sept. 22	Lebanon Valley	Carlisle, Pa.	36	0	W
Sept. 25	Villanova	Carlisle, Pa.	9	0	W
Oct. 2	Bucknell	Carlisle, Pa.	48	6	W
Oct. 9	Penn State	Wilkes-Barre, Pa.	8	8	T
Oct. 16	Syracuse	Buffalo, N.Y.	14	11	W
Oct. 23	Pittsburgh	Pittsburgh, Pa.	3	14	L
Oct. 30	Pennsylvania	Philadelphia, Pa.	6	29	L
Nov. 6	George Washington	Washington, D.C.	9	5	W
Nov. 13	Gettysburg	Carlisle, Pa.	35	0	W
Nov. 20	Brown (1)	New York, N.Y.	8	21	L
Nov. 25	St. Louis	Cincinnati, Ohio	32	0	W
			243	94	

(1) - Game played at the Polo Grounds, New York, N.Y.

1910
(8-6-0)
Captain: Peter Hauser

Date	Opponent	Where	C.I.S.	Opp.	
Sept. 21	Lebanon Valley	Carlisle, Pa.	53	0	W
Sept. 24	Villanova	Harrisburg, Pa.	6	0	W
Sept. 28	Muhlenberg	Carlisle, Pa.	39	0	W
Oct. 1	Western Maryland (1)				
Oct. 5	Dickinson	Carlisle, Pa.	24	0	W
Oct. 8	Bucknell	Wilkes-Barre, Pa.	39	0	W
Oct. 11	Gettysburg	Carlisle, Pa.	29	3	W
Oct. 15	Syracuse	Syracuse, N.Y.	0	14	L
Oct. 22	Princeton	Princeton, N.J.	0	6	L
Oct. 29	Pennsylvania	Philadelphia, Pa.	5	17	L
Nov. 5	Virginia	Washington, D.C.	22	5	W
Nov. 12	Navy	Annapolis, Md.	0	5	L
Nov. 16	Harvard Law School	Cambridge, Mass.	0	3	L
Nov. 19	Johns Hopkins	Baltimore, Md.	12	0	W
Nov. 24	Brown	Providence, R.I.	6	15	L
			235	68	

(1) - Game cancelled.

1911
(11-1-0)
Captain: Sam Burd

Date	Opponent	Where	C.I.S.	Opp.	
Sept. 23	Lebanon Valley	Carlisle, Pa.	53	0	W
Sept. 27	Muhlenberg	Carlisle, Pa.	32	0	W
Sept. 30	Dickinson	Carlisle, Pa.	17	0	W
Oct. 7	Mount St. Mary's	Carlisle, Pa.	46	5	W
Oct. 14	Georgetown	Washington, D.C.	28	5	W
Oct. 21	Pittsburgh	Pittsburgh, Pa.	17	0	W
Oct. 28	Lafayette	Easton, Pa.	19	0	W
Nov. 4	Pennsylvania	Philadelphia, Pa.	16	0	W
Nov. 11	Harvard	Cambridge, Mass.	18	15	W
Nov. 18	Syracuse	Syracuse, N.Y.	11	12	L
Nov. 25	Johns Hopkins	Baltimore, Md.	29	6	W
Nov. 30	Brown	Providence, R.I.	12	6	W
			298	49	

1912
(12-1-1)
Captain: Jim Thorpe

Date	Opponent	Where	C.I.S.	Opp.	
Sept. 21	Albright	Carlisle, Pa.	50	7	W
Sept. 25	Lebanon Valley	Carlisle, Pa.	45	0	W
Sept. 28	Dickinson	Carlisle, Pa.	34	0	W
Oct. 2	Villanova	Harrisburg, Pa.	65	0	W
Oct. 5	Washington & Jefferson	Washington, Pa.	0	0	T
Oct. 12	Syracuse	Syracuse, N.Y.	33	0	W
Oct. 19	Pittsburgh	Pittsburgh, Pa.	45	8	W
Oct. 26	Georgetown	Washington, D.C.	34	20	W
Oct. 28	Toronto	Toronto, Ontario	49	1	W
Nov. 2	Lehigh	Bethlehem, Pa.	34	14	W
Nov. 9	Army	West Point, N.Y.	27	6	W
Nov. 16	Pennsylvania	Philadelphia, Pa.	26	34	L
Nov. 23	Springfield Y.M.C.A. College	Springfield, Mass.	30	24	W
Nov. 28	Brown	Providence, R.I.	32	0	W
			504	114	

1913
(10-1-1)
Captain: Gus Welch

Date	Opponent	Where	C.I.S.	Opp.	
Sept. 20	Albright	Carlisle, Pa.	26	0	W
Sept. 24	Lebanon Valley	Carlisle, Pa.	26	0	W
Sept. 27	West Virginia Wesleyan	Carlisle, Pa.	25	0	W
Oct. 4	Lehigh	Bethlehem, Pa.	21	7	W
Oct. 11	Cornell	Ithaca, N.Y.	7	0	W
Oct. 18	Pittsburgh	Pittsburgh, Pa.	6	12	L
Oct. 25	Pennsylvania	Philadelphia, Pa.	7	7	T
Nov. 1	Georgetown	Washington, D.C.	34	0	W
Nov. 8	Johns Hopkins	Baltimore, Md.	61	0	W
Nov. 15	Dartmouth	New York, N.Y.	35	10	W
Nov. 22	Syracuse	Syracuse, N.Y.	35	27	W
Nov. 27	Brown	Providence, R.I.	13	0	W
			296	63	

1914
(5-9-1)
Captain: Peter Busch

Date	Opponent	Where	C.I.S.	Opp.	
Sept. 19	Albright	Carlisle, Pa.	20	0	W
Sept. 23	Lebanon Valley	Carlisle, Pa.	7	0	W
Sept. 26	West Virginia Wesleyan	Clarksburg, W. Va.	6	0	W
Oct. 3	Lehigh	Bethlehem, Pa.	6	21	L
Oct. 10	Cornell	Ithaca, N.Y.	0	21	L
Oct. 17	Pittsburgh	Pittsburgh, Pa.	3	10	L
Oct. 24	Pennsylvania	Philadelphia, Pa.	0	7	L
Oct. 31	Syracuse	Buffalo, N.Y.	3	24	L
Nov. 7	Holy Cross	Manchester, N.H.	0	0	T
Nov. 14	Notre Dame	Chicago, Ill.	6	48	L
Nov. 21	Dickinson	Carlisle, Pa.	34	0	W
Nov. 26	Brown	Providence, R.I.	14	20	L
Nov. 28	New England All-Stars (1)	Boston, Mass.	6	13	L
Dec. 2	Alabama	Birmingham, Ala.	20	3	W
Dec. 5	Auburn	Atlanta, Ga.	0	7	L
			125	174	

(1) - Game played at Fenway Park, Boston, Mass.

UNIVERSITY OF PITTSBURGH ERA

1915
(8-0-0)
Captain: Guy Williamson

Date	Opponent	Where	Pitt	Opp.	
Oct. 2	Westminster	Pittsburgh, Pa.	32	0	W
Oct. 9	Navy	Annapolis, Md.	47	12	W
Oct. 16	Carlisle	Pittsburgh, Pa.	45	0	W
Oct. 23	Pennsylvania	Philadelphia, Pa.	14	7	W
Oct. 30	Allegheny	Pittsburgh, Pa.	42	7	W
Nov. 6	Washington & Jefferson	Pittsburgh, Pa.	19	0	W
Nov. 13	Carnegie Tech	Pittsburgh, Pa.	28	0	W
Nov. 25	Penn State	Pittsburgh, Pa.	20	0	W
			247	26	

1916
(8-0-0)
Captain: Bob Peck

Date	Opponent	Where	Pitt	Opp.	
Sept. 30	Buffalo (1)				
Oct. 7	Westminster	Pittsburgh, Pa.	57	0	W
Oct. 14	Navy	Annapolis, Md.	20	19	W
Oct. 21	Syracuse	Syracuse, N.Y.	30	0	W
Oct. 28	Pennsylvania	Pittsburgh, Pa.	20	0	W
Nov. 4	Allegheny	Pittsburgh, Pa.	46	0	W
Nov. 11	Washington & Jefferson	Pittsburgh, Pa.	37	0	W
Nov. 18	Carnegie Tech	Pittsburgh, Pa.	14	6	W
Nov. 30	Penn State	Pittsburgh, Pa.	31	0	W
			255	25	

(1) - Game cancelled.

1917
(10-0-0)
Captain: H.C. (Doc) Carlson

Date	Opponent	Where	Pitt	Opp.	
Sept. 29	West Virginia	Morganstown, W. Va.	14	9	W
Oct. 6	Bethany	Pittsburgh, Pa.	40	0	W
Oct. 13	Lehigh	Pittsburgh, Pa.	41	0	W
Oct. 20	Syracuse	Pittsburgh, Pa.	28	0	W
Oct. 27	Pennsylvania	Philadelphia, Pa.	14	6	W
Nov. 3	Westminster	Pittsburgh, Pa.	25	0	W
Nov. 10	Washington & Jefferson	Pittsburgh, Pa.	13	10	W
Nov. 17	Carnegie Tech	Pittsburgh, Pa.	27	0	W
Nov. 29	Penn State	Pittsburgh, Pa.	28	6	W
Dec. 1	Camp Lee All-Stars	Pittsburgh, Pa.	30	0	W
			260	31	

1918
(4-1-0)
Captain: George McLaren

Date	Opponent	Where	Pitt	Opp.	
Nov. 9	Washington & Jefferson	Pittsburgh, Pa.	34	0	W
Nov. 16	Pennsylvania	Pittsburgh, Pa.	37	0	W
Nov. 23	Georgia Tech	Pittsburgh, Pa.	32	0	W
Nov. 28	Penn State	Pittsburgh, Pa.	28	6	W
Nov. 30	Cleveland Naval Reserves	Cleveland, Ohio	9	10	L
			140	16	

1919
(6-2-1)
Captain: Jimmy DeHart

Date	Opponent	Where	Pitt	Opp.	
Oct. 4	Geneva	Beaver Falls, Pa.	33	0	W
Oct. 11	West Virginia	Pittsburgh, Pa.	26	0	W
Oct. 18	Syracuse	Syracuse, N.Y.	3	24	L
Oct. 25	Georgia Tech	Pittsburgh, Pa.	16	6	W
Nov. 1	Lehigh	Bethlehem, Pa.	14	0	W
Nov. 8	Washington & Jefferson	Pittsburgh, Pa.	7	6	W
Nov. 15	Pennsylvania	Philadelphia, Pa.	3	3	T
Nov. 22	Carnegie Tech	Pittsburgh, Pa.	17	7	W
Nov. 27	Penn State	Pittsburgh, Pa.	0	20	L
			119	66	

1920
(6-0-2)
Captain: Herb Stein

Date	Opponent	Where	Pitt	Opp.	
Oct. 2	Geneva	Beaver Falls, Pa.	47	0	W
Oct. 9	West Virginia	Pittsburgh, Pa.	34	13	W
Oct. 16	Syracuse	Syracuse, N.Y.	7	7	T
Oct. 23	Georgia Tech	Pittsburgh, Pa.	10	3	W
Oct. 30	Lafayette	Pittsburgh, Pa.	14	0	W
Nov. 6	Pennsylvania	Philadelphia, Pa.	27	21	W
Nov. 13	Washington & Jefferson	Pittsburgh, Pa.	7	0	W
Nov. 25	Penn State	Pittsburgh, Pa.	0	0	T
			146	44	

1921
(5-3-1)
Captain: Tom Davies

Date	Opponent	Where	Pitt	Opp.	
Sept. 24	Geneva	Beaver Falls, Pa.	28	0	W
Oct. 1	Lafayette	Easton, Pa.	0	6	L
Oct. 8	West Virginia	Pittsburgh, Pa.	21	13	W
Oct. 15	Cincinnati	Pittsburgh, Pa.	21	14	W
Oct. 22	Syracuse	Pittsburgh, Pa.	35	0	W
Oct. 29	Pennsylvania	Philadelphia, Pa.	28	0	W
Nov. 5	Nebraska	Pittsburgh, Pa.	0	10	L
Nov. 12	Washington & Jefferson	Pittsburgh, Pa.	0	7	L
Nov. 24	Penn State	Pittsburgh, Pa.	0	0	T
			133	50	

1922
(8-2-0)
Captain: Tom Holleran

Date	Opponent	Where	Pitt	Opp.	
Sept. 30	Cincinnati	Cincinnati, Ohio	38	0	W
Oct. 7	Lafayette	Pittsburgh, Pa.	0	7	L
Oct. 14	West Virginia	Pittsburgh, Pa.	6	9	L
Oct. 21	Syracuse	Syracuse, N.Y.	21	14	W
Oct. 28	Bucknell	Pittsburgh, Pa.	7	0	W
Nov. 4	Geneva	Pittsburgh, Pa.	62	0	W
Nov. 11	Pennsylvania	Philadelphia, Pa.	7	6	W
Nov. 18	Washington & Jefferson	Pittsburgh, Pa.	19	0	W
Nov. 30	Penn State	Pittsburgh, Pa.	14	0	W
Dec. 30	Stanford	Palo Alto, Calif.	16	7	W
			190	43	

1923
(5-4-0)
Captain: Lloyd Jordan

Date	Opponent	Where	Pitt	Opp.	
Sept. 29	Bucknell	Lewisburg, Pa.	21	0	W
Oct. 6	Lafayette	Pittsburgh, Pa.	7	0	W
Oct. 13	West Virginia	Pittsburgh, Pa.	7	13	L
Oct. 20	Syracuse (1)	New York, N.Y.	0	3	L
Oct. 27	Carnegie Tech	Pittsburgh, Pa.	2	7	L
Nov. 3	Pennsylvania	Philadelphia, Pa.	0	6	L
Nov. 10	Grove City	Pittsburgh, Pa.	13	7	W
Nov. 17	Washington & Jefferson	Pittsburgh, Pa.	13	6	W
Nov. 29	Penn State	Pittsburgh, Pa.	20	3	W
			83	45	

(1) - Game played at Yankee Stadium, New York, N.Y.

STANFORD UNIVERSITY ERA

1924
(7-1-1)
Captain: Jim Lawson

Date	Opponent	Where	Stan.	Opp.	
Oct. 4	Occidental	Palo Alto, Calif.	20	6	W
Oct. 11	Olympic Club	Palo Alto, Calif.	7	0	W
Oct. 18	Oregon	Palo Alto, Calif.	28	13	W
Oct. 25	Idaho (1)	Portland, Ore.	3	0	W
Oct. 31	Santa Clara	Palo Alto, Calif.	20	0	W
Nov. 8	U.S.C. (2)				
Nov. 8	Utah (3)	Berkeley, Calif.	30	0	W
Nov. 15	Montana	Palo Alto, Calif.	41	3	W
Nov. 22	California	Berkeley, Calif.	20	20	T
		ROSE BOWL			
Jan. 1, 1925	Notre Dame	Pasadena, Calif.	10	27	L
			179	69	

(1) - Game played at Multnomah Stadium, Portland, Ore.
(2) - Game cancelled.
(3) - Game played at Memorial Stadium, Berkeley, Calif.

1925
(7-2-0)
Captain: Ernie Nevers

Date	Opponent	Where	Stan.	Opp.	
Sept. 26	Olympic Club	Palo Alto, Calif.	0	9	L
Oct. 3	Santa Clara	Palo Alto, Calif.	20	3	W
Oct. 10	Occidental	Palo Alto, Calif.	28	0	W
Oct. 17	U.S.C.	Los Angeles, Calif.	13	9	W
Oct. 24	Oregon State	Palo Alto, Calif.	26	10	W
Oct. 31	Oregon	Palo Alto, Calif.	35	13	W
Nov. 7	Washington	Seattle, Wash.	0	13	L
Nov. 14	U.C.L.A.	Palo Alto, Calif.	82	0	W
Nov. 21	California	Palo Alto, Calif.	26	14	W
			230	71	

1926
(10-0-1)
Captain: Fred Swan

Date	Opponent	Where	Stan.	Opp.	
Sept. 25	Fresno State	Palo Alto, Calif.	44	7	W
Sept. 25	California Tech	Palo Alto, Calif.	13	6	W
Oct. 2	Occidental	Palo Alto, Calif.	19	0	W
Oct. 9	Olympic Club	Palo Alto, Calif.	7	3	W
Oct. 16	Nevada	Palo Alto, Calif.	33	9	W
Oct. 23	Oregon	Eugene, Ore.	29	12	W
Oct. 30	U.S.C.	Los Angeles, Calif.	13	12	W
Nov. 6	Santa Clara	Palo Alto, Calif.	33	14	W
Nov. 13	Washington	Palo Alto, Calif.	29	10	W
Nov. 20	California	Berkeley, Calif.	41	6	W
		ROSE BOWL			
Jan. 1, 1927	Alabama	Pasadena, Calif.	7	7	T
			268	86	

1927
(8-2-1)
Captain: Hal McCreery

Date	Opponent	Where	Stan.	Opp.	
Sept. 24	Fresno State	Palo Alto, Calif.	33	0	W
Sept. 24	Olympic Club	Palo Alto, Calif.	7	6	W
Oct. 1	St. Mary's	Palo Alto, Calif.	0	16	L
Oct. 8	Nevada	Palo Alto, Calif.	20	2	W
Oct. 15	U.S.C.	Palo Alto, Calif.	13	13	T
Oct. 22	Oregon State	Portland, Ore.	20	6	W
Oct. 29	Oregon	Palo Alto, Calif.	19	0	W
Nov. 5	Washington	Seattle, Wash.	13	7	W
Nov. 12	Santa Clara	Palo Alto, Calif.	6	13	L
Nov. 19	California	Palo Alto, Calif.	13	6	W
		ROSE BOWL			
Jan. 2, 1928	Pittsburgh	Pasadena, Calif.	7	6	W
			151	75	

1928
(8-3-1)
Captain: Biff Hoffman

Date	Opponent	Where	Stan.	Opp.	
Sept. 22	Y.M.I.	Palo Alto, Calif.	0	7	L
Sept. 22	West Coast Army	Palo Alto, Calif.	21	8	W
Sept. 29	Olympic Club	Palo Alto, Calif.	6	12	L
Oct. 6	Oregon	Eugene, Ore.	26	12	W
Oct. 13	U.C.L.A.	Palo Alto, Calif.	45	7	W
Oct. 19	Idaho (1)	San Francisco, Calif.	47	0	W
Oct. 27	Fresno State	Palo Alto, Calif.	47	0	W
Nov. 3	U.S.C.	Los Angeles, Calif.	0	10	L
Nov. 10	Santa Clara	Palo Alto, Calif.	31	0	W
Nov. 17	Washington	Palo Alto, Calif.	12	0	W
Nov. 24	California	Berkeley, Calif.	13	13	T
Dec. 1	Army (2)	New York, N.Y.	26	0	W
			274	69	

(1) - Game played at Kezar Stadium, San Francisco, Calif.
(2) - Game played at Yankee Stadium, New York, N.Y.

1929
(9-2-0)
Captain: Don Muller

Date	Opponent	Where	Stan.	Opp.	
Sept. 21	West Coast Army	Palo Alto, Calif.	45	0	W
Sept. 28	Olympic Club	Palo Alto, Calif.	6	0	W
Oct. 5	Oregon	Palo Alto, Calif.	33	7	W
Oct. 12	U.C.L.A.	Los Angeles, Calif.	57	0	W
Oct. 19	Oregon State	Palo Alto, Calif.	40	7	W
Oct. 26	U.S.C.	Palo Alto, Calif.	0	7	L
Nov. 2	California Tech	Palo Alto, Calif.	39	0	W
Nov. 9	Washington	Seattle, Wash.	6	0	W
Nov. 16	Santa Clara	Palo Alto, Calif.	7	13	L
Nov. 23	California	Palo Alto, Calif.	21	6	W
Dec. 28	Army	Palo Alto, Calif.	34	13	W
			288	53	

1930
(9-1-1)
Captain: Ray Tandy

Date	Opponent	Where	Stan.	Opp.	
Sept. 20	West Coast Army	Palo Alto, Calif.	32	0	W
Sept. 27	Olympic Club	Palo Alto, Calif.	18	0	W
Oct. 4	Santa Clara	Palo Alto, Calif.	20	0	W
Oct. 11	Minnesota	Minneapolis, Minn.	0	0	T
Oct. 18	Oregon State	Palo Alto, Calif.	13	7	W
Oct. 25	U.S.C.	Palo Alto, Calif.	12	41	L
Oct. 31	U.C.L.A.	Los Angeles, Calif.	20	0	W
Nov. 8	Washington	Palo Alto, Calif.	25	7	W
Nov. 15	California Tech	Palo Alto, Calif.	57	7	W
Nov. 22	California	Berkeley, Calif.	41	0	W
Nov. 29	Dartmouth	Palo Alto, Calif.	14	7	W
			252	69	

1931
(7-2-2)
Captain: Harry Hillman

Date	Opponent	Where	Stan.	Opp.	
Sept. 19	West Coast Army	Palo Alto, Calif.	46	0	W
Sept. 26	Olympic Club	Palo Alto, Calif.	0	0	T
Oct. 3	Santa Clara	Palo Alto, Calif.	6	0	W
Oct. 10	Minnesota	Palo Alto, Calif.	13	0	W
Oct. 17	Oregon State	Palo Alto, Calif.	25	7	W
Oct. 24	Washington	Seattle, Wash.	0	0	T
Oct. 31	U.C.L.A.	Palo Alto, Calif.	12	6	W
Nov. 7	U.S.C.	Los Angeles, Calif.	0	19	L
Nov. 14	Nevada	Palo Alto, Calif.	26	0	W
Nov. 21	California	Palo Alto, Calif.	0	6	L
Nov. 28	Dartmouth (1)	Cambridge, Mass.	32	6	W
			160	44	

(1) - Game played at Harvard Stadium, Cambridge, Mass.

1932
(6-4-1)
Captain: Ernie Caddel

Date	Opponent	Where	Stan.	Opp.	
Sept. 17	Olympic Club	Palo Alto, Calif.	6	0	W
Sept. 24	San Francisco (1)	San Francisco, Calif.	20	7	W
Oct. 1	Oregon State	Portland, Ore.	27	0	W
Oct. 8	Santa Clara	Palo Alto, Calif.	14	0	W
Oct. 15	West Coast Army	Palo Alto, Calif.	26	0	W
Oct. 22	U.S.C.	Palo Alto, Calif.	0	13	L
Oct. 29	U.C.L.A.	Los Angeles, Calif.	6	13	L
Nov. 5	Washington	Palo Alto, Calif.	13	18	L
Nov. 12	California Aggies	Palo Alto, Calif.	59	0	W
Nov. 19	California	Berkeley, Calif.	0	0	T
Nov. 26	Pittsburgh	Pittsburgh, Pa.	0	7	L
			171	58	

(1) - Game played at Kezar Stadium, San Francisco, Calif.

TEMPLE UNIVERSITY ERA

1933
(5-3-0)
Captain: Edgar Smith

Date	Opponent	Where	T.U.	Opp.	
Sept. 29	South Carolina	Philadelphia, Pa.	26	6	W
Oct. 7	Carnegie Tech	Pittsburgh, Pa.	0	25	L
Oct. 13	Haskell Institute	Philadelphia, Pa.	31	0	W
Oct. 20	West Virginia	Philadelphia, Pa.	13	7	W
Oct. 28	Bucknell	Lewisburg, Pa.	7	20	L
Nov. 4	Drake	Philadelphia, Pa.	20	14	W
Nov. 18	Washington & Jefferson	Philadelphia, Pa.	13	0	W
Nov. 25	Villanova	Philadelphia, Pa.	0	24	L
			110	96	

1934
(7-1-2)
Captain: Peter Stevens

Date	Opponent	Where	T.U.	Opp.	
Sept. 29	Virginia Tech	Philadelphia, Pa.	34	0	W
Oct. 5	Texas A&M	Philadelphia, Pa.	40	6	W
Oct. 13	Indiana	Philadelphia, Pa.	6	6	T
Oct. 19	West Virginia	Philadelphia, Pa.	28	13	W
Oct. 27	Marquette	Milwaukee, Wis.	28	6	W
Nov. 3	Holy Cross	Philadelphia, Pa.	14	0	W
Nov. 10	Carnegie Tech	Philadelphia, Pa.	34	6	W
Nov. 24	Villanova	Philadelphia, Pa.	22	0	W
Nov. 29	Bucknell	Philadelphia, Pa.	0	0	T
		SUGAR BOWL			
Jan. 1, 1935	Tulane	New Orleans, La.	14	20	L
			220	57	

1935
(7-3-0)
Captain: James Russell

Date	Opponent	Where	T.U.	Opp.	
Sept. 20	St. Joseph's	Philadelphia, Pa.	51	0	W
Sept. 27	Centre	Philadelphia, Pa.	25	13	W
Oct. 5	Texas A&M	Tyler, Tex.	14	0	W
Oct. 11	Vanderbilt	Philadelphia, Pa.	6	3	W
Oct. 19	Carnegie Tech	Pittsburgh, Pa.	13	0	W
Oct. 26	West Virginia	Morganstown, W. Va.	19	6	W
Nov. 2	Michigan State	Philadelphia, Pa.	7	12	L
Nov. 16	Marquette	Philadelphia, Pa.	26	6	W
Nov. 23	Villanova	Philadelphia, Pa.	14	21	L
Nov. 28	Bucknell	Philadelphia, Pa.	6	7	L
			181	68	

1936
(6-3-2)
Captain: William Docherty

Date	Opponent	Where	T.U.	Opp.	
Sept. 21	St. Joseph's	Philadelphia, Pa.	18	0	W
Sept. 25	Centre	Philadelphia, Pa.	50	7	W
Oct. 2	Mississippi	Philadelphia, Pa	12	7	W
Oct. 12	Boston College	Boston, Mass.	14	0	W
Oct. 16	Carnegie Tech	Philadelphia, Pa.	0	7	L
Oct. 31	Holy Cross	Philadelphia, Pa.	3	0	W
Nov. 7	Michigan State	East Lansing, Mich.	7	7	T
Nov. 14	Villanova	Philadelphia, Pa.	6	0	W
Nov. 21	Iowa	Philadelphia, Pa.	0	25	L
Nov. 26	Bucknell	Philadelphia, Pa.	0	0	T
Dec. 5	St. Mary's	San Francisco, Calif.	7	13	L
			117	66	

1937
(3-2-4)
Captains: Christin Pappas, Joe Drulis and Moe Katz

Date	Opponent	Where	T.U.	Opp.	
Sept. 24	V.M.I.	Philadelphia, Pa.	18	7	W
Oct. 1	Mississippi	Philadelphia, Pa.	0	0	T
Oct. 8	Florida	Philadelphia, Pa.	7	6	W
Oct. 12	Boston College	Boston, Mass.	0	0	T
Oct. 22	Carnegie Tech	Philadelphia, Pa.	7	0	W
Oct. 30	Holy Cross	Worcester, Mass.	0	0	T
Nov. 6	Michigan State	Philadelphia, Pa.	6	13	L
Nov. 13	Bucknell	Lewisburg, Pa.	0	0	T
Nov. 20	Villanova	Philadelphia, Pa.	0	33	L
			38	59	

1938
(3-6-1)
Captain: Richard Wheeler

Date	Opponent	Where	T.U.	Opp.	
Sept. 23	Albright	Philadelphia, Pa.	6	0	W
Oct. 1	Pittsburgh	Philadelphia, Pa.	6	28	L
Oct. 7	Texas Christian	Philadelphia, Pa.	6	28	L
Oct. 14	Bucknell	Philadelphia, Pa.	26	0	W
Oct. 21	Boston College	Philadelphia, Pa.	26	26	T
Oct. 28	Georgetown	Philadelphia, Pa.	0	13	L
Nov. 5	Holy Cross	Worcester, Mass.	0	33	L
Nov. 12	Villanova	Philadelphia, Pa.	7	20	L
Nov. 19	Michigan State	East Lansing, Mich.	0	10	L
Dec. 3	Florida	Gainesville, Fla.	20	12	W
			97	170	

The Pop Warner Memorial Trophy

This prestigious award is presented by the Palo Club of Palo Alto, Calif., to the West Coast's most valuable senior college football player.

Year	Player	School
1949	Eddie LeBaron	College of the Pacific
1950	Russ Pomeroy	Stanford
1951	Ollie Matson	University of San Francisco
1952	Jim Sears	U.S.C.
1953	Bob Garrett	Stanford
1954	George Shaw	Oregon
1955	Bob Davenport	U.C.L.A.
1956	Jon Arnett	U.S.C.
1957	Joe Francis	Oregon State
1958	Joe Kapp	California
1959	Chris Burford	Stanford
1960	Bill Kilmer	U.C.L.A.
1961	Chon Gallegos	San Jose State
1962	Terry Baker	Oregon State
1963	Vern Burke	Oregon State
1964	Craig Morton	California
1965	Mike Garrett	U.S.C.
1966	Pete Pifer	Oregon State
1967	Gary Beban	U.C.L.A.
1968	O.J. Simpson	U.S.C.
1969	Don Parish	Stanford
1970	Jim Plunkett	Stanford
1971	Jeff Siemon	Stanford
1972	Mike Rae	U.S.C.
1973	Lynn Swann	U.S.C.
1974	Anthony Davis	U.S.C.
1975	Chuck Muncie	California

1976	Ricky Bell	U.S.C.
1977	Guy Benjamin	Stanford
1978	Jerry Robinson	U.C.L.A.
1979	Charles White	U.S.C.
1980	Ken Margerum	Stanford
1981	Marcus Allen	U.C.L.A.
1982	John Elway	Stanford
1983	Ron Rivera	California
1984	Jack Del Rio	U.S.C.
1985	Rueben Mays	Washington State
1986	Dave Wyman	Stanford
1987	Mike Perez	San Jose State
1988	Rodney Peete	U.S.C.
1989	Tim Ryan	U.S.C.
1990	Greg Lewis	Washington
1991	Tommy Vardell	Stanford
1992	Glyn Milburn	Stanford